Charles W. King
James W. Robinson

the NEW PROFESSIONALS

The Rise of
Network Marketing
As the Next Major Profession

PRIMA SOHO
An Imprint of Prima Publishing
3000 Lava Ridge Court • Roseville, California 95661
www.primalifestyles.com • (800) 632-8676

PRIMA SOHO is a trademark of Prima Communications, Inc.

PRIMA PUBLISHING and colophon are trademarks of Prima Communications Inc., registered with the United States Patent and Trademark Office.

Library of Congress Cataloging-in-Publication Data
King, Charles W.
    The new professionals : the rise of network marketing as the next
major profession / Charles W. King, James W. Robinson
      p. cm.
    Includes index.
    ISBN 0-7615-1966-1
    1. Multilevel marketing. I. Robinson, James W. II. Title.
HF5415.126.K555 2000
658.8'4—dc21
                                    00-042101

00 01 02 03 HH 10 9 8 7 6 5 4 3 2
Printed in the United States of America

How to Order
Single copies may be ordered from Prima Publishing, 3000 Lava Ridge Court, Roseville, CA 95661; telephone (800) 632-8676 ext. 4444. Quantity discounts are also available. On your letterhead, include information concerning the intended use of the books and the number of books you wish to purchase.

Visit us online at www.primalifestyles.com

the NEW PROFESSIONALS

CONTENTS

FOREWORD

If you are thinking about getting involved in a network marketing opportunity, you must read *The New Professionals* by Charles King and James Robinson. It is the best, most authoritative and up-to-date source of information on the state of multilevel marketing (MLM) at the turn of the twenty-first century.

As the authors state in these pages, network marketing has long suffered from an information vacuum. Trade organizations have not kept reliable statistics. Business schools and mainstream financial publications have failed to acknowledge the industry's existence. Major media outlets have focused on MLM only when there were juicy scandals to report.

That these unhappy circumstances are changing today is largely due to the personal efforts of two men, the authors of this present volume. A graduate of the Harvard Business School with a doctorate in business administration and a professor of marketing at the University of Illinois at Chicago (UIC), Charles King has done ground-breaking research into MLM, amassing the most complete and reliable data available on this elusive industry. As senior vice president and counselor to the president of the U.S. Chamber of Commerce, James Robinson has been an unusually influential evangelist for network marketing, through his bestselling books *The Excel Phenomenon*, *Empire of Freedom*, and *Prescription for Success*.

King and Robinson write as objective and scholarly observers of network marketing, not as self-interested participants. They have assembled an impressive array of facts, demonstrating beyond a doubt that MLM will be an important vehicle for people seeking self-employment, business ownership, and financial independence in the twenty-first century. They also offer useful snapshots of leading companies, showing a judicious awareness of the strengths and weaknesses of each one.

Over the years, I have perused many MLM books, the good, the bad, and the ugly. *The New Professionals* is the closest thing I have found to a one-stop-shopping source of accurate information about MLM. For the serious entrepreneur conducting due diligence on the industry, it is an indispensable tool. For the curious beginner, just setting out to explore the mysteries of MLM, it is an illuminating and highly readable introduction.

—Richard Poe
author of *Wave 3: The New Era in Network Marketing,*
The Wave 3 Way to Building Your Downline, and
Wave 4: Network Marketing in the 21st Century

the NEW
PROFESSIONALS

CHAPTER 1

A New Approach to Work, Family, and Lifestyle

A corporate CEO sells his company at the height of his success and power. A senior government official suddenly walks away from the perks and prerogatives of high office. A woman executive who spends years successfully breaking through the glass ceiling in her industry walks into the office one day and says, "I quit." A nationally recognized heart surgeon gives up his practice.

Lawyers, doctors, dentists, university professors, stockbrokers, company managers, professional athletes, real estate developers, and small business owners—all of whom poured years of hard work into preparing for and building lucrative careers—walk away from the success and money and don't look back.

What are these people doing? What do they have in common? Where are they going? And why?

They've all joined the ranks of the New Professionals. And many of them have decided to embrace an industry they had once laughed at, sneered at, and swore they'd never touch—network marketing.

Network marketing is the low-cost, and now high-tech, industry that invites you to build your own business and earn a potentially high income while working from home on your own schedule. You earn immediate income and serious long-term residual income by selling products and services directly to consumers and convincing others to do the same.

Network marketing—known in the past as *multilevel marketing* and historically disparaged as pyramid schemes for schemers and suckers—is today emerging as the most powerful distribution method and the most appealing enterprise model in the new economy. It's an approach to sales and entrepreneurship so powerful that traditional companies, struggling to find new ways to reach a fragmented market while containing the prohibitively high costs of full-time sales forces and national advertising campaigns, are now borrowing its best features to apply to their operations.

> Network marketing is an approach to sales and entrepreneurship so powerful that traditional companies are now borrowing its best features to apply to their operations.

Network marketing—once known as the last refuge for the hapless and hopeless, those who had failed at everything else—has entered the new millennium with a fresh image as a place for winners. Today, it's a high-touch, high-tech field, international in scope, that is growing in sophistication, complexity, and diversity; an industry where knowledgeable workers are welcome, professionalism is prized, and search engines and stock options are replacing pep rallies and prayer circles.

No wonder that serious professionals from many fields are taking either their first look, or a fresh look, at network marketing. Each year, thousands of people are leaving well-established, lucrative careers to pursue new opportunities with the broad range of interesting companies that comprise this industry. In the process, these New Professionals are not only changing the face of network marketing but are also having a broad impact on the business world as a whole.

Their success is altering attitudes about working at home and solving problems that mainstream companies never could—such as breaking through the glass ceiling, combating discrimination, offering full opportunities for people with disabilities, allowing retirement-aged people to stay on the job, and better balancing the demands of family and career. Many have ended the need for long commutes at dawn and dusk and increased their productivity and job satisfaction, while simultaneously reducing their isolation from family and community and cutting their contribution to air pollution and traffic jams.

The New Professionals in network marketing and other fields were often highly successful in their chosen careers but were unfulfilled. They represent a growing economic and social force, global in scope. In the United States, 15 percent of the workforce is now self-employed—a share exceeding those who belong to labor unions. Twenty million Americans now "telecommute," performing some or all of their professional duties from home. In Los Angeles, the nation's second largest city and largest regional economy, less than half of the workforce is now employed in traditional Monday-through-Friday, nine-to-five jobs.

Half of all stocks are owned by families earning under $100,000 a year, indicating that in an era of "merger mania," the most important merger of all has been the bonding of Main Street with Wall Street. Average Americans have become serious investors, spurred by ease of online trading. Many others are starting small businesses on the side or buying into them. Secretaries with stock options are a common sight throughout the start-up companies of the new economy. Fading from view is the idea that a professional performs one set of tasks for one paycheck. They and their families are instead taking a diversified and highly entrepreneurial approach to the generation of income and accumulation of wealth. Invest a little money here, join with some partners to start a new venture there, start a home-based business for the spouse and children here, do some consulting work there—it's all part of a new approach to work and lifestyle.

We believe *The New Professionals* is the first book to seriously examine these trends and how network marketing is shaping and being shaped by them. Our goals are clear:

- To provide valid documentation of the credibility of network marketing

- To prove that network marketing is a rich and varied profession, embracing an interesting array of business models, marketing plans, product and service lines, technologies, and international markets

- To show that network marketing is a credible channel of distribution and highly effective in the extremely fragmented e-commerce economy

- To critique the current economic and lifestyle conditions facing many professionals, suggesting that network marketing responds to many complaints. We will begin and end our book here and in the middle chapters provide you with the substance and documentation you need to make a reasoned judgment about the potential of network marketing in your own life and career.

Our goal is neither to sermonize or proselytize but to stimulate a serious discussion for serious professionals. Here's what to expect:

- We will define network marketing and distinguish it from its older parent, which is called *direct selling*. How does one get paid in the business?

- We will trace the historic roots of the industry, the key milestones, the pioneers, and the struggle for legal and public acceptance.

- We will outline the scope of the industry today. Network marketers comprise an estimated 81.7 percent of participants in the direct selling industry that, as of 1998, claims 9.7 million independent businesspeople in the United States and 30.9 million worldwide. Direct sales entrepreneurs sell $23.17 billion of goods and services annually here and $80.4 billion around the globe. How have they accomplished this? How big an economic force will they become in the future?

- We'll identify the advantages of this business model over both traditional professions and other forms of small business ownership. No other business requires such a low cost of entry with virtually no significant overhead. There are no bank loans, second mortgages, or employee headaches. No other business allows its practitioners such flexibility over their schedule. That's why many top professionals find in network marketing an ideal lifestyle that doesn't force them to choose between raising a family and pursuing a financially rewarding career.

In addition, we'll discuss how the network marketing industry is changing and why your image of it may be seriously out-of-date. We'll illuminate the positive trends that will shape and define its future:

- Major companies in the industry are publicly traded on Wall Street, with some offering lucrative stock options to top distributors.

- These firms have professional management and are pouring millions into R&D to devise exclusive, proprietary products.

- Services and technology products will comprise an increasing share of sales, alongside more traditional personal care and household products.

- There are fewer rallies and "house parties." More professional workshops and online training are replacing them.

- Unlike other sales channels, network marketing will not only survive the e-commerce revolution but will thrive because of it. Forget about the image of having to load product in your trunk for delivery to customers or attending an endless number of "coffee klatches" with neighbors and friends. The new network marketer will recruit online, order products online, authorize fulfillment online, and get credited and paid online.

- It's a global movement in which participants can now run sophisticated international businesses from their home office command centers anywhere in the United States or the world.

- As noted, while we all admire "rags-to-riches" stories as a vital part of America's promise, network marketing is now attracting an unprecedented number of professionals from many fields who have earned stature, respect, and success in those fields and are bringing these qualities to the industry. They are rapidly changing the culture of network marketing. You'll meet some of them in this book.

But the rise of the New Professionals can be only partly explained by the tremendous improvements in network marketing. For most of us, the lure of a good opportunity is not by itself a sufficient motivator for action. We have to be pushed toward it by a shortcoming in or dissatisfaction with our current situation. As you'll see in chapters 2 and 3, it is just such a push-pull effect that is fueling today's substantial growth in network marketing.

The world of work is changing, and it will never be the same.

The old model whereby you trade forty years of your time, talent, and singular devotion to a company or profession in exchange for a secure and steadily growing income, peer recognition, and employer loyalty has been shattered. It will not be reassembled.

A few hearty souls in society say good riddance to that comfortable but stale old order. But for most, it's an unsettling and fearful prospect—at least until our eyes are opened to the new possibilities replacing the old verities.

The concern and confusion are understandable. The late twentieth century was marked by ceaseless change alongside bountiful, but vacuous, material prosperity. It is very tempting to forsake opportunity for security and to prize the comfort of constancy above the relentlessness of change.

It is not surprising that in a society that values security above almost everything else, many would try to cling to that old work model even when there's not much left to cling on to.

For years, this was the deal: You kiss your family good-bye and commute every day to a job or an office, work hard and well, bring tasks home when needed, and travel when required. You strive for advancement and recognition in your organization or profession. Your superiors measure your success according to the standards they have established, or if you have your own business or practice, your customers and clients do based on the rate at which they keep coming back.

Unlike other sales channels, network marketing will not only survive the e-commerce revolution but will thrive because of it.

This occupation is normally your sole or primary source of income, and if you were unable or did not want to continue, the income would stop. It's a straight transaction of time for money. You do this for thirty-five or forty years. Then you stop working entirely, drawing a small portion of your prior income from your employer in the form of a pension. You hope that this pension, coupled with private savings and social security, will permit a frugal but comfortable life.

Your part of this bargain may sound a little depressing, but think about how much you have been getting in return. Customarily, your organization would

- Provide you with slow but steady income growth
- Pay for vacations and holidays
- Organize health, dental, and vision care for your entire family
- Set up and manage a pension for when you get old
- Insure your life should you die while still working for the company
- Handle all the bookkeeping associated with paying your taxes and insuring you against unemployment and workplace injury
- Provide you with a fully equipped office or work station, train you in the latest technologies, and pay for advanced education
- Sometimes offer fitness and childcare services and stock in the company
- For your psyche, recognize your good efforts through corporate promotions and recognition
- Probably even let you keep and use, for personal travel, the frequent flyer award mileage you earn when traveling on company business

It's not such a bad deal—especially if your colleagues are fun, the work is challenging, and you can get passionate about the lofty mission that any firm or organization worth its salt will try to formulate and instill in you. If not, maybe a company over in the next state will offer you a better deal. It may even help you sell your house, move your family, and find you a new mortgage.

Lest you think we are striking an overly cynical or condescending tone so early in what we hope is a narrative full of hopeful possibility, please note: not everything in that old employment equation was or is about money and security. They account for only part of the alluring appeal of the one job/one paycheck/one profession work model.

Another aspect is the desire to be part of a cause larger than yourself. It's the intellectual stimulation that comes with being surrounded by others in your field and the lifelong professional and personal relationships you acquire. It's being part of a great organization and taking part in the big decisions that lead it to its growth and success. It's about being proud to tell people who you work for and what your title is, and getting that "Ah!" of recognition and respect when you tell them.

It's about loyalty and dedication. Who among us is not impressed when we read about a corporate CEO who started in the mailroom forty years ago and worked his way to the top? Or a family doctor who delivered thousands of babies and their children too? Or an airline pilot who defended the United States in war and then made a hundred thousand takeoffs and landings, delivering passengers safely all over the world before hanging up his wings after decades in flight?

There is no shame, and much honor, in serving a profession or an organization with skill and dedication your entire adult life and then happily retiring with respect and some degree of income security.

There's just one problem. It's getting harder and rarer to find the opportunity to do that working in the traditional companies and serving in the old professions. As economic pressures in those companies and professions grow, they in turn place greater time pressures on their employees and practitioners. The losers are the children, the spouses, and the quality of life. It's like a jigsaw puzzle with the most important pieces of the picture missing—for many professionals there's big hole in the center of what was supposed to be the perfect portrait of success and happiness.

The old employment model is breaking apart. Only the foolish, complacent, or lazy refuse to see it and seize the opportunities to protect themselves and their families.

Many of those who thought they could escape that trap by becoming their own bosses in small businesses, franchises, or consultancies instead find they are caught in an even tighter vise. With their life savings often on the line, they work incredible hours. Customers and clients pay them like small businesses, but they are taxed, regulated, and sometimes sued like they were big businesses with bottomless resources.

We will show you how the old employment model is breaking apart. Only the foolish, complacent, or lazy refuse to see it and seize the opportunities to protect themselves and their families. Consider these signs of the professional world's increasing inability to provide either stability or challenge in today's economy:

- In an era of historic economic prosperity, we are seeing unprecedented downsizings and layoffs.

- Companies are scaling back traditional benefits such as health care coverage, telling employees to go find it on their own.

- Firms are outsourcing more functions than ever before to avoid overhead costs of full-time workers. In many cases, they will hire you only as an independent contractor. Have you ever known what it feels like to pay *both* halves of your social security and Medicare payroll taxes? Get ready to find out!

- The high-tech, global economy has made it possible for domestic industry to move not only manufacturing jobs offshore but white-collar tasks as well. Every day, six hundred Filipinos in smart business attire report to work at one of America Online's service departments for its U.S. customers—at the old Clark Air Force base outside of Manila.

- Merger mania has only just begun. When was the last time you heard of a merger that actually *increased* the number of professional and managerial jobs in a newly consolidated firm?

- Many doctors report that the economic realities of modern practice have driven them far away from their traditional and time-honored role as caregivers. They invested years of their life at enormous expense to establish practices, only to find themselves treated like run-of-the-mill employees. Others say they spend more time filling out paperwork and fending off lawsuits than they do providing care. Other professionals, in fields ranging from law to education, report similar disenchantment and disappointment.

- The population is aging. Professionals could soon spend more years in retirement than on the job. How many will be financially prepared for such welcome longevity based on their current occupations?

- With deeply troubling trends among young people, from gun violence to rising drug abuse, professionals of all kinds wonder how they can face up to the increasing uncertainty and time demands of the new economy and still be caring, loving, and attentive parents. "Why do we have to choose?" they ask. There has got to be a better way.

Many are finding a better way in the new world of network marketing. They are finding a knowledgeable profession with a tremendous range of interesting products, companies, and business approaches to choose from.

It's a business that they can build with their families from their own homes, on either a part-time basis as a supplemental income stream or a full-time basis with serious, long-term residual income.

It's an industry that has embraced information and Internet technology, enabling businesspeople to minimize time-consuming and unpleasant tasks and instead devote full attention to selling and recruiting.

It's a business in which there are no employee headaches, no payroll, and very little overhead—yet in which they can build sales organizations that span the globe and open up rewarding opportunities for world travel.

They are finding a profession in which they are surrounded by success and optimism and in which more money is made by helping others make money—a refreshing change from the dog-eat-dog mentality of global capitalism or the green-eye-shade mentality of corporate bureaucracies.

In sum, they are finding an opportunity to fill in the missing pieces of that "portrait of success and happiness" they have been working so hard to perfect: financial independence, long-term income security, time freedom, control over their lives, and attachment to a cause greater than themselves.

But how did they do it? Where did they start? How did they choose a company? How do you know whether network marketing is right for you? After we look at the economic and social conditions that are pushing New Professionals to new approaches and document the viability and trends in network marketing as a whole, we'll then do something rarely, if ever, attempted in the existing literature on the industry. First, we'll present individual company sketches that define their differences in business approach. Which ones are the pacesetters, the rising stars? Then, we'll have a no-holds-barred discussion of the kind of professionals who are most likely to succeed in network marketing—and those who will not. This should help you personally answer those questions.

For fifteen years, Lloyd Tosser of Tempe, Arizona, poured his heart and soul into the insurance business. He lived to regret it. "I had worked hard to get to what I considered the 'pinnacle' of my insurance career only to have it yanked away from me," he says. The company he worked for was bought out by a larger firm, drove agents away with the changes, and ended up dissolving Lloyd's division.

> New Professionals are finding an opportunity to fill in the missing pieces of that "portrait of success and happiness" they have been working so hard to perfect.

But at the time Lloyd and his wife Deborah also happened to have purchased a legal protection plan from Pre-Paid Legal Services, Inc.—the Ada, Oklahoma, network marketing company with an innovative product that offers customers unlimited access to top attorneys for a small monthly fee. As for many other professionals, it was a positive experience with a quality product or service that first sold them on the company and helped them overcome misgivings about network marketing.

"We used our Pre-Paid Legal plan two times, and in both cases it worked great," Lloyd says. "It's very unusual to find a product that actually works the way it's supposed to and when you need it. We were so impressed we thought why not sell the product as well?"

Reaching a new and lasting pinnacle of success, what the Tossers appreciate the most is not the money but the way their network marketing business rewards their efforts. It has also led to profound and positive changes in their lifestyle.

"It seems like a simple opportunity, but it's a rare one," Lloyd says. "The harder you work, the more money you make. Sounds almost silly, doesn't it? But how many companies are left in America where you are rewarded for working hard, where there's no upper limit, and where you aren't constantly looking over your shoulder waiting for someone to take it all away from you?

"Deb and I work for ourselves now. We're not stuck in morning traffic, white-knuckling the steering wheel while eating an Egg McMuffin. We have a one-minute commute from the bedroom to the office. If we want to work late, we can. If we want to take the day off we can.

"It's up to us now. We're in control of our own lives."

By the time you finish this book, it will be up to you. Do you want to become a New Professional?

Risks and Rewards in the New Economy

T oday we are witnessing the steady destruction of the traditional employment economy, in which workers sell their time to a company in exchange for money and sell their experience in exchange for security. This traditional structure is being replaced by a single, massive interconnected economy in which money, people, companies, ideas, and technologies are totally fungible. In this new economy, spectacular growth and severe dislocations are occurring side by side. It is an economy that is choking off the more traditional methods of generating secure income but at the same time is spawning new opportunities.

Business Week recently assessed this development and its impact on workers:

> Just as the New Economy is dismantling the old rules of commerce, the new workforce is shredding the contracts between employers and employees. Employers are giving up rigid wage scales in favor of flexible compensation. They are learning to live with high turnover and abolishing seniority-based pay. . . . What will remain is an altered employment relationship in which increasingly independent workers negotiate their own way through their careers.

New Professionals understand these changes and are altering their careers and their strategies for generating wealth and income accordingly. Network marketing has become an important component of their new approach. For many it is a successful substitute for compensations they used to find in traditional employment, particularly long-term income security, steady advancement and recognition of achievement, and attachment to an emotionally satisfying mission. Alongside these values, they also find rewards rarely found in their former occupations: time freedom, flexible schedules, and the satisfaction of building a business on their own, a business that makes room for and strengthens the family.

THIS IS NOT YOUR FATHER'S ECONOMY

The changes reshaping the traditional economy and the search for a better opportunity have taken John Hargett and his family over a long and winding road.

"I've seen both sides of traditional business as a business owner and a corporate executive," he explains. "In the early 1980s, my family owned a wholesale grocery business. I spent eight years fighting high interest rates, employee problems, taxes, and larger competitors. All this for fifteen-hour days and hypertension!"

Acting on a tip from his father, who had retired from the pharmaceutical industry, John then entered the corporate world, working for an expanding company in the generic prescription business. "The first five years were incredible," he reports. "I was promoted early on to the position of vice president for the western United States. This title and responsibility gave me a much larger income and a job security that led my wife, Brenda, and me to build a new custom home for our family."

But then disaster struck the Hargetts. The company went through a hostile takeover, and John's position was eliminated. He spent nine months looking for a comparable position, but a downturn in the industry made such positions nonexistent. He ended up settling for a lesser job at 35 percent less pay, working for a small drug company.

"The combination of being out of work for nine months and the reduction in pay cost my family all our savings, our 401K, and the down payment on the home we were building. My oldest daughter was forced to leave college. We put our current home up for sale, but the housing market was depressed and no one was buying." Finally, with no other options left, in 1993 the family filed for bankruptcy. "Our home was eventually foreclosed on," John explains, "and Brenda went back to work. Then I found out that my company was up for sale. I knew I was about to go through the same process of elimination all over again."

> New Professionals find rewards rarely found in their former occupations: time freedom, and the satisfaction building a business on their own.

One day during these difficult times, Brenda came home and told John that she had learned that a coworker was involved in a company that sold preventive health care products through network marketing. She told John they would soon get a call inviting them to a briefing. John told her he was planning to say no when the call came because of his preconceived image about the industry.

"I knew preventive health had a great future because of the aging of our population," he explains. "What was challenging was the concept of network marketing."

But at work John saw the handwriting on the wall. He knew his job could soon be eliminated. So despite misgivings, he became a distributor for Rexall Showcase International, the network marketing arm of Rexall Sundown of Boca Raton, Florida.

John worked at the business every spare moment he could find. "My immediate goal was to double what I was making in my corporate job so we could buy a home and put our daughter back in college. Within two years, this was accomplished," he reports.

Shortly after that, John left his corporate job to develop his new business full-time. Three months later he learned that the company he had worked for was sold, and the entire sales force, of which he had been a part, was eliminated. "My regret is that not one individual believed they were at risk. Some spent up to a year looking for work rather than invest in owning a business like mine."

Today, after just four years, John and Brenda Hargett have a network marketing organization that extends throughout the United States and parts of Asia. They are among the top twenty earners at Rexall Showcase. "This business has provided our family not only with a more beautiful home than before but also with a lifestyle that never could have been accomplished in so short a time in traditional business," John says.

He reflects on the lessons he has learned and what others should draw from his experience. "My father worked for thirty-eight years for the same pharmaceutical company and retired with a terrific pension. My mom stayed at home to raise four sons. It was a good life.

"I wanted to be like my dad. He had always told me to go to college, get a good education, plug into one of the best corporations in America, work hard, and keep your mouth shut and you'll be blessed.

"Up until the early 1990s, my dad's philosophy actually worked. But all that has changed."

LOOKING FOR THE RIGHT OPPORTUNITY

There is nothing unusual or new about John Hargett's desire to control his own destiny by being his own boss. The lure of that dream has energized millions throughout history and has helped inspire a steady flow of immigrants to U.S. shores. Yet many achieving that dream in the traditional small business sector are finding conditions not much better than those who are dependent on corporate America for secure, high-paying jobs. Franchises and small or family-owned businesses for most represent an imperfect alternative to the corporate world or their professions. They can be high-cost, high-risk ventures that are more likely to double, rather than halve, the time you must spend on the job away from your family.

Joan Florence knew all along that there was a better path than working for a big company. Born and raised in Cullman, Alabama, Joan was one of ten children—five of whom, including Joan, became nurses. She was good at her profession and recognized for it when she landed a job in blood services nursing with the American Red Cross in Birmingham.

Yet after more than a decade in nursing, Joan saw an opportunity to jump into the weight loss business, which, in the mid-1980s, was a lucrative and popular place to be. A franchise opened up in Tuscaloosa, so she moved there, invested her savings, and joined the growing legions of women who own and operate their own small businesses.

As in nursing, Joan was successful. She made that business profitable virtually from the day she bought it to the day she sold it.

"But I learned that being your own boss isn't all that it's cracked up to be," Joan says. "There is a lot of volatility in the weight loss business. I had employee problems. I had overhead expenses. There are regulations and taxes and liability. You're affected by the ups and downs in the economy, changing consumer trends, and even the weather."

For a time, Joan was not only running her own business but also helping her brother run his—a two-hour drive away. "I was just getting burned out," she recalls.

Early in 1996, she received a tape in the mail from a friend who was in a different kind of business—network marketing. "But I was so busy, the tape just sat there for

three or four months before I even bothered to listen."
When she did listen, she was impressed.

Starting at ground level in the fall of 1996, Joan began
sending tapes to everyone she knew and following up to determine interest. "Within months, the business started taking off.
It grew very fast, reaching all across the country." Such quick
growth entitled Joan to not only handsome commissions but
also company bonuses. "By the end of my first year, my check
for October had already reached $16,000 in bonuses, and I
sold my weight loss business."

To Joan, the most striking thing about this business is
how it differs from her franchise business. "I work out of
my home, according to my own schedule, and there are no employees. In most small busi-
nesses you may think you're the
boss, but the employees are really running you. In this business you have great teammates
and a professional company
backing you up, without any of
the headaches!"

> Franchises or family-
> owned businesses can
> be high-cost, high-risk
> ventures that are more
> likely to double the
> time you spend away
> from your family.

Joan Florence and John Hargett each had to confront the realities of an economy in which,
even when you make substantial
money, you always have to
worry whether it's going to dis-
appear overnight—an economy in which you work harder
and harder to maintain a steadily diminishing quality of life.

AN EMPTY PROSPERITY?

If you simply look at the numbers economists love to cite,
it's hard to argue with the performance of the American
economy. Inflation barely exists. Unemployment is at a

thirty-year low. Consumer demand and confidence are high. Millions of Americans who never invested in the stock market before are building sizable personal portfolios. In February 2000, we broke the record for the longest-running expansion in American history—107 months and counting. It seems like the good times are going to roll on forever!

But there's trouble churning just beneath the surface.

In 1998, at the depth of the Asian financial crisis, six leading economists gathered at the headquarters of the U.S. Chamber of Commerce in Washington, D.C., to help businesspeople assess the impact of Asia's problems on the U.S. economy. Prime Minister Goh of Singapore visited later in the day, and when he learned of the presence of these six economists, he joked, "If you have six economists here, then that means you'll get twelve opinions about what's going to happen!"

Indeed, few economists predicted the crisis in the first place. A year earlier at the prestigious World Economic Forum annual meeting in the Swiss Alps, the political and economic intelligentsia of the entire world had gathered to predict the future, and a discussion of impending turmoil in Asia wasn't even on the agenda!

This underscores the unpredictability of the global economy. To rewrite the old adage, it seems like the more things change, the more things change. Where will you fit in as industries continue to change and consolidate? What will happen to your job as corporations become empowered to move white-collar tasks offshore, thanks to Internet technology? Your CEO might be in merger negotiations right now. What will that mean to you? When is the last time you heard of a merger that led to an *increase* in professional positions in that organization?

The good times may keep rolling on, but they might roll right over you. That's a reality driving many to become New Professionals.

WILL YOU BECOME A "JUST-IN-TIME" EMPLOYEE?

Despite the happy-face economic statistics that still accurately describe the U.S. economy in many respects, many Americans are worried about their income security. They're beginning to realize they have bought homes and cars they can't afford, delayed implementing a serious savings plan, and overextended themselves in both work and debt. Their concerns are not surprising when you consider what is happening in corporate America.

A report in the *Los Angeles Times* concludes, "For many corporations, downsizing has become a strategy that is used in good times and bad. Senior managers, under considerable pressure from stockholders to increase profits, often take the easiest way by cutting employment costs."

All told, the U.S. Department of Labor reports that despite sustained economic growth, 3.6 million workers were laid off during the last two-year period for which statistics are available. These workers had held their jobs for three years or longer. An estimated six million more who had been with the companies less than three years also lost their jobs. In the first ten months of 1998 alone, 523,000 jobs were cut, a pace exceeding the previous year by 200,000.

Whether the job cuts are attributed to big mergers, loss of Asian export sales, or the need to economize to satisfy investors, the list of major corporations cutting staff is growing longer and longer. In 1998 the downsizing hit list included:

AT&T	18,000
Motorola	15,000
Raytheon	14,000
Seagate	10,000
Xerox	19,000
BankAmerica	18,000

Travelers Group	18,000
First Union	17,480
Sunbeam	16,400
United HealthCare	15,400

As 1998 drew to a close, 9,000 workers were slated to lose their jobs as a result of the merger between oil giants Exxon and Mobil. Boeing announced a two-year downsizing program that would trim its workforce by 53,000. In 1999, megamergers such as Daimler-Chrysler, MCI-Sprint, and many others brought additional job insecurities to tens of thousands of well-paid professionals.

In the 1980s, the concept of "just-in-time" delivery was popularized in American industry. In this business practice, companies achieve shipping, warehousing, and production efficiencies by ordering raw materials and components only as they are needed and turn them into finished products only as they are ordered. A more efficient transportation system and sophisticated information technology made this commonsense idea possible.

Stanford University Management Professor Jeffrey Pfeffer sees a parallel in the increasing industry practice of layoffs as a strategy of first resort, calling the result for workers "just-in-time employment."

"There are some companies that wouldn't hold workers one minute more than they're needed," he told the *Los Angeles Times*. "They will hold inventories of goods for a long time, but they don't want to hold inventories of people."

Financial manager and commentator John Dorfman notes the cruel irony that announcements of mass firings often trigger increases in a company's stock price. "It's a knee-jerk reaction," he writes. "Practically every time a company announces job cuts, investors bid up the stock. It peeves me to no end."

Furthermore, Dorfman points out that if companies are trying to impress investors, the impression usually doesn't stick around for very long. "Not only are job cuts callous and evidence of bad corporate planning, they aren't even good for the stock's performance over the following year or two." His own survey of companies that had previously downsized discovered that seven out of ten had stocks performing more poorly than the market as a whole.

> In 1998, companies farmed out 15 percent of all manufacturing. In 2000, they will outsource more than 40 percent.

Echoing Dorfman's conclusion in its own survey, the *Los Angeles Times* reports, "Experts say they're surprised that so many companies are using layoffs as a first resort, especially since studies have shown that downsizing alone doesn't achieve the desired financial results." The paper cites Cornell University Professor Theresa Welbourne, who emphasizes that a company should consider the workplace climate it creates when laying off employees. "Downsizings often lead firms into downward spirals. Your high performers seek out other jobs, and that eventually has an impact on the company's earnings."

Being laid off is perhaps the most extreme manifestation of the overall upheaval in the corporate employment environment. The *Times* cites survey findings that discovered that "more than half of all working Americans have been downsized, have worked for a company that has merged or been bought out, or have moved to a different city because of their job."

Outsourcing tasks to reduce company overhead has exploded, with serious consequences for workers. In 1998, companies farmed out 15 percent of all manufacturing. In 2000, they will outsource more than 40 percent.

But the phenomenon of outsourcing along with accompanying layoffs is no longer confined to blue-collar workers on the factory floor. In recent years, workers with at least some college education made up the majority of people whose jobs were eliminated. Better-paid workers—those making at least $50,000 per year—now account for twice the share of lost jobs that they did in the 1980s.

It is no wonder that employees feel less attachment, loyalty, and commitment to their companies—and more competition with their colleagues, as a "them or me" mentality consumes the workplace. In one survey, 75 percent of employees say companies are less loyal to employees than they were ten years ago. Seventy percent agree that most working people compete more with coworkers now, rather than cooperate with them.

There are also indications that the climate of economic fear has spread from the workplace to the community and the home. When *USA Today* asked baby boomers between the ages of 32 and 50 to write to the newspaper about how they felt about the security of their white-collar professional jobs, the responses included bitter and poignant tales of lost respect, broken marriages, and even thoughts of suicide. One respondent sadly chronicled the decline of his once-friendly and prosperous suburban neighborhood: "A bunker mentality has replaced neighborhood fellowship. A nomadic existence has usurped the concept of roots—of living in one place for a lifetime. The security that comes from stability is what boomers want most. And it is the very thing that today seems so hard to possess."

Another reader, who worked for a big oil company for twenty-five years before losing his job, put it bluntly: "They can call it reengineering, restructuring, downsizing, but it still means you're fired."

That significant layoffs are occurring in the midst of a growing economy and a booming stock market seems like a contradiction. So does this: At a time when some employees are being let go, others are being brought into the country under special work visas to fill jobs companies say they can't fill with domestic workers.

Other employees claim they are being required to work increasing amounts of overtime. One phone company worker was actually fired after twenty-four years on the job for refusing overtime work because as a single father he had to care for his children. Thus, many employees who survive the spate of downsizings find their work environment more competitive, time-consuming, and tense. Succeeding in the corporate "rat race" forces many to put family and quality of life in second place.

To be fair to employers, several points must be kept in mind.

First, the competitive environment requires that companies hold a tough line on costs, or else everyone's job at the firm could be at risk.

Second, research shows that most laid-off workers find new jobs within a short period of time. Although some earn less, many others actually earn more than they did in their previous position.

Third, many companies are attempting to adapt to individual employee needs, offering overtime work to those who have the time to earn more, while allowing others to cut back their hours, work four-day weeks, or work from home to balance employment and family responsibilities.

Fourth, rigid government hiring and firing rules, burdensome regulations, spiraling payroll taxes, and an explosion of employee-related litigation mean that the company's cost of maintaining a worker now extends far beyond that worker's actual salary. Unions and trial lawyers fight to preserve this status quo.

In fact, at times federal, state, and local governments seem to be doing their best to put traditional employment in America on the endangered species list.

Minimum wage levels are being raised, making it harder to bring new American workers into entry-level jobs. New health care mandates and the threat of liability are making it costlier and riskier to provide health coverage for employees. In California, an anachronistic rule requiring overtime after an eight-hour day (instead of a forty-hour week) has been reinstated.

Ergonomics could become the most monumentally complex workplace rule of the next decade. The Occupational Safety and Health Administration (OSHA) is determined to go forward with a rule that could potentially be the most expensive regulatory protocol in U.S. history.

More than just an added cost or some new paperwork burden is at stake when government imposes new regulations like this. By relentlessly seeking to regulate the modern workplace further, government will further tax the patience of American business when it comes to sustaining the huge costs of maintaining traditional employment opportunities.

Much can be admired about a system that has produced a strong, productive economy with very low unemployment and virtually no inflation—an economy that is envied by all around the world. U.S. Chamber of Commerce president and CEO Thomas J. Donohue puts it bluntly: "Don't ask business to apologize for being the one institution in this country that has really worked!"

Indeed it has. American free enterprise has brought untold prosperity and opportunity to our society and to countries around the world that have emulated the U.S. system. But that system is undergoing profound change, and many Americans have come to realize they must change with it. Millions of Americans are leaving that uncertain environment or building alternatives around it so that they can achieve more secure, prosperous lives for themselves and their families. They want to take charge of their own lives once again. They are the New Professionals.

FRANCHISES AND FAMILY-OWNED BUSINESSES: THE IMPERFECT ALTERNATIVE

For millions of Americans, the answer has been the same as it was for Joan Florence: be your own boss by starting a small business or buying into a franchise. The path of entrepreneurship attracts so many because it affords an opportunity to build something on your own. Ideas and creativity count. Hard work pays off. You have the right to succeed and the right to fail. You feel in charge of your destiny.

The men and women who own and run the small businesses and who are self-employed represent a significant economic and social force that brings much of the creativity, energy, inventions, and new jobs to our country. Consider these developments:

- More than 22 million small businesses are operating in the United States today, businesses that collectively employ half of all the workers and create two out of every three new jobs.

- Women own more than 33 percent of these businesses and are starting them at a rate faster than men. Compare that to the corporate world where, according to *Business Week*, women account for just 11.2 percent of the officers of the top 500 firms. In just thirty-two of those companies do women constitute 25 percent or more of top management. At 125 firms there are no women in those ranks.

- An estimated 15 percent of American workers are self-employed. The 12.1 million who are self-employed exceed the number of Americans who belong to private-sector unions. We hear a great deal about those unions in the news but not nearly so much about this strong and growing independent workforce.

Starting a small business and being your own boss represents an obvious response to the growing uncertainty and the deteriorating quality of life found in mainstream employment. It proves to be satisfying accommodations for millions of people. Yet many others find that this supposed solution creates new sets of problems.

In 1996, just over 170,000 new businesses were formally created in the United States. That same year, 72,000 businesses failed. Most small businesses shut their doors within the first five years of their establishment.

Starting a small business can drain your family's life savings and force you to go deeply into debt—even mortgaging your house—to get the necessary financing. You'll likely need that financing if, for example, you want to buy a good franchise in a substantial business; they can cost you from $100,000 to $500,000 and more!

According to a recent survey of sixteen top franchise opportunities in 1999, the estimated total investments required, including franchise fees, were as follows:

Taco John's Restaurants	$310,000–$550,000
Dunkin' Donuts	$124,470–$808,559
Golden Corral Steaks	$1,200,000–$3,400,000
Marco's Pizza	$160,000
Dairy Queen	$147,240–$585,140
Great Harvest Bread Co.	$150,000
Burger King	$320,000–$1,900,000
Jimmy John's Gourmet Sandwich	$76,400–$203,400
Rita's Real Italian Ices	$115,000–$218,000
Cousins Subs	$156,700–$239,000
Heavenly Ham	$98,000–$236,000
Mazzio's Pizza	$309,000–$976,000
The Pizza Ranch	$273,500–$428,500
Baskin-Robbins USA	$189,427–$406,655
Perkins Family Restaurant	$1,500,000–$2,500,000
McDonald's	$413,000–$672,2000

If you have little or no track record, it can be very difficult to get needed bank loans to finance franchises or other
small business start-ups. A recent survey by the U.S. Census
Bureau found that even with the current low interest rates,
nearly 49 percent of small businesspeople said it had become
more difficult to get financing than in the past. And, even
with what is reputed to be a strong economy, the number of
small businesses reporting a growth in sales fell to its lowest
level since 1968. This is an ominous development because
smaller enterprises account for just over half of the output of
the entire American economy.

To add to the small businessperson's headaches, governments at all levels continue to pile on burdensome and often
contradictory layers of regulations. Safety inspectors from
OSHA have recently put out the word that they are going to
start applying rules designed for big companies—companies
that have at their disposal large human resources and safety
staffs, not to mention teams of corporate lawyers—to small
ventures as well. We've already seen in congressional hear-
ings how the IRS had been targeting smaller business and
family farms, which don't have the resources to fight back.

Look for payroll tax hikes, new health care mandates,
and additional mandatory increases in the minimum wage to
add substantially to the cost of maintaining employees. And
should one of those employees become disgruntled or seek
to exploit an employer, he or she can always find an eager
lawyer to help take the employer to the cleaners on a contin-
gency fee basis.

Thankfully, the United States is home to millions of entrepreneurs who are courageous, stubborn, or both and who
continue to fuel the vital small-business engine of its economy. Yet, as Joan Florence and many others have discovered,
"being your own boss" did not lead to the kind of income security, time freedom, and lifestyle they dreamed of. It may
have been an important step on the journey to financial independence, but it was not in itself a satisfactory destination.

GETTING ON THE RIGHT SIDE OF CHANGE

Renowned network marketer Todd Smith has seen small business from virtually every angle and has been successful at everything he has done. He has carefully considered the upsides and downsides of different business and career approaches—especially in the new economy.

A native of Elgin, Illinois, Todd plunged right into the working world upon graduating from high school and soon found himself earning a degree from the "School of Hard Knocks."

"In the summer of 1981, I got a job digging ditches and laying cable for the local cable TV company," Todd recalls. "I got laid off on my birthday! Then at Christmas time I got a temporary job with UPS to help handle the holiday rush. Guess what happened to me after Christmas?"

Laid off from two jobs in six months, Todd decided that entrepreneurship—being his own boss—had to be his ticket to success. He moved to Chicago at the urging of his older brother and started a silkscreen printing business that sold designer T-shirts, caps, and other items. "We started with a $3,000 investment and within four and a half years, we did a million dollars' worth of business and employed 25 people," he explains. It was an important learning experience for a young man still in his early twenties. "Sure I was my own boss," he points out, "but I was working 90 hours a week and pulling just $35,000 a year in personal income out of the business."

So at age 23, Todd started selling real estate. Soon he became the second-highest-producing real estate agent in Illinois, with an annual income of more than $400,000 in his peak year by the end of the 1980s.

But with a young and growing family, Todd found himself questioning the meaning of success. "I just got burned out," he explains. "I couldn't take my wife out on a date on a Friday night without the pager going off ten times. I'd come out of church on Sunday, and there'd be fifteen messages on my answering service. In the meantime, real estate was changing. Commissions went down a point, then another point, then down again.

"I finally reached a point where I made a decision. This was not what I wanted to do for the rest of my life. I wanted something different.

"I was very methodical about my search for a new venture," he reports. "I took out a yellow legal pad and listed everything I learned and wanted from a business.

> When you are freed of all the headaches inherent in the old model, you are able to focus all your attention on customers, sales, and income.

"I wanted something I could start part-time, something that could be built while maintaining my real estate income. I wanted to be in business for myself but be backed by strong products and a strong infrastructure. Where was this ideal business? I knew I would find it somewhere."

One day Todd saw a magazine ad that "hit all the hot buttons," he remembers. But when he found out it was to start a network marketing distributorship for Nu Skin Enterprises, Inc., Todd was skeptical and disappointed. But he kept an open mind.

"I came to understand the power of generating a leveraged income, that it could be done part-time, and that I could use all my contacts in real estate to full advantage. And I learned it was a portable business, which was vitally important because we had already decided we wanted to move to Florida and focus on our family's quality of life."

Todd began his Nu Skin distributorship in May, 1990, and within four months built an organization of more than 1,600 distributors and generated $200,000 in sales volume. His first check after four months of part-time effort was for $31,600.

He later moved on to Rexall Showcase International, where he is among that company's top income earners. But it's more than money that pleases Todd.

"As for myself, I have zero stress. My commute to work is however many steps it takes to walk from the bedroom to the office in my home. And the way I look at it, I'm really in two businesses. One is transforming the health, longevity, and vitality of people through unique products that work. And the other is transforming the finances and lifestyles of ambitious people through a unique business opportunity."

From his position of success as a New Professional, Todd Smith now believes that "the majority of the population could be self-employed in the near future whether they are ready or not. You can no longer depend on your employer or your job to provide for your security or even to be around tomorrow. How long could you last?

"If you are an employee who works for someone else, you should find a new model to take control of your finances."

The same is true for business owners or those with their own medical, legal, and other professional practices. "If you own a business, you're not exempt," Todd says. "Most are being crushed with overhead, taxes, and employee headaches. Owning a traditional small business can be a financial death trap—you pay a fortune to get in, and all you pull out is an average income."

Just as with the situation facing employees working for someone else, the old model of owning your own business and being your own boss is gone, too.

Many people confront this new economic landscape and ignore the changes. They continue to rely on that which can no longer be relied on for their financial security and quality of life. Others play the blame game, lashing out bitterly at corporations, the government, or the state of the world in general. But Todd Smith and other New Professionals remind us: "You can protect yourself and free yourself from dependence on the old models. You have options."

Along with every period of tumultuous change come exciting new possibilities for those willing to see them and seize them. Many New Professionals are finding a new business model in network marketing, one that blends the best attributes that traditional employment and small business ownership used to provide but that also offers advantages found nowhere else:

- It is a home-based business opportunity. There is no store, no lease—just a phone, a fax, and a personal computer. Your commute lasts for as long as it takes you to walk down the hall.

- It entails no employees, payroll, schedules, payroll taxes, workers compensation claims—no employee headaches.

- It offers a potential for a rapid increase in income and for high income, because when you are freed of all the headaches inherent in the old model, you are able to focus all your attention on customers, sales, and income.

- You develop a secure diversified income, a residual income that pays you over and over for the same activity and that pays you for the efforts of others you bring into the business.

Putting yourself on the right side of global economic change does not necessarily mean throwing your current career and lifestyle overboard. It does mean managing your career in a flexible, diversified, and entrepreneurial fashion. The days of working one job for one paycheck are dying. An entrepreneurial career means diversifying your activities and developing several streams of income. For some, that may mean a job or practice with a network marketing business on the side. Others may pursue their business full-time and invest some of the profits in other businesses, stocks, or properties. But for all it can mean retaking control of your financial and personal life—successfully navigating a stormy ocean of change.

Investment guru and author Robert Kiyosaki sums it up this way: "It's time for people to begin minding their own business. A job means you're being paid to mind somebody else's business. In this new economy, you're paid to mind your own business.

"The idea that you can go to school, get good grades, find a safe, secure job, and have the company and the government take care of you is fundamentally of the Industrial Age. It was a good program—as long as you were born prior to 1930."

Richard and Mary Reed of Minnesota came to understand this reality. They say they have always been entrepreneurs at heart, but coming from conventional and conservative backgrounds, Richard went the corporate route, while Mary tested the waters in different types of business. "We always believed in network marketing but never had a whole lot of success finding the right company," Mary says.

When Mary started a business through Pre-Paid Legal Services, Richard continued on with his successful corporate career. But after twenty-five years at it, he grew tired of that life—tired of making big money for others. He was also becoming realistically fearful that a younger person could replace him. Mary recalls, "When we attended an awards trip a couple of years ago for the top producers in Richard's company, we looked around at the crowd and didn't see any happiness. What we saw and heard was the dread of going

> An entrepreneurial career means diversifying your activities and developing several streams of income.

back home and starting on next year's goals. There were bigger goals, split-up accounts and territories, more travel, and
fewer rewards."

The Reeds knew it was now time to venture out on their
own. "We've really enjoyed the freedom of working for ourselves and being able to contribute to the launching of our
company in Minnesota," says Mary.

"It's a great feeling to be able to look the doubting relatives in the eye and proudly tell them that your company has
been number one on the American Stock Exchange and on
the *Forbes* list of best small companies in America. None of
the companies any of them has ever worked for has that
credibility.

"The awesome part is it's just beginning!"

At a time of great economic upheaval, network marketing is stepping in with an opportunity for people to make a
transition to new opportunities and a more secure income.
As the pace of this economic change accelerates and as more
people realize they need, and indeed have, better options, the
ranks of the New Professionals will grow at a tremendous
rate in the United States and around the world.

But as we'll see in the next chapter, a lot more than
money is driving this growth.

The Quest for
Time Freedom

What does it mean to be impoverished? How do you know when you've gone bankrupt? It depends on your definition.

Is it possible to make a six-figure income, pay all your bills on time, be sought after for your consulting services by the biggest companies in America—and still be in a state of poverty? Tom Bissmeyer knows from personal experience that it is.

"I was taught the old school method of success," he explains. "Get a good education, work hard, keep your record clean, and everything will work out fine. So that's what I set out to do."

After getting both bachelor's and master's degrees in business and finance, Tom went to work for an international accounting and consulting firm. "This was my first exposure to the fact that hard work wasn't the only thing that would get you promoted. It also depended on who you knew." After being recruited away to be part of a capital acquisition team for a large real estate development company, Tom seemed poised for success. It was the mid-1980s, the economy was booming, and Tom and his team raised more than $100 million in financing in one year. The reward for their efforts, however, was a very small bonus.

"This taught me another valuable lesson about the business world," he explains. "If you truly want to be paid what you're worth, then you had better be the one writing the check!"

With that lesson learned, Tom decided to go into business for himself and, through strong effort and some lucky breaks, built a successful speaking, training, and consulting business. He advised some of the top companies in America and became a sought-after lecturer on financial planning.

There was just one problem. "I soon found myself working seven days a week," Tom explains. "Often I would do corporate consulting during the week and contract speaking on the weekends. This went on for several years. I found myself traveling in excess of 250 days a year."

From a financial perspective, Tom could not complain. His earnings were well into the six-figure range. "But from a family and life perspective, I was bankrupt," he admits. "Even though I was providing for my family economically, I sure wasn't being the kind of husband and father I wanted to be to my family."

A collision was coming. Tom remembers hearing his daughter's first words over the telephone and learning about her first steps during a call from his wife, Lynne. When the couple's second child was born in 1992, Tom was determined to take part. He took three weeks off. "My family needed me and I wanted to be there, but I lost over $40,000 in income because I wasn't working."

He felt trapped. "I realized I had built a monster that was eating me alive. I didn't have any idea how to achieve a balance between work and the other parts of my life. If I slowed down even for just a second, income slowed right down behind me," Tom said.

At least becoming a consultant was a choice Tom made himself. In today's economy, many companies are making that choice for you. As discussed in the last chapter, the new corporate ethic is to shed as much long-term cost and obligation as possible to meet both the test of global competition and the test of Wall Street, which habitually celebrates company downsizing and layoffs with a rise in the stock price. Outsourcing and turning employees into consultants is, from the company's point of view, an effective way to get services without all of the overhead and obligations that a regular full-time employee can bring.

Some professionals greet this development favorably. More flexibility, a greater feeling of independence, the ability to take on more than one project, and diversify work and income can indeed be some of the benefits. But Tom Bissmeyer has a warning for all those who choose or are forced to enter the consulting world.

"I realized that there is something out there that is worse than a boss; it's called clients. They drove my schedule and my travel. They didn't care if it was my child's birthday, my anniversary, or something else important in our lives. They basically said if you want to continue to be our consultant, you must be available when we need you and where we need you. If not, we can easily find someone else."

By 1992, Tom had had enough. "I always considered myself a student of success. I became convinced there was a perfect business out there that would allow me to continue to work for myself, generate above-average income, control

> **M**any of us have been in the position of trying to convince ourselves to make an important decision where the evidence and logic are so compelling that the necessity to act just screams out at us. But still we hesitate and resist.

my own travel schedule, and build a leveraged income. I was determined to find it!"

But you don't find mid-six-figure incomes like the one the Bissmeyers enjoyed just like that. Through a process of analysis and elimination, Tom began to sort out the possibilities. "I looked at other types of consulting that wouldn't require as much travel, but I would still have had all the client issues to deal with. I looked at franchising, but I just couldn't get excited about putting half a million dollars on the line and managing a bunch of teenagers for a living."

As he winnowed out less attractive options, Tom took his first serious look at network marketing. He had been exposed to the business before but, like many upscale professionals, accumulated a good deal of mental baggage about it. Nonetheless, he decided to keep an open mind and for the first time really study the industry and its track record.

"The more I began to read and learn about the industry, the more excited I became," Tom reports. "I really began to dig. I looked at several companies and studied the compensation plans closely.

"Network marketing seemed to offer everything I was looking for: something I could begin part-time and then move into full-time; a leveraged income as opposed to one dependent solely on my own efforts; an unlimited income potential if I were willing to work really hard at it; and a flexible schedule that would allow me to spend time with my family and keep those parts of my current career I really enjoyed, such as public speaking.

"I could choose whom I would work with. The capital needed to enter the business was extremely low. I could not only work out of my home, but because this kind of business is a portable business, Lynne and I could also choose where we wanted that home to be!"

Many of us have been in the position of trying to convince ourselves to make an important decision about our lives and careers where the evidence and logic are so compelling that the necessity to act just screams out at us. But still we hesitate and resist and often fail to take that first step. Tom felt those same pressures and anxieties. The analysis he had created was so overwhelming, but he still worried, "What are my friends going to think? What are my colleagues going to say? What if I fail?"

His resolve to act was made all the more difficult by the fact that this was a person on whom society had already hung a great big "success" sign—a high income, prestigious clients, notoriety as a sought-after speaker, a loving wife, and two children, one girl and one boy. Perfect.

But Tom overcame his doubts and complacency, and he stopped living by others' definition of success. He entered network marketing in the spring of 1993. "I believe one of the biggest keys to early success in network marketing for successful professionals is to develop a strong 'why.' My why was so big that I was able to look right past the naysayers."

Success came to Tom Bissmeyer—again. But he wouldn't want anyone to think it was easy. "It took a lot of hard work to get it going, and I had plenty of setbacks along the way. There were many times I felt like quitting during the first couple of years. By having a strong why, I was able to stay focused during the tough times."

Tom's toughest decision after starting his network marketing business was to go full-time after nine months, even though he had yet to rise to the level of his consulting and speaking income. "I just took a leap of faith," he says.

It paid off. Today, Tom is one of the most successful network marketers in the country, earning an income approaching seven figures. "And I fully anticipate it will double within the next couple of years," he adds.

But more important is the balance Tom has restored to his life. "I have complete control of my schedule now," he explains. "I take my children's school calendar and plan my business activities around that—what a reversal!"

Recently the Bissmeyers fulfilled another dream by relocating to the foothills of the Rocky Mountains. "One of the greatest joys of this business is that I can work out of my home," Tom says. One of those seemingly very ordinary but special moments occurred recently that keeps coming back to Tom as a reminder of how his life has changed for the better: "I was in my home office doing a three-way phone call with a distributor. The entire family was in the office with me. My wife was on the computer e-mailing some friends. My daughter was at my desk doing her homework. My son was drawing a picture. Our dog was lying in front of the fireplace.

> Can you count on politicians in Washington to make necessary changes now to forestall the need for more drastic changes later?

"I thought I had to sacrifice those important family moments in order to be successful and provide for my family. I was wrong. Boy, was I wrong!"

Tom Bissmeyer knows that the trap he was in has snared many other successful professionals. "I am amazed by the number of well-paid professionals who tell me that they are unhappy with their careers and their lives," he says. "When they tell me their goals, they are remarkably similar to the ones I had been chasing but found elusive.

"I can sincerely relate to their frustrations because I had them, too. I really believe I have found a better way to live and work, and that's why one of my missions is to tell the professional world that there is a better way."

Tom Bissmeyer is but one of the 76 million baby boomers—those born between 1946 and 1965—who find themselves increasingly focused on the quality of life as well as the material abundance of life. For scores of professionals, time has become a cruel commodity. There's too little of it now. There will seem to be too much of it later.

They face "time poverty" now in traditional careers—endless hours of commuting, working, and traveling that pull them away from family, community, physical fitness, and relaxation. Yet they will spend more years in retirement than any generation in human history, struggling to stay out of financial poverty. Many will be forced to depend on collapsing government entitlement programs and meager personal savings in a vain struggle to maintain some semblance of their abundant material lifestyle.

Aspiring New Professionals invariably ask this question: How can we better balance the conflicting time demands of career and family now, while building a secure and plentiful income as well as a sense of purpose in life during what we hope is a lengthy retirement? This question takes on a special urgency when one places the demographic trends and problems plaguing government entitlements alongside the economic uncertainties discussed in the last chapter.

THE DEMOGRAPHIC TIME BOMB

The aging of the boomers and the likelihood that many will live to age 90, 100, and even longer presents society with enormous implications. Like the upheavals imposed by the rise of the global economy and the destruction of traditional corporate employment, the aging of the society is driving many to change their assumptions and patterns of work and lifestyle.

Boomers are turning 50 at the rate of 10,000 a day. Beginning in 2011, when the first boomers reach the age of 65, the ranks of America's elderly will explode. At the same time, overall population growth will continue to decline, and the ratio of working-age Americans to retired Americans will decline, perhaps as low as two workers for every retiree. The elderly are living longer, and at the same time young adults are having fewer children.

The aging of America, a pattern that is being replicated all over the world, presents profound challenges. It also serves as one more powerful trend driving many professionals to the alternative career and lifestyle model offered by network marketing.

Boomers represent the most affluent generation in human history. They've grown accustomed to a life of hard work that brings rich rewards, and they don't want to have to give it all up. Yet they are coming to understand that because they are so large in number, there is no way the government's social safety net of retirement and medical insurance programs can possibly survive the onslaught of boomer retirees intact.

Many now realize how poorly prepared they are for retirement. By one estimate, 96 percent of all pension plans will pay at most 20 percent of our current salary when we retire. Can you live on that?

According to *Success* magazine, a person 35 years old today making $60,000 will need $150,000 a year at age 65 just to maintain his or her current lifestyle. That means this person would have to save $44,000 a year—100 percent of after-tax income—to live at that level in retirement.

Many Americans are taking some steps to prepare. Twenty-five million participate in 401k plans that collectively have amassed a trillion dollars in assets. Thirty-seven percent of U.S. households invest in mutual funds. Yet, only an estimated 2 percent who reach the age of 65 are financially independent.

If you are one of the majority of people who have not put into place an effective strategy to retire in good health and sound finances, you've picked the worst possible time to be in that condition. That's because all around the world a demographic time bomb is ticking away. When it explodes, rich and poor countries alike will be flooded with retirees looking to governments and a proportionally shrinking population of younger workers to provide for their income, medical, and lifestyle needs.

Statistics from the Bureau of the Census are usually dry and antiseptic, but in this case they tell a dramatic story:

- America's population continues to age. In 1860, half the population was under the age of 20. In 1994, half were 34 or older. By the year 2030, half will be 39 or older.

- From 1900 to 1994, the elderly population—those aged 65 and older—increased eleven times over, compared to just a threefold increase for those under the age of 65. Until the year 2010, the rate of growth of the elderly will be relatively modest but will then explode from 2010 to 2030 as the baby-boom generation retires.

A person 35 years old today making $60,000 will need $150,000 a year at age 65 just to maintain his or her current lifestyle.

- Since 1960, the number of Americans aged 65 or older has increased 100 percent, compared to 45 percent for the population as a whole. The number of people aged 85 and over has increased 274 percent.

- By 2000, America will be home to 35.3 million people aged 65 or older—12.8 percent of the population. By 2030, 70.1 million Americans will be 65 or older—20.1 percent of the population.

- By the year 2000, 12.4 million will be between the ages of 75 and 84; 4.3 million will be 85 or older. By 2030, those numbers will explode to 23.3 million and 8.8 million, respectively!

- Globally, 357 million people were aged 65 or older in 1994—about 6 percent of the world's population. The world's elderly are growing at a rate of 2.8 percent a year, compared with 1.6 percent growth for the population as a whole. Over half of the world's elderly live in poorer developing nations today. By 2030, two-thirds of the elderly will live in those countries.

Much of America's aging process has been brought about by the welcome news of longer life expectancies. When the nation was founded, life expectancy at birth was just 35 years. In the mid-1800s, it was 42; by 1900, it was about 48. And as we entered the new millennium, it reached 78! Social and financial impacts aside, this has been a remarkable human achievement, owed in large part to medical advances as well as a free economic system that has improved living standards.

But longer life spans are not the only demographic shift we're seeing in our country and many others. Lower birthrates mean that fewer workers are available to take the place of retirees—and that presents a tremendous challenge for the "mature" developed economies of the West. In Japan, a country with one of the longest life expectancies in the world, the percentage of the population aged 65 and over has already exceeded 16 percent—and by 2030 the overall population in that country is projected to be less than it is today.

How do you sustain economic growth and collect sufficient taxes to support growing numbers of retirees who have ever-increasing medical needs, when relatively fewer and fewer workers are coming into the system?

In 1950, there were sixteen workers for every retirement-age Social Security beneficiary in the United States. By 1960, the ratio had narrowed to 5 to 1. Today it is just over 3 to 1. And by the year 2030, it will be 2 to 1.

The United States is not alone in grappling with a declining ratio of workers to retirees. According to the *Los Angeles Times,* here is the current situation in some of the world's major economies:

Country	# of Workers	# of Retirees	Ratio
Britain	27 million	9 million	3:1
Canada	14 million	4 million	3.5:1
France	25 million	11 million	2.3:1
Germany	32 million	11 million	2.9:1
Italy	20 million	21 million	0.95:1
Japan	70 million	17 million	4.1:1
U.S.	147 million	44 million	3.3:1

Life expectancy in each of these countries actually exceeds that of the United States. As citizens live longer and birthrates hold steady or decline, expect these ratios to decline throughout the world's most advanced countries, severely testing both their prosperity and their social cohesion. The Census Bureau concludes:

> Demographers have called out an early warning that the Baby-Boom generation is approaching the elderly ranks. American society has tried to adjust to the size and needs of the Baby-Boom generation throughout the stages of the life cycle. Just as this generation had an impact on the educational system (with "split shift" schools and youth in college) and the labor force (with job market pressures), the Baby-Boom cohorts will place tremendous strain on the myriad specialized services and programs required of an elderly population.
>
> A window of opportunity now exists for planners and policymakers to prepare for the aging of the Baby-Boom generation.

SOCIAL INSECURITY

Will those planners and policymakers heed the early warning and act judiciously to shore up the programs designed to support retirees in their old age? Can you count on politicians in Washington to make necessary changes now to forestall the need for more drastic changes later? And even if they find the political backbone to do so, will government programs under any scenario provide the income security you need to retain a semblance of your current lifestyle? These are questions New Professionals have already asked—and answered.

Started in 1935, Social Security worked reasonably well for the first half-century of its existence. In fact, it helped substantially reduce poverty among the elderly. It worked because there were many more workers paying in than there were retirees pulling money out—not to mention the fact that the initial retirement age of 65 actually exceeded a man's life expectancy at the time!

With so many boomers in the workforce, as well as a long string of payroll tax increases, the Social Security trust fund will continue to take in more than it sends out until 2013. Then the draining of the fund starts, as fewer workers pay into the system and boomers begin to retire. Interest on the current surplus will close the gap for a while, but by 2030, without changes in the system, Social Security will become insolvent. Even if the big budget surpluses now projected in Washington actually materialize, they will only buy a few extra years for the current system.

The burdens on the system are growing, yet many Americans are highly dependent on the program's benefits:

- For 63 percent of beneficiaries, Social Security provides at least 50 percent of their total income.

- For 26 percent, it provides 90 percent of total income.

- For 14 percent, it is the only source of income.

The problem for workers and retirees is that each time politicians try to fix these problems, they come up with only two responses: increase taxes and reduce benefits.

For the typical American, Social Security is already an expensive program with low benefits and a poor rate of return on investment:

- The average monthly benefit for today's retiree is $663 for those retiring at 62 and $925 for those retiring at 65. The maximum monthly benefit is just over $1,300 per month.

- Employers and their employees each pay a tax of 7.65 percent (for Social Security retirement and disability as well as Medicare) on the first $72,600 of income, for a combined payroll price tag of 15.3 percent.

- Self-employed entrepreneurs, the engine of our economy, are hit particularly hard. They pay the whole tax themselves. Moreover, the amount of income subject to the Social Security payroll tax was hiked on January 1, 1999, and further scheduled increases have already been signed into law.

- Low inflation is on the whole a positive development, but it means that benefit increases tied to the inflation rate have in recent years been minuscule.

- The retirement age is going up. It will gradually increase to 67.

- A particularly sore point for investment-savvy boomers is the fact that the average rate of return for their dollars "invested" in Social Security is less than 2 percent—worse than even a passbook savings account. Most believe they could do much better in the stock market, which explains the growing interest in a partial privatization of the system.

What a bargain! Higher taxes, a poor rate of return, delayed retirements, and benefits that for most won't come close to sustaining their current lifestyle. On top of that, the system will one day be faced with insolvency due to the aging of the population. The question facing boomers is, Can you get ahead of all this through savings and investments alone? For most the answer is no.

The same dilemma confronts prospective retirees all over the world. The *Los Angeles Times* recently reviewed the status of various government retirement programs and the taxes required to pay for them:

Japan: **Retirement age to increase from 60 to 65; shared payroll tax to rise to 29.8 percent by 2026**

Britain: **Maximum benefit from government pension reduced from 25 percent of wages to 20 percent; retirement age for women to be increased from 60 to 65**

Canada: **Shared payroll tax to rise from 5.85 percent to 9.9 percent in 2003; benefits to be gradually reduced, particularly for upper-income retirees**

France: **Retirement age to increase from 60 to 65; benefits to be calculated on best 25 years of earnings rather than 15; workers to pay into the system for 40 years, up from 37.5**

Germany: **A 1 percent increase in the federal value-added tax to be imposed to help pay for pensions; benefits to be reduced from 70 percent of previous earnings to 64 percent**

Italy: **Retirement age, now 57 for women and 62 for men, to increase to 65 for both; civil servants to work until age 67**

HEALTH CARE: AN ADDITIONAL CONCERN

Inevitably accompanying the impacts of aging societies are concerns about the growing expense of and lack of access to health care. Consider these disturbing reports and developments:

- Nearly 15 percent of the entire output of the U.S. economy is spent on health care, a share that will rise to 20 percent by 2020 and a greater share than that of other major developed nations, where the average is 8 percent.

- Despite this enormous cost, 44 million Americans—over 16 percent of the population—have no health insurance. A million people lost coverage in 1998, following 1.7 million in 1997.

- An estimated 10.7 million American children are unprotected by health care coverage.

- The majority of Americans—61.4 percent—depend on employers for health insurance. Yet many smaller companies, finding costs skyrocketing and the potential for more government regulation and increased liability increasing, are preparing to bail out of the system if necessary. According to a Public Opinion Strategies survey conducted in February, 1998, 57 percent of small employers say they would be very likely or somewhat likely to stop providing health care coverage should major new regulatory measures, now under consideration in Washington, be enacted into law. Forty-six percent of those surveyed say they would be likely to stop providing coverage if health premiums rise another 20 percent. Since more than half of working-age Americans are employed by these smaller firms, the findings portend a substantial future threat to the mainstay of our health care financing system—employer-sponsored coverage.

- An analysis in *Inc.* magazine concludes that "companies with fewer than 100 employees get little attention in the [health] insurance marketplace; they are the small fish that everyone throws back." Even a low number of claims won't stop massive premium increases for many small companies, the magazine reports.

- Sixty-one percent of insured Americans now get their coverage from managed care organizations, and, fair or unfair, many of them don't like it. A *Newsweek* poll in December, 1998, found that more than half of Americans believe HMOs are harming the quality of medical care. A recent *New York Times* survey found that 58 percent believe that managed care organizations are impeding doctors' ability to control treatment. Many doctors deeply resent what they view as the intrusion of accountants, insurance companies, lawyers, and health care bureaucrats in their relationships with patients. That approach is driving many to network marketing, where they can reaffirm the tradition of caregiving that brought them to medicine in the first place.

- Under intense pressure to hold down costs and at the same time increase service options, some insurance companies are bailing out of the system. Reacting to the announcement in December, 1998, that Prudential Insurance Company would sell its ailing health care operations to Aetna, the *Los Angeles Times* called the move the latest in a "flood of defections from the ravaged managed care business. Prudential is the most dramatic example yet of an insurance company exiting the troubled health care arena. The proposed sale alarmed doctors and consumer groups, who fear the new company would have the power to force patients to accept fewer services and doctors to accept lower fees."

Millions of working Americans are finding the cost of health insurance rising, its availability slipping, and the quality of care declining. If that were not enough, the government's Medicare program, designed to cover all seniors, is actuarially unsound. The last thing it can afford is an onslaught of millions of retiring baby boomers after the turn of the century.

Medicare is caught in the same demographic squeeze as Social Security. In 1995, there were 3.9 workers paying taxes to cover each Medicare beneficiary. The Medicare trustees estimate that by 2030, there will be just 2.2 workers for every beneficiary. Meanwhile, abuse of the system is rampant. A recent inspector general's report found that the Medicare program wastes $1.03 billion a year by overpaying for certain prescription drugs.

Senator John Breaux of Louisiana, who chairs the national Bipartisan Commission on the Future of Medicare, says it bluntly: "We have problems today with 39 million people on Medicare. What are we going to do when [millions of] baby boomers start walking through that Medicare door in the year 2010 and saying, 'Here's my card, where's my treatment?' We are going to have a system that is insolvent and can no longer afford to pay for the treatment."

Stanford University Professor Victor Fuchs told *Business Week*, "Although people justifiably worry about Social Security, paying for the old folks' health care is the real 800-pound gorilla facing the economy." By 2020, the share of the U.S. gross domestic product spent on seniors' care alone will double to 10 percent.

> Without changes in the system, Social Security will become insolvent. Even if the big budget surpluses actually materialize, they will only buy a few extra years.

As is the case with the projected insolvency of Social Security farther down the line, the familiar government response to Medicare's dilemma is to raise taxes and cut benefits. But add the crises facing both programs together and it's impossible to envision closing the gap with taxes. The payroll tax rate on young Americans that would be required to maintain these programs "as is," figures Hudson Institute fellow William Styring, would "probably be 37 percent by 2020 and 51 percent by 2030."

Those rates, he continues, "are not only unthinkable but politically impossible and an economic wrecking ball that would kill an incentive for the young to work, save, and invest."

The more likely reality that will face boomers and their families will be "fend for yourselves!" According to *Business Week,* Professor Fuchs "estimated that annual health care spending per senior will soar from $9,200 in 1995 to almost $25,000 (in 1995 dollars) in 2020—a hike that would strain the resources of both the government and seniors themselves, who on average shoulder over a third of their own health bills."

Considering the myriad financial pressures and increased demands placed on the U.S. health care system, Hudson's William Styring believes there's only one logical prognosis to be issued, as stark as it is—the "financial collapse of the U.S. health care system."

KEEPING A SENSE OF PURPOSE

While many professionals contemplate the prospect of financial poverty in their later years, they are also concerned about staying active and maintaining a strong sense of purpose when they retire. New Professionals believe they have found that network marketing addresses these concerns.

As we will discuss in detail in later chapters, with its emphasis on a flexible business opportunity, access for all, and the value of residual income, network marketing responds to the boomers' desire to be financially secure when they retire. There is no mandatory retirement age in this industry and no less-than-golden parachutes. If you're successful, the checks keep coming until you depart this earth and bequeath that income to your heirs. You can take a lengthy trip, have major surgery, and even be confined to a bed or wheelchair, and still have a network marketing business work for you. Just as important, network marketing allows senior citizens to maintain an interesting activity that challenges them and gives them a purpose. Maintaining a sense of purpose and embracing a set of interesting and challenging goals are important for everyone, but particularly for those in or near retirement.

It's a troubling but well-documented fact that suicides among the elderly, especially men, are on the rise. In fact, the Census Bureau reports that elderly men are more likely to commit suicide than to die in motor vehicle accidents. Sometimes they take their elderly spouses with them.

George and Elnor White were married for fifty-eight years. In November 1998, the *Washington Post* reported, their bodies were found in the garage of their suburban Baltimore home. Elnor was killed by her husband with his World War II army pistol. He then turned it on himself. "In homicide-suicides involving older couples, depression is often as much the killer as any bullet," the newspaper concluded. "With cruel speed it transformed . . . one of Maryland's most respected trial lawyers into a despairing, paranoid man, a man certain that the future held only penury and pain for himself and his wife. No balance sheet, no doctor, no loved one could convince him otherwise."

The *Post* goes on to report that in Florida, "where retirees make up about 20 percent of the population, an elderly homicide-suicide is reported on average at least once a month." This troubling trend underscores the need for countries with growing legions of elderly to open up and make room for their experience and continuing contributions—for their sake and for the benefit of society as a whole.

Indeed, in a report called "The New Millennium American," analysts at PaineWebber note that the desire to remain productive, useful, and challenged is a central part of the profile of the baby boom generation:

> Unlike their parents who grew up amid the hardships of the
> Depression and World War II, baby boomers today do not
> view a leisurely retirement as their reward for years of hard
> work and sacrifice. Boomers have always been work centered
> and will remain so. . . . For many boomers, work is a career

and a way of life, not a job; it provides a social network of professional contacts and is the source of inner satisfaction as well as a way to pay the mortgage.

The authors go on to cite public opinion research that reveals:

- A large majority—75 percent—of baby boomers expect to keep working after they retire from their current careers.

- But only 15 percent want to do so in their former occupation at reduced pay.

- Another 28 percent want to work part-time in a different occupation.

- 10 percent want to start a new business.

"Boomers will not retire," the analysts conclude. "They will retread. As they will grow older, they will restructure their lives so as to relieve stress and work on their own terms."

Driving aging boomers' search for new projects and directions is the sense among many that as life progresses, their current goals are going unfulfilled. The PaineWebber report found that "in recent years, many baby boomers have increasingly felt the pang of unmet expectations. Now that most of them are in their forties—and despite continued material prosperity—many boomers feel that they haven't 'made a difference' or 'made the world a better place.'"

The analysts continue: "Many boomers have still not found inner happiness—to the contrary they are probably the most stressed generation in history." Reviewing survey research, they identify this stress as coming from these factors:

The normal responsibilities of middle age—career, finances, caring for children and elderly parents. Additional

pressures come from a sense of no job security and the failure to save for retirement.

The disappointment of their expectations. "Boomers are for the most part middle-class, middle-aged, and middle of the road, a state that many of them revolted against when they were growing up."

Too many decisions to make. "The downside of the Information Age is that people are overloaded with information and choices." In a recent survey of all Americans, a full 40 percent said that the lack of time was a bigger problem for them than the lack of money.

Echoing a point discussed in the last chapter, the PaineWebber authors conclude that we have indeed entered a period of cradle-to-grave entrepreneurialism. "More and more Americans are being forced to behave like entrepreneurs in managing their careers, supervising their children's education, and planning their retirement," they write. "Many people of 'retirement age' are likely to choose the stimulation of work over the monotony of having nothing to do."

Network marketing is thus ideally positioned to fill not only an "income gap" for its business builders but also a "meaning gap" for those at or near retirement as well as for middle-aged boomers dissatisfied with their current contribution to society. It's easy to dismiss the industry's oft-repeated refrain of "making a positive difference in people's lives" as corporate sloganeering. But it's a vision that attracts many highly skilled but disillusioned professionals to network marketing opportunities. They see a deeper personal happiness that can flow from being part of something larger than themselves.

TIME POVERTY AND ITS TOLL ON FAMILY

The aging of society impacts more than just the elderly; in fact, it portends huge consequences for succeeding generations of younger Americans. Many elderly or near-elderly are concerned not only about their income and health security in later years but also about being a burden on children and grandchildren. Those family members in turn wonder how they can properly maintain their elders in comfortable surroundings.

Longer life expectancies are creating several phenomena seldom seen before:

- The old are taking care of the very old. According to the Census Bureau, more and more people in their fifties and sixties are likely to have surviving parents, aunts, and uncles. They "will face the concern and expense of caring for their very old, frail relatives since so many people now live long enough to experience multiple chronic illnesses," the bureau reports.

- Furthermore, a sizable proportion of the baby boomers have remained childless (26 percent as of 1990). That will translate into big increases in the number of seniors who are unable to count on children for care and must therefore be institutionalized.

- A so-called sandwich generation has emerged, consisting of those boomers who find themselves paying for their children's college education and the care of their elderly parents or grandparents all at once. How many of us are financially equipped to do that and at the same time save and invest for our own retirements?

These accumulating financial pressures, coupled with the insecurities now inherent in the workplace, have in recent years pushed the concerns of children to the background. The traditional family is under serious strain:

- Since 1970, the number of unmarried couples with children under 16 years of age has increased 548 percent.

- In 1993, 31 percent of all babies were born to unwed mothers—up dramatically from 10.7 percent in the 1970s. In 1950, it was just 3.9 percent.

- There are nearly eight million single-parent households with children at home.

A majority of working-age women are now employed outside the home. This has been a positive development for most women, but the impact on children of both single-parent households and working-couple households is unmistakable. Denied the close supervision and nurturing of times past, many youth are drawn into or are victims of destructive behavior.

Youth crime is on the rise, even as crime rates overall level off. More than 1.5 million young people in the United States are arrested for crimes each year. Young men under the age of 18 commit 17 percent of all violent crimes.

Drug use among young people is on the way back up after a hopeful but short-lived dip in the mid-1980s. A recent comprehensive survey of junior and senior high school students uncovered these troubling findings:

- Since 1991, the proportion of eighth graders who had taken any illicit drug in the previous twelve months has almost doubled, from 11 percent to 21 percent.

- At the same time, the proportion of tenth graders taking those drugs rose by two-thirds, from 20 percent to 33 percent.

- The proportion of twelfth graders taking an illicit drug in the past twelve months has increased from 27 percent to 39 percent.

Researchers are discovering further consequences for children when parents find they must both work harder and longer outside the home. "Parents are right to be concerned about the squeeze on family time," the *Washington Post* concluded in an in-depth report. "Specialists say that children benefit intellectually and socially when the whole family is together—by listening to adult conversation, learning to relate to siblings, and getting a clearer sense of the family's moral values."

A recent study by Search Institute, an organization specializing in research on children, examined 270,000 sixth to twelfth graders in 600 communities nationwide. According to the *Washington Post,* the institute discovered that "children who spent at least four evenings a week at home with their families and had frequent, in-depth conversations with their parents were less likely to have sex and use alcohol or drugs." Another study that involved the taping of dinner conversations between parents and children in the Boston area for eight years uncovered this interesting result: "Preschoolers who were exposed to mealtime discussions among parents and siblings did better on vocabulary and reading tests in elementary school than those who weren't."

> **W**ith its emphasis on a flexible business opportunity, access for all, and the value of residual income, network marketing responds to the desire to be financially secure upon retirement.

Many busy parents, intuitively aware of research findings like these, have made well-intentioned efforts to reserve so-called quality time with their children. But further research shows that the notion of scheduling their children as if they were just another entry on their appointment calendars doesn't work and misses the point. In a recent report, *Newsweek* states:

Experts say that many of the most important elements in children's lives—regular routines and domestic rituals, consistency, the sense that their parents know and care about them—are exactly what's jettisoned when quality time substitutes for quantity time. . . . Parents who race in the door at 7:30 P.M. and head straight for the fax machine are making it perfectly clear where their loyalties lie, and the kids are showing the scars.

Working women appear particularly conflicted by the dilemma of reconciling the demands of work and home. "I think she's doing okay," one working woman told *Newsweek* about her young daughter. "If it were up to me, I'd spend more time with her. I wish I were able to stay home, but that's just not possible."

Eager to aid the family finances, pursue career aspirations, and raise a family all at once, many women attempt to carry a near-impossible burden. While *Newsweek* found that men are picking up a greater share of child-rearing and household responsibilities, the burden still falls most heavily on women, whether or not they are also working outside the home.

> Network marketing is ideally positioned to fill not only an "income gap" but also a "meaning gap."

Specifically, women employed outside the home were found to devote an average of 6.6 hours per week to the most essential childcare responsibilities, such as bathing, feeding, reading, and playing. The average employed man devotes just 2.5 hours to these activities.

As we saw in the case of the Bissmeyers, the right opportunity in network marketing offers working parents a chance to put their family first, while still enjoying the financial benefits and personal satisfaction that comes from building their own business. Why should anyone make the awful choice between a rewarding career and good parenting when there is a way to do both?

TIME FREEDOM—
THE PERK OF THE NEW CENTURY

Perhaps more than any other single factor—more than the uncertainties present in the new economy and concerns about being economically and emotionally prepared for long years in retirement—the quest for time freedom is driving successful professionals away from traditional careers to alternatives such as network marketing. With the pool of available workers shrinking, this quest is not only fueling the growth of this industry but also forcing others to overthrow their own "9 to 5" work cultures.

Business Week confirms what our personal discussions with hundreds of New Professionals uncovered:

> Most workers' No. 1 concern has nothing to do with getting free flying lessons or health insurance for their pets. It doesn't even have to do with chopping the hours they work or fattening their paychecks. Rather, employees' top priority is getting the flexibility to control their own time and when, how, and where they do their jobs—giving them the freedom to finesse their own work-life balance.

The primary response to the growing demand for the time freedom perk is telecommuting. Thanks to low-cost information technology and communications, small business owners, the self-employed, and even many in the corporate and professional worlds are doing more work out of their homes. This has become a promising path for those trying to meet family responsibilities and avoid long commutes.

Link Resources has been conducting an ongoing survey of people who work at home and found they have been steadily increasing in numbers throughout the 1990s. At least one-third of all adult workers perform some work at home in at least one of the following categories, as detailed by *Inc.* magazine:

- Primarily self-employed home workers (12.1 million as of 1995) for whom self-employment is the primary source of income

- Part-time self-employed home workers (11.7 million) who hold multiple jobs and spend part of their time working from home

- Telecommuters (6.6 million), employees who work from home part- or full-time during normal business hours

- Corporate after-hours home workers (8.6 million), who use computers, phones, and faxes to do company work at home after normal business hours

In recent years, telecommuting in particular has become a popular and highly valued mode of work for professionals. Research using more recent data than the Link survey finds an estimated 20 million American telecommuters, those who perform some or all of their work tasks at home.

Telecommuting's acceptance by mainstream business is highly relevant to network marketing companies as they attempt to attract legions of distributors with much the same pitch: By working out of the home, you can better balance family and professional responsibilities, avoid long commutes, live where you want, and, in many cases, exercise more control over your own time and schedule. The embrace of telecommuting by top companies and professions helps break down a stigma that suggests if you work out of your home, it's because you can't find a prestigious job, you're "just a housewife," or you must not be very important or successful.

Jim reports that in the upper-middle-class neighborhood where he lives in Los Angeles, of the eight 30- to 50-year-old professionals living on his block, only one gets into his car and commutes to a job each day. The rest, including Jim, now work primarily out of their homes. They are not unemployed, underemployed, lazy, ill, or retired—they are New Professionals.

The appeal to employees is obvious. But why are big companies like AT&T, IBM, Arthur Andersen, and others stepping into this still largely uncharted terrain?

Why should anyone make the awful choice between a rewarding career and good parenting when there is a way to do both?

"Telecommuting has gotten an added boost from a strong economy in which employers must make accommodations to attract the best and brightest workers," *Business Week* concludes. "There are also environmental and political pressures as companies respond to Clean Air Act provisions that aim to cut traffic. And businesses want to pare real estate costs by creating 'hoteling' arrangements in which, say, ten people share a single cubicle on an as-needed basis."

While a stigma used to be attached to working at home ("He says he's a consultant, but he's really unemployed"), the concept has now put down strong roots in America's work culture. Good evidence of this could be seen in January, 2000, when OSHA announced that companies who permitted telecommuting would be held responsible and liable for the safety of their employees' home offices. The government would even launch some inspections of people's homes to insure that their dens complied with traditional workplaces' strict health and safety codes.

A storm of protest ensued. The business community said that if companies were going to start getting fined or sued because of clutter, inadequate lighting, or an inoperable smoke alarm in employees' homes, they would kiss telecommuting goodbye. Employees, protective of their opportunity to work at home and resentful of the prospect of government inspectors rummaging through their houses, joined businesses in howls of outrage. OSHA withdrew its ruling two days later, a quick and rare reversal on the part of government regulators.

Whether you work for yourself or someone else, working at home can be a perfect accommodation between the competing demands of career and family. It is one of the most powerful magnets drawing New Professionals to network marketing.

Yet how long will it take for your company to catch on? "For all the hype about the new economy, most jobs are still modeled on the clock-punching culture of the industrial past," reports *Business Week*. "Like wired-up assembly-line drones, people are expected to show up Monday through Friday and do their work in eight-, nine-, or ten-hour chunks of time."

When it comes to the quest for time freedom, network marketing remains light-years ahead of traditional employment and business ownership. Helping people regain control of their lives and allowing them to better balance the competing priorities of career and family is a major attraction to and contribution of modern network marketing. The promise of time freedom, without sacrificing an abundant material lifestyle, is not only attracting more successful professionals to its own ranks but also contributing to welcome changes in traditional occupations themselves.

Six years ago, when Jack Hawk was all of 25 years old, he thought he already had everything he wanted out of life. He and a partner built a respectable insurance business, owning three agencies in Kansas City, St. Louis, and his hometown, Omaha, Nebraska.

But something was missing. "I was spending every waking moment either on the road visiting one of our offices, in an insurance appointment, dealing with clients, hiring employees, training agents and staff, or doing payroll for thirty employees," Jack says. "I had no time for my wife and three young children."

Then Jack ran into business problems that brought crushing legal bills. He ended up closing his insurance business and found himself $500,000 in debt. "I was depressed and felt like a failure," he reports.

> Research finds an estimated twenty million Americans are telecommuters, or people who perform some or all of their work tasks at home.

But in the fall of 1996 while on a family trip to Denver, Jack decided to look up an old friend who might have some ideas as to what he could do next. They connected, and Jack was introduced to network marketing. "I was hooked on the business," he reports. "My first few checks went to pay my attorney fees from my bankruptcy."

Now a full-time network marketer with Pre-Paid Legal Services, Jack has turned around not only his finances but his family life as well. "My wife, Camille, a licensed attorney, is quitting her job to stay home with our daughter. I rarely miss my sons' soccer games. In fact, I hardly ever miss their practices. I am their coach!

"I have an office in my home. I don't have employees, leases, payroll, expensive computer networks, loans, or expensive CPAs. In the old business there were only so many hours in the day. If I wanted to expand into another market and generate more money, I would have to hire more people. Today I can get the same leveraged effect without having to hire anyone. I just show the product and the business opportunity and get the same net effect. Instead of putting them into *my* business, I put them into *their* business."

Economic change and uncertainty; the prohibitive costs and burdens of small business ownership; the growing time and financial pressures on once attractive professions; the aging of society and the prospect of long years of cash-poor retirement; and the compelling desire to become reattached to family, community, and larger causes—these factors together comprise the socio-economic backdrop that is giving rise to the New Professionals. It is now time to turn our discussion to an in-depth examination of network marketing itself. How has an industry that traces its roots to a rag-tag collection of door-to-door salespeople transformed itself to a modern, high-tech, global business that is ideally positioned for the marketing realities of the Internet age and the lifestyle demands of highly educated, successful professionals?

Turn the page!

CHAPTER 4

The Rise of
Network Marketing

The cliché widely acclaimed throughout the network marketing community is that the network marketing industry is coming of age. Clearly, industry folklore and statistics document that the 1990s saw dramatic changes across the network marketing industry, including these:

- A surge in the number of new start-up companies entering the industry—and ultimately dropping out—after their initial "bath of fire" in this very competitive arena

- Impressive expansion of the established leader firms

- Broadening of the products and services offered in the network marketing channel

- Significant growth in the industry sales volume

- Involvement of more and different types of sales distributors

- Innovations in industry business practices integrating new technologies, particularly in the areas of telecommunications, computerization, and the Internet

- Massive international expansion and global growth

- Impressive increase in positive public recognition, improved credibility and acceptance, and an industry commitment to increased professionalism across the network marketing environment

We'll examine these interesting developments—and separate fact from fiction—in the next chapter. But many readers will first want answers to these questions: What is network marketing? From where does it trace its roots? How does it differ from direct selling, and how do both network marketing and direct selling differ from other ways in which goods and services are bought and sold? The goal of this chapter is to present:

- A brief review of direct selling, the basic environment in which network marketing is a part
- The concept of network marketing
- The history of network marketing since the 1930s–1940s
- The profile of network marketing and its participants as the industry undergoes significant developments and makes its way into the new century as an attractive alternative for New Professionals

We offer this information in the belief that today's serious professionals are knowledge workers. They want to know the following: How did the industry that they are considering joining develop? What were its ups and downs? Who were its pioneers? What are the basic concepts on which this form of business operate, and how are these concepts put into practice by different companies?

There's a further purpose for this discussion. Probably no other industry in U.S. history has been more misunderstood. There are so-called business experts—analysts, journalists, investors, competitors, and regulators—all over the country issuing opinions about it, casting judgments on it, and questioning its fundamental legitimacy with barely a modicum of understanding about how it really operates. We hope to close the rather wide gap among many between their opinions about network marketing and their knowledge of network marketing. Our goal is not persuade all those "experts" to like it or convince every professional to join it. But we do hope to foster a recognition that this is a genuine industry that legitimately meets the distribution, product, and entrepreneurial needs of a growing number of companies, consumers, and business professionals.

We have already noted that a common theme among top network marketers is that a negative image of the industry—sometimes based on a bad experience, but more often on misinformation and lack of knowledge—is what stood in their way, delaying and nearly scuttling their entry into the business. The objective industry analysis presented in the next two chapters—a discussion of its past, present, and future prospects—will hopefully help other New Professionals avoid such a period of confusion. In this way they can make a sound personal decision about the industry and whether it is right for them.

> We hope to close the rather wide gap between opinions about and knowledge of network marketing.

THE EVOLUTION OF DIRECT SELLING

Direct selling has been an integral part of the economic landscape since the earliest days of recorded business history. Nicole Woolsey Biggart, in *Charismatic Capitalism*, did an outstanding job in documenting the major milestones in the evolution of direct selling in the United States from colonial America into the 1980s. The Direct Selling Association, the national association of more than 140 leading firms that manufacturer and distribute goods directly to consumers, broadly defines direct selling as the sale of a consumer product or service in a face-to-face manner away from a fixed retail location in the home or the office.

Using this definition, Biggart traced direct selling in the United States to the "Yankee peddlers"—colonial peddlers/salesmen who sold tools, tea, and liniment from door to door. These itinerant merchants, often from northern European backgrounds, were initially based in New England, near the center of the colonial economy. Over time, immigrants from Eastern Europe migrated south and worked the southern colonies. Until the 1840s, peddlers were an important distribution channel in serving both rural, isolated farmers, and the emerging retailing phenomenon, the general store.

> Direct selling is the sale of a consumer product or service in a face-to-face manner in the home or the office.

With the arrival of the railroad and improved communications, manufacturers expanded to larger markets. Country storekeepers could order directly from manufacturers in distant cities and receive the merchandise. An expanding retail channel began to develop in rural communities. Many peddlers opened retail stores. Alfred D. Chandler reported in his book *The Visible Hand,* "The new stores along with improved transportation and the rise of the modern wholesaler to supply them, all but ended the peddler as an instrument of distribution in the United States."

The independent salesperson, however, continued as a sales channel but with different functions. After the Civil War, independent salespersons begin to sell only the goods of a single manufacturer, and the direct selling company sales force thus began to develop.

With the development of the department store and its broad array of competing products, manufacturers were losing control of their distribution channel. Some manufacturers wanted exclusive representation to differentiate themselves from competition. Biggart observed that "some believed that a sincere personal appeal or knowledgeable demonstration would show the goods to better advantage. Manufacturers tried to recapture the advantages of personal selling . . . but under conditions that gave them some measure of control."

Over the 1900–1920 era, the dynamics of managing the direct sales force changed. The typical "home office" sales organization involved a loose, barely organized sales team. The direct salespeople were recruited by circulars and advertisements in newspaper and magazines. The salesperson would order products through the mail from the host company and sell them however he could. (In those days, most salespeople were men.) The salesperson's commission was the difference between the price he paid and the price he charged the customer. The salesperson paid his own expenses. The only contact the salesperson had with the home office was by mail. He received no training in sales techniques or product knowledge except through the mail. There was no local mentoring or supervision.

In 1915, the Fuller Brush Company, a manufacturer of brushes and household products, reorganized as a "branch office" company. Fuller Brush opened local offices (branches) that recruited, trained, and supervised the regional sales groups. The branch manager was either a company employee or an independent salesperson who received a "manager's commission" on the branch's sales and a standard commission on his personal sales. The branch office companies paid the expense of the field facilities to develop better control of recruiting, training, and supervising the sales organization.

Industry historians estimate that more than two hundred thousand people were selling door-to-door in 1920. By the end of the 1920s, we see the formation of some legends in the direct selling industry, such as the California Perfume Company (Avon Corporation); Electrolux, a maker of vacuum cleaners; W. T. Raleigh, ultimately a manufacturer of spices and household products; and the West Bend Company, a cookware manufacturer. In 1925, the National Association of Direct Selling Companies (NADSC), a predecessor of today's Direct Selling Association (DSA), became the trade association and spokes-organization for the direct selling industry.

> Industry historians estimate that in 1920 more than two hundred thousand people were selling door-to-door.

In the 1930s, the direct selling industry continued to expand. Frank S. Beveridge, an executive with Fuller Brush, founded Stanley Home Products. Encyclopaedia Britannica was launched by Sears Roebuck and Company through its catalog division and sold to a direct selling company that would specialize in knowledge products in 1933. Industry sources noted that under the economic trauma of the Depression years, companies looking to reduce distribution costs also turned to direct sales.

The 1940s proved to be a particularly eventful decade for the direct selling industry. Biggart reported that three key developments occurred in the 1940s that would significantly impact the future developments of the direct selling culture.

First, the direct selling industry embraced the concept of the "independent contractor." It developed distributor contracts that specified the distributors were in business for themselves and thus were required to pay all costs of doing business including transportation, purchase of samples, and promotional materials. The result was that the independent contractor status positioned the direct sales distributor as a cheaper labor supply.

More specifically, the direct selling companies were freed from the responsibility for "employee welfare" and enforcement of government-defined codes of work practices. The direct selling companies were also relieved of the associated expenses of minimum wage, Social Security, unemployment compensation, income tax withholding, and so forth, that were evolving in President Franklin Roosevelt's social reform movement of the New Deal.

The second development of the 1940s was the creation of the "party plan." Stanley Home Products was an early pioneer in perfecting this sales program. A Stanley Home Products distributor would ask a "hostess" to invite a group of her friends to her home for a "party." After establishing an interactive atmosphere, the Stanley distributor would start showing and demonstrating products and get the guests involved with the product. At the end of the party, the guests were invited to purchase products in which they were interested. The hostess who had staged the party was usually credited with a percentage of the gross sales to be applied to her own purchases.

The party plan was an excellent innovation in creative direct selling.

The party plan was an excellent innovation in creative direct selling. The product demonstration and sales close were interwoven in a social party of friends. The hostess did most of the recruiting and managed the mechanics of party administration. The direct sales distributor multiplied his or her sales impact by talking to a group versus presenting to one prospect. The party atmosphere was based on an invitation from the hostess, a gathering among friends and acquaintances, a setting in a private home, and an implicit commitment to make the party a success, show interest in the products, and, potentially, make a purchase.

ENTER NETWORK MARKETING

The third development, which transformed the structure of the direct selling industry, was the creation of the multilevel distribution channel. The earliest history of multilevel marketing (MLM) is based largely on oral documentation bordering on folklore. Historians of the industry agree, however, that the 1930s and early 1940s marked the beginning of this new era in direct selling.

The pioneers among the traditional direct selling companies such as Watkins, Fuller Brush Company, and Stanley Home Products reportedly used "referral marketing" for recruiting new salespeople. The first published reference to referral marketing was reported by Biggart as a predecessor to contemporary referral/network marketing.

In that case, in 1929, a branch sales office introduced "friendship selling." The firm's own salesmen were used to canvass their friends and recruit new sales candidates. The logic was straightforward. Who knew the skills needed to be a successful salesperson in that company? Someone who was a successful salesperson in that company was a knowledgeable expert.

When a new recruit was signed as a direct salesperson and purchased a company sales kit, the salesman who introduced the "new hire" to the company was paid a $5 prize, or "finder's fee," and given a small percentage of the new recruit's gross sales as a commission override for the first sixty days. The "sponsoring" salesperson clearly had a financial incentive to train and support the new hire during those sixty days to maximize the override commission.

While the identity and birth date of the first multilevel marketing company is open to debate, several of the early multilevel marketing companies, using marketing plans similar to those of contemporary network marketing companies, have been identified. Doris Wood, MLM practitioner and co-founder of the Multi-Level Marketing International Association (MLMIA), reports that Wachter's Organic Sea Products Corporation is the "oldest, continually operating, privately held network marketing company in the world."

Carrie Minucciani, president and third-generation grand-daughter of the founder, tells a story of romanticism and entrepreneurial zeal. "Wachter's Sea Products Corporation was founded in 1932 by Dr. Joseph V. Wachter, a scientist. Joseph Wachter, originally a young musician in Europe, experienced failing health and launched an international tour to explore the world in what he thought were his last years.

"While in Alaska, Joseph Wachter became fascinated by the native Indian cultures and their nutritional habits and methods of natural healing. Miraculously, young Joseph regained his full health and dedicated himself to the study of these unfamiliar foods . . . harvested from the gardens of the sea."

Ultimately settling in San Francisco, Wachter organized Wachter's Organic Sea Products Corporation to "bring the benefits of sea plants to humankind" through direct selling to consumers. There is some question about exactly when Wachter's adopted a multilevel compensation plan. It was clearly in the 1930/1940 era when the multilevel/network marketing channel movement was being conceived. Wachter's two sons, Joseph V. Wachter Jr. and Earl A. Wachter, continued their father's product research and organizational development.

In 2000, Wachter's is still headquartered in the San Francisco Bay area, owns its own manufacturing facility, and maintains tight internal quality control of the production processes. The firm is organized around nine product divisions and manufacturers and distributes an extensive line of more than 150 health, nutrition, and personal care products in more than twenty-six countries. The firm still maintains its multilevel compensation program, paying on at least four levels of downline sales. The firm's Web site (www.wachters.com) declares, "Wachter's compensation plan is one of the most lucrative in the industry, with a 67.5 percent payout."

In our interview with Carrie Minucciani, she summarized, "Wachter's will continue its mission and will be family owned and operated into the fourth generation. Our children are standing by."

The early multilevel marketing pioneer who had the greatest impact in creating the new sales channel was Nutrilite, founded by William Casselberry, a psychologist, and Lee Mytinger. Since 1934, the firm had been selling the products of the California Vitamin Company directly to customers. In 1941, the firm began to sell Nutrilite XX through the C&M Marketing Plan, a network marketing program.

The C&M Marketing Plan was probably the first "breakaway" compensation plan design in the history of the MLM industry. The compensation plan included these elements: a 3 percent distributor bonus on the sales of people personally sponsored, a breakaway wholesale organization when group sales volume reached $15,000, and "override" royalties paid by the company to the sponsors on the sales volumes of all breakaway groups.

History has documented that Nutrilite played a seminal role in the launch of the network marketing industry as it exists today. It provided the business model, the breakaway compensation plan, that would be copied and widely used in the initial stage of industry development.

Frank Beveridge left Fuller Brush, organized Stanley Home Products in 1933, and subsequently transitioned into network marketing. W. T. Raleigh also adopted the network marketing structure.

Within Stanley Home Products, three key distributors would resign and organize new selling organizations that would have dramatic impact on the competitive structure of the direct selling industry. Mary Kay Ash founded Mary Kay Cosmetics. Mary Crowley created Home Interiors and Gifts. Brownie Wise built the Tupperware party plan program.

Nutrilite was also the training ground for two key industry leaders, Rich DeVos and Jay Van Andel, former Nutrilite distributors. When Nutrilite management problems threatened product supplies in the 1950s, DeVos and Van Andel formed their own manufacturing company, the American Way Association (the parent of Amway), in Ada, Michigan. Amway, of course, became the largest network company in the world with sales of over $5 billion in 1998.

The 1950 to 1960s saw the network industry expanding dramatically to include Shaklee (1956), Amway (1959), Mary Kay (1962), and National Safety Associates (1970). In the 1970s, the growth of the network marketing channel was gaining momentum.

NETWORK MARKETING, MULTILEVEL MARKETING: WHAT'S IN A NAME?

Before describing the position and condition of the industry today, let's pause to explore how network marketing got its name and how it works.

Network marketing and *multilevel marketing* are synonymous terms. Industry folklore documents that multilevel marketing was the initial title given this channel of distribution in the 1940s. Multilevel marketing was descriptive of compensation plans in which commissions were paid on sales made at "multiple levels" or "multiple tiers" down a vertically structured sales organization.

Doris Wood, of the MLMIA, published one of the first formal definitions for this sales channel: "Multilevel marketing is a legal system of merchandising products through multiple levels of distribution (distributors). These distributors purchase at wholesale and act as the middleman between the manufacturer and the consumer who pays retail."

By comparison, traditional door-to-door direct sales compensation programs paid on only one level based on a specific, single buyer/seller sales transaction.

Since its inception, MLM has been given many labels: word-of-mouth marketing, people-to-people sharing, friends doing business with friends, conversational marketing, interactive distribution, personal marketing, relationship marketing, people-to-people sharing, and others. Critics argue that the industry uses different terms and buzzword titles to distinguish this selling process—and distance it—from the much maligned and illegal Ponzi schemes, financial pyramid selling programs, chain letters, and consumer fraud scams.

> Network marketing places the appropriate emphasis on person-to-person communication, relationship building, and nurturing processes.

Network marketing is the preferred term for the new millennium. Network marketing places the appropriate emphasis on person-to-person communication and relationship building and nurturing processes at the core of this marketing channel. Network marketing based on interpersonal communication can be linked directly to information technology, the focus on distribution processes related to efficiently serving consumers and maximizing satisfaction, and the global, multicultural economy, which is highly dependent on person-to-person communications.

NETWORK MARKETING VERSUS DIRECT SELLING

How, precisely, is network marketing distinguished from direct selling? This question is one of the most frequently asked in all of the sales discipline! It is also one of the most challenging questions to answer clearly. Network marketing and direct selling share some significant similarities *and* some important differences.

Network marketing and direct selling both:

- Use the face-to-face, one-on-one interpersonal communication process in transmitting ideas from person to person
- Transmit information, explain, and demonstrate ideas about products/services
- Operate away from a fixed retail location (e.g., a department store, retail specialty store, retail discount store, supermarket)
- Typically operate in an office or home

Direct selling and network marketing differ on several key dimensions, described separately in the following sections.

Closing the Sale/Getting the Order Versus Relationship Building

Direct selling has historically been criticized for focusing on closing the sale and getting the order. "Nothing happens until a sale is made" is the charge of the direct selling culture.

During Charles King's college years, he was a part-time direct salesperson for an encyclopedia company. The organization trained him in classic direct, door-to-door selling, typically selling door-to-door in a middle-class, upwardly mobile suburban subdivision.

King described that direct selling process: "The initial prospecting objective was to get an invitation to make a product presentation in the consumer's home. The presentation was designed to showcase the product and answer informational and motivationally based questions. The process then turned to handling objections. Ultimately, the focus shifted: introduce the sales contract, close the sale, get the purchase contract signed, collect the first payment and *get out*—before the customer changed his or her mind about the purchase."

Closing the sales transaction with a purchase payment was the focus from the first knock at the door through the presentation into close and departure!

Obviously, the direct selling process has matured and become much more sophisticated, with its pitch softened since the 1960s to early 1970s. But many direct sales programs are still hard sell, close-the-deal oriented.

A massive literature exists today outlining the selling process, including prospecting, making the product presentation, identifying key product features and benefits, handling objectives, closing the sale, completing the order, executing the winning follow-through, and more. A whole industry of sales trainers and sale force management consultants exists to develop and fine-tune that selling process.

Information Sharing and Relationship Building

In network marketing, the emphasis focuses on information sharing and developing and maintaining an ongoing personal relationship over time. The network marketer is typically interacting with friends and family or new contacts who hopefully may evolve into friends.

> There is a psychological commitment to preserving and building the social network.

The objective, to be sure, may be to present the product/service concept and relevant information to the prospective buyer and get the friend to buy and try the product. The long-term goal, however, is to develop and maintain those interpersonal relationships beyond the initial selling transaction. There is a psychological commitment to preserving and building the social network.

Independent Contractor Status

The network marketer, usually called a distributor, sales associate, or consultant, is almost universally an independent contractor. The demographics of the direct selling force, as reported in the 1998 Direct Selling Growth and Outlook Survey, indicated 99.8 percent of all direct salespeople, including network marketers, worked as independent contractors.

The network marketing independent contractor is a free agent who can sell anywhere, in any territory or region of the United States or in any foreign countries where the distributor's company operates. The independent contractors operate their own selling operations, have virtually no bosses or field supervision, have "time freedom" to set their own work schedules, pay their own expenses, and receive commissions for products/services sold by them directly or by their sales group.

The network marketer must, however, operate within the policies and procedures prescribed by the company. The company policies and procedures typically define specific regulations regarding product claims that can be made, the use of advertising, specific sites/locations where sales can or cannot be made, the specifics of the compensation plan, various administrative procedures, and so forth.

The professional salesperson, in contrast, may be an employee for a manufacturer, with a contractual employment relationship including salary/commission and fringe benefits. This salesperson would work under the supervision of a local, regional, or national sales manager.

Organization Business Building

Network marketing offers the opportunity for the independent distributor to build a sales organization on which the distributor can make commissions based on the sales of the downline group that he or she has built.

As a business builder, the distributor recruits prospects and then trains them on "best business practices" in network

The distributor recruits and trains prospects in network selling and in duplicating those techniques to build their own downline sales organizations.

selling and duplicating those techniques to build their own downline sales organizations. The upline business–building distributors mentor their downline sales organizations. The business-building distributor creates his or her success on the successful performance of the downline organization. The upline leaders are responsible for recruiting, training, and coaching their downline group.

As reward for mentoring and managerial effort, the upline distributor earns an override commission on the sales productivity of the downline group that has been recruited and trained.

The Structure of the Sales Compensation Plan

In direct selling, the commission plan typically pays only based on the individual sales transaction. In the encyclopedia sales example, King was paid a 48 percent commission on the retail sales transaction amount when the order was approved and processed by the publisher. Then it was the "end of the transaction—on to the next!"

Similar to this direct selling process, in network marketing, a commission is also paid on the initial product or service sale. Therefore, the network marketer does actively sell product to customers as in direct selling and makes a commission from those sales.

Network marketing compensation plans, however, are also designed to capitalize on repeat purchases by that initial customer. The original distributor who developed the customer relationship continues to earn commissions on the repeat purchases of those customers.

As emphasized earlier, for those distributors who are organizational business builders, they earn an override commission on the sales of the downline group they have recruited and trained as network marketing distributors. While each network marketing company typically has a compensation plan designed for its particular product line and marketing strategy, plans often pay commissions on many downline generations of distributors—sometimes thousands, tens of thousands, hundreds of thousands of distributors—representing millions of dollars of product sales volume.

Within this broad network marketing compensation structure, individual companies each have their own distributor compensation plans designed around their particular products, marketing strategies, and the financial goals of the firm. The compensation plan, often called the *marketing plan* of a company in network marketing, is critical for the distributor to study and understand. It explains how the company calculates the distributor's commissions based on certain sales performance criteria.

In overview, the industry has a complex terminology that describes various types of compensation formula, such as the breakaway plan, the binary plan, the matrix plan, the unilevel plan, and hybrid plans involving selected elements of several of these generic programs. A literature does exist that broadly describes these various generic compensation structures. The leading textbook in the network marketing field, *Direct Sales: An Overview,* by Dr. Keith B. Laggos, presents a comprehensive, five-chapter overview of different compensation plans. It is available in major bookstores.

In the current exciting competitive environment, aggressive network marketing companies are reevaluating traditional compensation structures to make them more attractive in recruiting and motivating distributors. The New Professional investigating network marketing should carefully review the compensation plans of all candidate companies and understand how they operate before joining any network marketing organization.

THE NETWORK MARKETING CHANNEL: A DESCRIPTION

The fundamental role of the network marketing channel is to accelerate the movement of products and services—provide "speed-to-market"—using the most efficient distribution technique in the marketing discipline: word-of-mouth communication.

In concept, traditional consumer product distribution channel sends a product through these hands and these steps:

Manufacturer—Corporate salesperson—Food broker—Regional wholesaler—Local wholesaler—Retail grocery store

> The role of the network marketing channel is to accelerate the movement of products using the most efficient distribution technique: word-of-mouth communication.

The channel is expensive to set up, often requiring millions of dollars to achieve retailer representation and store saturation. Once the channel structure is in place with various channel members participating, an extensive logistical system of transportation, warehousing, and inventory management functions is required to supply and service the channel members. All of these channel members, in turn, must charge a margin percentage to cover their operating costs and profits. In addition, the typical packaged food product will be promoted through regional or national advertising campaigns potentially involving massive budgets. For example, Proctor and Gamble, an icon in packaged food marketing, spent approximately $3 billion in advertising in 1998.

Network marketing, in contrast, involves a much more direct, shorter, and less expensive channel:

Manufacturer—Network of wholesale/retail distributors—
Consumer

Through network marketing's use of word-of-mouth communication and direct manufacturer-to-consumer delivery, significant economies can be realized based on:

- More rapid penetration of the target market, thereby decreasing the market development investment and accelerating the positive channel sales and cash flow during the production introduction stage

- Reduction of advertising costs replaced by word-of-mouth communication

- Elimination of margin costs for unnecessary middlemen

THE NETWORK MARKETING PROCESS: SPECIFIC ACTIVITIES

The network marketing process involves three basic activities:

1. *Product usage.*

The distributor buys and uses the product and services that he or she represents. Through product or service usage, the distributor learns about and experiences their benefits. In industry parlance, the distributor, as a product/service user, "becomes the product of the product." The distributor has an economic gain in buying from the company at a reduced wholesale price. In some compensation plans, the distributor may also earn a commission or performance bonus on that personal consumption if it is included as part of the distributor's total group sales volume.

2. ***Retail/wholesale sale of the product to customers.***

    The distributor may sell the product/service directly to customers. Based on these sales transactions, the distributor can earn:

    a. a retail profit (price charged to the customer minus the cost of goods purchased from the manufacturer or network marketing company) or

    b. a sales commission or performance bonus on products or services sold, paid directly by the supplier company.

3. ***Creation and management of a sales organization.***

    The distributor can build a sales organization through recruiting, training, and managing a downline of sales people. As a reward for the sales management effort, the upline distributor/sales manager of that downline sales organization is paid a blend of overrides, commissions, and bonuses on the sales of the entire sales group she or he has recruited, trained, and managed.

A QUESTION OF LAW AND LEGITIMACY: IS NETWORK MARKETING A "REAL" BUSINESS?

The legal environment for the network marketing industry has been one of continuing change over the past sixty years. Richard Poe, in his classic description of the industry's maturation, *Wave 3*, pinpointed 1979 as "the end of the 'tough, pioneering' days, . . . when the Federal Trade Commission (FTC) ruled Amway was a legitimate business—not a pyramid scheme."

Analysis of the legal record indicates that since 1979, however, intensive attacks on the network marketing industry have continually been made by state attorneys' general offices, the FTC, and the Securities and Exchange Commission (SEC) at different points in history—most recently in 1999 ongoing into 2000. Legal observers report these investigatory surges have been prompted by several factors:

- Outstanding growth by some highly visible newcomer network marketing companies that demanded regulatory attention

- Increased interest of the regulatory community in the network marketing industry in general

- Recognition by the regulators that the network marketing industry could be a lucrative legal "hunting ground" for significant fines and penalties to fund further regulatory budgets

- Entry of many new start-up network marketing companies with no limited credibility that might be vulnerable from the view of the regulators

- Network marketing business practices by both some established companies and some new start-up companies that pushed the envelope of acceptable business practices from the regulators' perspective

Jeffrey A. Babener, a leading network marketing attorney representing many of the major firms in the industry, has extensive experience in dealing with the regulators and in-court litigation. He has noted that the industry regulatory record has been characterized by "cycles in which the legal climate has vacillated between challenge and support. . . . Although still not without legal—and practical—challenges, in general, legitimate direct sales companies are well received throughout the United States."

The legal and regulatory framework related to network marketing, however, is still a constantly changing mosaic of overlapping laws that lack uniformity, varying from state to state. It is essential, therefore, that the New Professional investigating network marketing as a business alternative have a broad understanding of the legal climate related to the distribution channel.

A LEGAL CHECKLIST
FOR DOING DUE DILIGENCE

What should the New Professional know and consider as he or she decides to enter this industry and choose a particular network marketing company? Here is a brief legal background and a summary checklist of key issues that have been identified in the case law, relevant statutes, and industry codes of ethics to aid the New Professional's "due diligence" process:

- In the entrepreneurial sector, federal and state regulatory agencies have had an ongoing war under way with pyramid schemes, chain letters, and other forms of endless chains, lottery games, and Ponzi Schemes, all of which have posed as legitimate direct sales operations. These high-profile cases have often negatively influenced the public's perceptions of legitimate network marketing companies.

- The SEC and the FTC defined early guidelines regarding illegal pyramids and other unlawful entrepreneurial chains in the legal court cases of *Dare to Be Great* (1973) and *Koscot Interplanetary Inc.* (1975).

- Based on the historic Amway litigation from 1974 to 1979, Amway Corporation prevailed against the FTC and established the multilevel/network marketing industry as a legitimate channel of distribution. The decision produced the "Amway Safeguards Rule," which details the most significant set of legal standards to determine the legitimacy of a network marketing company.

Against this legal backdrop, here is a checklist of key issues to use in evaluating network marketing companies on their legality and legitimacy:

- Network marketing companies must be bona fide sales organizations that market bona fide products to consumers.

- Products sold must have a "real-world" marketplace and realistic and intrinsic value measured by the price-quality relationship.

- Product prices should be competitive and not inflated.

- Compensation plans must not require or encourage "front-end buy-in" inventory loading by distributors.

- Distributors must engage in retail selling and qualify under the "ten retail customer policy"; that is, distributors must make ten sales to retail customers as a qualification for eligibility to receive commissions and bonuses on the sales/purchases by other distributors in their downline.

- Distributors should emphasize retail sales to nonparticipant consumers outside the network marketing organization.

- Distributors must personally use or sell a minimum of 70 percent of their previously purchased product inventory before placing a new order. The goal is to minimize inventory accumulation.

- Compensation plans must not encourage or require mandatory purchases of peripheral/accessory products or services.

- Commissions are paid solely on products/services purchased by the distributors for personal use or sale to other distributors or nonparticipating retail purchasers.

- Compensation plans must not pay commissions to distributors for headhunting or recruiting where the emphasis is on recruiting rather than selling the product.

- Sign-up costs should be low, requiring no substantial cash investment. Sales kits should be sold at cost or near company cost to distributors.

- Companies should provide an official "buy-back" policy for unsold, unopened, restockable product that can also include a reasonable restocking charge. The buy-back policy should apply to distributors who overbuy or choose to terminate from the sales organization before all of the product is used or sold.

- Distributors who are "business builders" developing a downline sales organization are responsible for providing bona fide supervision, distributive selling support, product training, or soliciting training/coaching/mentoring to the downline sales organization to move the product or service to the ultimate consumer.

- Network marketing companies should not make any earnings representations unless those claims are based on a track record of sales performance.

DIRECT SELLING AND NETWORK MARKETING IN THE UNITED STATES TODAY

Now let's look at the state of the industry today. How much business do today's network marketers do? What products and services do they sell? Where do they sell them? How much time do they spend building their independent businesses and what are their general backgrounds?

The DSA annually surveys manufacturers, both members and nonmembers, who use the direct selling channel regarding the sales of products and services made by their companies. As you will see, the network marketing share of that channel is the most significant.

The "Whys" of Direct Sellers and Network Marketers

Why do people get involved in direct selling? People from all walks of life—female homemakers, upwardly mobile blue-collar workers, middle managers, small business owners, college professors, attorneys, dentists, persons with disabilities, and others—work part- and full-time in direct selling. In the 1997 Survey of Attitudes Toward Direct Selling by Wirthlin Worldwide, direct selling representatives (current and former) were found in 19 percent of the sample homes, with 6 percent of the homes reporting current representatives.

> Distributors must use or sell a minimum of 70 percent of their previously purchased inventory before placing a new order.

Historically, the mantra of the industry promoters was "BMTF"—big money and time freedom. The industry folklore said people get into direct selling and the network marketing industry to make impressive incomes and have time freedom to do whatever else they want to do as their own bosses. Although some direct sellers and network marketers undoubtedly have gotten involved for those reasons, the DSA and confidential research reports by network marketing companies tell a broader story. The reality is most people have entered direct selling and network marketing for a variety of additional reasons beyond BMTF.

Current direct selling representatives gave Wirthlin Worldwide these primary reasons for becoming a direct sales representative in rank order of importance (on a scale of 1 to 5, with 5 indicating a very strong reason):

Opportunity to meet new people	4.1
Receiving recognition for your accomplishments	3.6
Money-making potential	3.6
A way to purchase products at a discount	3.4

A collection of other proprietary research from network marketing companies report direct sellers and network marketers also join the industry to:

- Buy specific, quality products at a discounted/wholesale price

- Meet a short-term financial objective (e.g., buy a car, take a vacation, etc.)

- Get involved in a "work hard"/"high reward" business venture: "the harder one works, the more money one can potentially make"

- Build a source of ongoing, supplemental income

- Develop a new entrepreneurial career path based on "sweat equity" and a relatively small financial investment

- Meet new people and have increased social involvement

- Improve self-development

- Contribute to the development of others

- Participate in a business with a friend or family member

The most recent DSA 1999 National Salesforce Survey reconfirmed these conclusions. While 32 percent of the respondents reported their main reason for becoming a direct sales representative was to earn additional income, 68 percent of the respondents named other reasons: 20 percent reported "believe in the product/good product," 10 percent chose "Discount/wholesale/free products," with the remaining 38 percent listing a range of reasons already itemized in the earlier research.

At the University of Illinois at Chicago, since 1994, co-author Charles King and a team of network marketing authorities have conducted the UIC Certificate Seminar for Network Marketing for network marketing practitioners. The program was the first ever sponsored by a major university and continues to be the premier university program of its kind in the world. It covers the proven techniques for planning, building, and managing a network marketing distributor organization.

> **M**ost people have entered direct selling and network marketing for a variety of reasons beyond BMTF.

In that program, one session focuses on the "whys" of network marketing. Participants define the mission of the network marketing industry from the distributor's perspective. The mission statements written by those very intensely involved participants give some powerful insights about their views of network marketing. Some illustrative mission statements:

- "Through relationship marketing, we empower others to achieve a high level of self-mastery using integrity, honesty, compassion, accountability and ethics. We give people personal freedom and financial independence to lead an abundant life."

- "To nurture and protect the environment where people, regardless of background, education, or experience, with minimum capital investment, can achieve personal and financial independence helping others do the same."

- "Through the cooperative efforts and applied faith of individuals of every age, sex, race, education, and religion, network marketing stands alone as the greatest vehicle in the world for personal freedom, entrepreneurial success, and enhanced family life."

- "Promote the understanding and acceptance of network marketing to become the premier choice which empowers people to maximize their potential, increase their freedom, and create personal wealth."

DSA Announcement:
1999 Direct Retail Sales and Number of Salespeople

Neil Offen, president of the Direct Selling Association, announced the preliminary data for the direct selling industry for 1999 at the Direct Selling Association Convention in Boca Raton, Florida in June, 2000.

- Direct retail sales totaled $24.54 billion in 1999, up 5.9 percent over 1998.

- The number of direct salespeople increased to 10.3 million in 1999, up 6.2 percent over 1998.

Offen summarized, "This is the sixteenth record year in a row for direct selling. I congratulate you on this industry-wide achievement. All of you are helping to keep the American Dream, being one's own boss and directly relating effort to reward, alive and well in our country."

The detailed 1999 data are not available pending additional analysis.

Historical Growth in Direct Sales
and the Sales Force: 1993–1998

Direct dollar sales and the number of distributors engaged in direct selling and network marketing for the 1993–1998 period, the most complete data available, are summarized in Table 4.1.

Table 4.1 makes the following points:

Table 4.1 *Direct Sales in the United States, 1993–1998*

Year	Retail Sales ($U.S. Billions)	Number of Salespeople (Millions)
1993	14.98	5.7
1994	16.55	6.3
1995	17.95	7.2
1996	20.84	8.5
1997	22.21	9.3
1998	23.17	9.7

NOTE: *These statistics are estimates of the entire direct selling industry, including both DSA reporting members and estimates for the nonparticipating firms.*

Table 4.2 *Multilevel Versus Single-Level Compensation Programs, 1998*

	Multilevel	Single-Level
Percentage of firms	80.4	19.6
Percentage of dollar sales	73.5	26.5
Percentage of salespeople	81.7	18.3

- From 1993 to 1998, direct sales grew from $14.98 billion to $23.17 billion, a more than 54 percent increase.

- Likewise, the number of distributors involved in network marketing distributors increased over the five-year period from 5.7 million to 9.7 million, an increase of more than 70 percent.

Compensation Structure

Table 4.2 compares network/MLM versus single-level compensation programs.

Table 4.2 makes a couple of important points. First, network marketing compensation programs now dominate the direct selling industry on all significant measures of performance. In 1994–1995, Neil H. Offen, then executive director of the DSA, reported the DSA had faced a "growing schism between traditionally structured members and the multilevel members. The membership was then divided roughly 50:50, with almost all new applications for DSA membership being multilevel."

Second, multilevel compensation plans:

- Are used by 80.4 percent of all direct selling firms

- Generate 73.5 percent of total direct sales

- Include 81.7 percent of all direct salespeople

From the information presented in Tables 4.1 and 4.2, we are able to determine the specific sales and occupation impact of network marketing today, versus the direct selling industry as a whole:

- $23.17 billion total direct sales (73.5 percent of sales dollars accounted for by the network marketing channel = $17.03 billion in network marketing dollar sales

- 9.7 million distributors (81.7 percent network marketing salespeople = 7.2 million network marketing salespeople

Percentage of Sales by Major Product Groups

Table 4.3 presents the percentage of total dollar sales by major product group reported for 1998.

Conclusions from Table 4.3 include these:

- The product/service mix moving through the direct sale channel has shifted somewhat in recent years. Home/family care products continue to be the dominant category moving through the direct sales channel, accounting for

Table 4.3 *Percentage of Total Dollar Sales by Major Product Groups, 1998*

Product Group	Percentage
Home/family care products (cleaning products, cookware, cutlery, etc.)	32.2
Personal care products (cosmetics, jewelry, skin care, etc.)	25.9
Services/miscellaneous/other	18.2
Wellness products (weight loss products, vitamins, etc.)	17.9
Leisure/educational products (books, encyclopedias, toys/games, etc.)	5.8

over 32 percent of the $23.17 billion industry sales volume in 1998 but down from 38.8 percent in 1995.

- Personal care products were in number two position with 25.9 percent, but this figure is also down from 34.4 percent in 1995.

- Services/miscellaneous products have assumed a growing percentage, achieving an 18.2 percent share of direct sales up from 10.4 percent in 1995, 4.8 percent in 1985, and 4.0 percent in 1980.

Selling Strategy

The selling strategy or method used to generate sales reported as a percentage of total dollar sales are presented in Table 4.4.

From Table 4.4 we can draw the following conclusions:

- In terms of selling strategies used, individual/one-on-one selling accounted for 71.9 percent of the total dollar sales moved in the channel.

Table 4.4   *Selling Strategy as a Percentage of Total Dollar Sales, 1998*

Strategy	Percentage
Individual/one-on-one selling	71.9
Party plan/group selling	26.3
Customer placing order directly with firm (in follow-up to a face-to-face solicitation)	1.6
Other	0.2

- When "customer placing order directly with firm (in follow-up to a face-to-face solicitation)," at 1.6 percent is viewed as an extension of individual/one-on-one selling, the total goes up to 73.5 percent.

- By comparison, party plan/group selling moved only 26.3 percent of the total dollar sales and has been declining in recent years under the pressure of consumer "time poverty."

Location of Sales

Table 4.5 reports the location of sales as a percentage of total dollar sales.

Conclusions from Table 4.5 include these:

- Direct sales in the home continue to dominate as the primary sales location, accounting for 69.5 percent of total direct sales dollars.

- The "near-follower" locations were "over the phone" and "in the workplace," totaling 10.9 percent and 10.7 percent respectively.

- The combined "in the home," "over the phone," and "in the workplace" responses represented over 91 percent of total direct sales dollars.

Table 4.5 *Location of Sales as Percentage of Total Dollar Sales, 1998*

Location	Percentage
In the home	69.5
Over the phone (in follow-up to a face-to-face solicitation)	10.9
In the workplace	10.7
At a temporary location (fair, exhibition, shopping mall, etc.)	6.1
Other location (representative's office, direct mail, etc.)	2.8

Demographics of the Direct Sales Population

Table 4.6 presents a brief demographic profile of the direct sales population.

The demographic profile of the U.S. direct selling population has been researched by the Direct Selling Association most recently in two different studies, the 1999 Direct Selling Growth & Outlook Survey and the 1999 National Salesforce Survey. The surveys report relevant 1998 distributor profile data.

The Direct Selling Association (DSA) summarized: the "typical" direct selling representative is "a 43-year-old Caucasian woman who is married, has completed some college courses, does not have any temporary or permanent disabilities and uses English as the primary language in her home. Her average annual gross income before taxes from her direct selling activity is less than $12,000 and she does not have any additional employment outside of direct selling."

The detailed data are presented in Table 4.6.

Table 4.6   *Demographics of the Direct Sales Population*
Percentage of Total Direct Sales Population 1998

Type of Employment			
Independent contractor	99.8%	Employee	0.2%

Hours of Work per Work			
Less than 30 hours	82.8%	40 hours or more	10.8%
30–39 hours	6.4%		

Gender			
Female	57.9%	Two-person teams	15.7%
Male	26.4%		

Total Number in Household			
Mean	3.3		

Total Number of Children in Household			
Zero	45%	Three	10%
One	18%	Four or more	6%
Two	20%	Refused	1%

We can conclude the following points from Table 4.6:

- Independent contractors control the direct sales force, representing over 99.8 percent of the industry.

- Although women still account for the majority of the direct sales population at 57.9 percent, the current trend has clearly been toward increases in men and two-person teams (typically male and female). In 1996, for example, women accounted for 70.4 percent of the direct sales

Table 4.6   *(Continued)*

Race

Caucasian	83%	Native American	1%
African American	8%	Other	1%
Hispanic	4%	Refused	2%
Asian	1%		

Age

Mean	43.4	45–54	24%
18–24	5%	55–64	12%
25–34	22%	65 and over	6%
35–44	30%	Refused	1%

Education

Less than high school	3%	Associate degree	9%
High school graduate	23%	College degree	25%
Some college	30%	Postgraduate	10%

Disability

Have a disability	6%	Temporary	10%
Permanent	87%	Don't know/refused	3%

force, while men and two-person teams were 19.3 percent and 10.3 percent, respectively.

- Most direct seller/network marketers work their business part-time, or at least fewer than forty hours a week, by choice or necessity.

- Analysis of gender across different sales approaches produced these conclusions: women represent 92 percent of the party plan direct sellers, with men accounting for only

8 percent; by comparison, men represent 30 percent of the one-on-one direct sellers.

- Direct sellers have relatively small families. The average family household included 3.3 members; 45 percent of the households had no children and 38 percent had two children or less; only 16 percent of the families had 3 or more children.

- Caucasians accounted for 83 percent of direct sellers; African Americans accounted for 8 percent overall; 4 percent of Hispanics were involved in direct selling. Within the party plan segment, African Americans accounted for only 3 percent and Hispanics only 1 percent of participants.

- The average age of direct sellers was 43.4 years; 76 percent of direct sellers were in the 25–54 age range; 12 percent were in the 55–64 bracket; 6 percent were 65 or over.

- On education, 23 percent of all direct sellers were high school graduates; 74 percent had some college; 25 percent had a college degree; 10 percent had a postgraduate education.

- 6 percent of direct sellers had a permanent or temporary disability.

GOING GLOBAL: INTERNATIONAL DIRECT SELLING

The World Federation of Direct Selling Association (WFDSA) coordinates statistical information collected from approximately fifty different DSAs around world. The statistical data reporting challenges are significant. The DSA organizations operate:

- In different languages and cultures related to statistical reporting

- With widely different levels of operational sophistication across DSA countries

- Based on varying currency exchange rates

- Using different data collection systems and reporting timing cycles

Despite these difficulties, the WFDSA information does provide an informative description of the global direct selling industry.

The direct selling industry, according to Neil Offen, president of the U.S. DSA, experienced dramatic growth in developing the international market place in the 1990s.

- In June 2000, the World Federation of Direct Selling Associations (WFDSA) reported its latest International Statistical Survey of Direct Selling Companies. Adding the updated 1999 preliminary data for the U.S., reported by Offen, generated these conclusions. Global direct sales volume was over $84 billion. This number, however, does not reflect the dramatic true unit sales growth because of the economic crisis in Korea, Malaysia, Thailand, Indonesia, and several other markets. The negative economic climate has also impacted on Japan, the largest direct sales market in the world by sales volume. Japan's direct sales have been flat for several years, reflecting the Japanese currency fluctuations and the economic uncertainty of the era.

- On a global basis, direct sales distributors now exceed over 4 million people, up more than 39 percent from 1996. Approximately 18 million people have joined the global network marketing community since 1993, about a 132 percent increase.

- Conservative industry estimates forecast that more than 200 million new distributors will be recruited around the world over the next ten years.

Table 4.7   *Estimated Direct Global Retail Sales and Sales Force, 1993–1999*

Year	Retail Sales ($U.S. Billions)	Numbers of Salespeople (Millions)
1993	61.67	14.9
1994	67.57	17.7
1995	74.90	21.0
1996	79.32	24.9
1997	80.47	30.9
1998	81.87	33.7
1999	84.51	34.6

Table 4.7 presents the most current WFDSA global sales and sales force data for 1993 through 1999.

From the WFDSA country statistics for 1997–1998 and 1999—the most recent available—a list of the "billion dollar (U.S.$) +" direct selling countries has been assembled. These are listed with their most recent sales information and the distributor population in Table 4.8. While these country-by-country numbers may not meet the rigorous standards of academic economists, they do give a broad comparative perspective across the leading direct selling countries.

Several impressive conclusions emerge from Table 4.8:

• Over $84 billion (U.S.) were sold through the direct selling channel in 1999 worldwide.

• Over 34.6 million direct selling salespeople were engaged in the industry in 1999.

• There is heavy concentration of direct selling activity: countries have direct sales of over $1 billion (U.S.).

Table 4.8   *The "Billion Dollar +" Countries in Direct Selling*

Country	Retail Sales ($U.S. Billions)	Numbers of Salespeople (Millions)
Japan	$31.00 (1999)*	2.000*
United States	$24.54 (1999)*	10.300
Germany	$3.57 (1998)*	0.455
France	$3.57 (1998)*	0.200
Brazil	$2.68 (1999)*	1.165
Mexico	$2.65 (1999)*	1.700
Italy	$1.85 (1999)*	0.260
Korea	$1.40 (1998)*	0.818
United Kingdom	$1.34 (1999)*	0.424
Taiwan	$1.22 (1998)*	2.781
Australia	$1.20 (1997)	0.650
Malaysia	$1.12 (1999)	2.000
Argentina	$1.10 (1998)*	0.394
Canada	$1.05 (1998)	1.300
Total	**$78.29 (92.6%)**	**23.447 (67.8%)**
All other countries	$6.22 (7.4%)	11.139 (32.2%)

Cross Check:

$78.29 (92.6%)	23.447 (67.8%)
6.22 (7.4%)	11.139 (32.2%)
$84.51 (100%)	34.586 (100%)

Estimated international retail direct sales	$84.51 (100%)	34.586 (100%)

WFDSA retail sales estimates include both DSA and nonmember companies.

Data from WFDSA International Statistical Survey, worldwide direct sales data, June 2000.

- The "billion dollar (U.S.$) countries" account for over 92 percent of global direct sales but only about 67 percent of the distributors worldwide.

- Japan is the leading direct sales country, accounting for 36.7 percent of worldwide direct selling sales.

- The United States is in second position with a 29.0 percent market share of global direct sales.

- Combined, Japan and the United States represent 65.7 percent of worldwide direct sales.

- Germany and France each account for roughly a 4 percent market share of global direct sales.

- Brazil, Mexico, Italy, Korea, and the United Kingdom each hold between 3.2 and 1.5 percent market share of worldwide direct selling sales.

The Power of the Asian Block in Network Marketing

The Asian block countries have a strong interpersonal communication culture and a well-established competitive infrastructure of direct sales activity. Table 4.9 presents the most recent information identifying the major direct selling countries in Asia.

Several significant issues should be noted:

- Reflecting the economic power of this Asian block in the direct selling industry, these countries represent approximately $35.83 (U.S.) of estimated direct sales volume, over 42 percent of total world sales. The countries account for almost fourteen million direct sales people, more than 39 percent of the worldwide direct selling community.

- Japan is the largest direct selling country in the world and dominates the Asian block.

- Korea, Taiwan, and Malaysia are also members of the "billion dollar +" group of direct selling companies.

- Despite their strong positioning in the direct selling industry and the enormous potential for long-term devel-

Table 4.9 *Asian Countries in Direct Selling*

Country	Retail Sales ($U.S. Billions)	Numbers of Salespeople (Millions)
Japan	$31.00 (1999)*	2.000
Korea	$1.40 (1998)*	0.818
Taiwan	$1.22 (1998)*	2.781
Malaysia	$1.12 (1999)	2.000
Thailand	$0.55 (1998)*	2.500
Indonesia	$0.21 (1998)	2.580
Philippines	$0.17 (1997)	1.008
Hong Kong	$0.11 (1999)*	0.077
Singapore	$0.05 (1999)*	0.014
Total	$35.83	13.778

WFDSA retail sales estimates include both DSA and nonmember companies.

Data from WFDSA International Statistical Survey, worldwide direct sales data, June 2000.

opment and expansion in direct sales, most of these Asian block countries have Third World economies. Their inherent economic instabilities may slow direct sales growth in the near term.

POISED FOR THE FUTURE

Network marketing is deeply rooted in the American past. Today it is a sales and entrepreneurial movement that is sweeping the globe. While its sales account for a small fraction of total consumer sales, its impact up to now extends far beyond dollars and cents. It is worth underscoring the Wirthlin Worldwide finding that 19 percent of American homes have at least one member who is or has been engaged in some form of direct selling. Consider, then, Taiwan, which has a total island population of less than just 21.5 million people and 2.78 million direct sellers! These and other statistics indicate significant engagement or at least experimentation with this form of entrepreneurship.

As we have seen and will see throughout this book, many New Professionals are coming to view network marketing as one of the best opportunities to reconfigure their lifestyles, work cultures, and financial game plans. Were the network marketing industry of the 1990s simply frozen in place, it is unlikely that we would be seeing a significant migration of more highly skilled and successful people to it. Direct selling and network marketing would remain as much a social activity for part-timers rather than a more comprehensive career and life plan.

But the industry has not been frozen in place. It is undergoing substantial and mostly positive changes—exciting developments that are leading many top professionals to take their first serious, unbiased look at the least expensive and most promising model of entrepreneurship in existence today.

Network marketing today has a new face, and describing it for you means it's time for a new chapter!

CHAPTER 5

The New Face of
Network Marketing

Network marketing is an industry rich in history with a long, albeit controversial, past—one that is deeply rooted in the traditions of face-to-face salesmanship, an occupation honored in many societies but frequently disparaged in our own.

By the 1990s, as documented in chapter 4, the industry had achieved a level of acceptance and legitimacy it never knew before. Today its impact on the economy and society extends well beyond its still relatively small claim on total consumer sales or the workforce, attracting a broad array of individual participants for diverse reasons. It is clearly positioned as an attractive alternative professional lifestyle for workers and an effective alternative distribution channel for consumer product and service companies struggling to be heard in a fragmented, Internet-driven marketplace.

Why? How did it come to pass that that an industry that traces it roots to the door-to-door Fuller brush salesman, the Avon lady, the Tupperware party hostess, and the flag-waving Amway distributor become such a potent channel of distribution for a growing number of top product and service companies? What has made network marketing such an attractive avenue of entrepreneurship for so many skilled and seasoned professionals?

Only part of the answer rests in changes outside the industry—economic, social, and technological changes that are forcing both companies and professionals to seek new distribution and income-generating opportunities. Much of the answer resides in what is happening to network marketing itself.

Industry standards in product development, marketing, management, financial systems, technology, and business ethics have risen substantially in recent years, giving network marketing a "new face" based in reality and not the customary and expected industry hype.

Network marketing has become a business that is international in scope, powered by new technology, rich with innovative, proprietary products—and that is thoroughly compatible with the New Professional's renewed focus on family, lifestyle, retirement planning, and time freedom.

In this chapter, we will outline seven major trends that are quickly coming to define the new face of network marketing, trends that will fuel its growth as well as its economic and social impact for years to come. But to understand these trends fully, it is first necessary to clear up some of the misperceptions about the industry, perpetuated by some of the people in it, that tend to exaggerate its accomplishments to date.

From the outset, we promised a clear-eyed view of industry achievements and potential so that aspiring New Professionals can thoughtfully evaluate both their interest and prospects in network marketing. This industry has been subjected a great deal of criticism, stereotyping, and even undue harassment by competitors and regulators over the years, but some of these attacks have been brought on by network marketers themselves.

THE "LIES" OF NETWORK MARKETING

The early history of network marketing was written by strong sales personalities with powerful communications skills. These "Type A" individuals transformed the prospecting and product sales approach from the traditional "pitch and patter" of door-to-door selling into a fervent, emotionally laden hard sell. This hard sell promised not only a decent product and a good income but also an opportunity to change lives, overcome addictions, repair failing marriages, revitalize America, and change the world!

The "sales story" had to be charismatic, captivating, and compelling to close the sale and to keep recruits motivated. Exaggeration and hyperbole were the tone of the day.

Product claims usually could not be verified. Company monitoring of salespeople was ineffective—or nonexistent. Network marketing was not alone in its lack of sensitivity to consumer interests. The modern consumer protection movement and customer satisfaction ethic remained in various stages of infancy throughout the economy.

> This industry has been subjected to a great deal of criticism, stereotyping, and even undue harassment by competitors and regulators.

In this culture of overstatement, some network marketers exploited the market; others were victimized. Stephanie Mehta, a staff reporter for the *Wall Street Journal*, identified a 1984 article used to recruit distributors that appears to have fueled a major wave of misinformation and factual distortion that has plagued the industry for the past fifteen years and is still referenced.

Mehta explains that the article, "by multilevel consultant Beverly Nadler, states without attribution that Harvard teaches multilevel marketing. It also states that between 50% and 65% of all goods and services will be sold through multilevel methods by the 1990's." The *Journal* never reported this statement.

Mehta reports that Nadler couldn't be reached to comment. But in her 1992 book, *Congratulations, You Lost Your Job,* she admitted that she didn't verify some information in her original article.

John Milton Fogg's classic criticism of this industry weakness, "The Lies of MLM,"—should be on the "must read" list for every networker and prospect in the culture. Fogg documented several of the most common "lies":

- "The *Wall Street Journal* says that by the year 2000, 60–70% of all goods and services will be sold through network marketing." The reporters and staffers at the *Wall Street Journal* denied that statement was ever made. It is logically invalid and a factual misstatement.

- "MLM is taught at the Harvard and Stanford business schools and in other leading colleges and universities." Harvard administrators and professors denied that they ever taught network marketing in the college's curriculum. Harvard Business School professor Thomas Bonoma emphasized in the *Marketing News*, "We do not teach such methods [MLM]. . . . [T]hey are not part of the curriculum. . . . [T]hey are not taught at this or any other reputable business school in the country."

- "Some 20 percent of all millionaires in America were created through network marketing." At Fogg's writing in the early 1990s, he reported that "90 percent of the millionaires were created through real estate." Fogg acknowledged that some network marketers earn a million dollars a year, while others earn a million dollars over their network marketing careers. "But 20 percent of all the millionaires in the United States," he wrote, "please, use some common sense."

- "John Naisbitt, in his best selling book, *Megatrands,* says network marketing is the wave of the future." Fogg countered, "John Naisbitt never mentioned network marketing in *Megatrends, Megatrends 2000* [the latest edition], or anywhere else."

Fogg summarized his exposition with this powerful charge to network marketers: "I urge each of you to squash the lies you find out there. Tell the truth. Honesty is and always will be the very best of policies. Integrity is our most precious asset."

Income Claims and Emphasis on Money

Network marketing has been criticized for its preoccupation and overemphasis on "making money." Critics argue there is too much focus on "getting rich quickly, with no work."

The fact is, however, that the network marketing industry contains many examples of people who, from relatively modest beginnings, have developed substantial fortunes. For example, Dexter Yeager, arguably one of the wealthiest practitioners of the network marketing distributor culture, began as an Amway distributor, building the most powerful downline organization in Amway, and then expanded into the "tool" business, producing sales aids and ultimately building a diversified family financial empire. Mark Yarnell, a minister, launched his network marketing career with Nu Skin in the mid-1980s and achieved a multimillion-dollar annual income by the mid-1990s with a worldwide distributor organization estimated at over 250,000 people. Building on that success, Mark has become a best-selling author, educator, and industry speaker.

Jeff Roberti, the leading income earner in National Safety Associates (NSA) in the 1990s; the late Ken Pontious, the top distributor in Enrich; Todd Smith and Randy Schroeder at Rexall Showcase; Brian Bumpas with Mannatech; Craig Byrson, Dave Johnson, Richard Kall, Laura Kall, Russ Karlan, and Craig Tillitson from Nu Skin—and the list goes on and on—have all achieved multimillion-dollar annual income status.

Nu Skin reports that, in the United States in 1998, its top income earners, the "Blue Diamonds," earned, on average, over $480,000 per year. In 1995, Nu Skin organized its Millionaire Club for distributors who had earned a million dollars or more in commissions from Nu Skin International. As of June 2000, that elite group has 264 members.

While the "big-money income earners" are obviously newsworthy, hundreds of thousands of other network marketing distributors make substantial incomes, if not in the millionaire class. Tens of millions of additional people worldwide make important contributions to their personal income, improve their psychological and physical health, enhance their lifestyles, and broaden their human experience—because of the network marketing culture!

Do all network marketers make "Big Money"? Of course not. The point is that some network marketers can and do make impressive incomes. The opportunity for achieving wealth is there!

As noted in chapter 4, however, 68 percent of all network marketing distributors become involved in the field for a wide range of different reasons beyond "making money." A lower commitment to "business building" is evident, as the Direct Selling Association (DSA) reported in its distributor profile that only 5 percent of the distributor population works full-time or forty hours or more per week in network marketing; 52 percent work nine hours or less per week.

The lower time investment, however, does impact the income earned. As noted in the DSA's income profile, the average distributor earns less than $12,000 per year. Many network marketing companies publish income claim disclaimers to reduce misconceptions about the "get rich quick" myth. Amway, for example, states clearly in "The Amway Sales and Marketing Plan" that every potential distributor must review, "The Average Monthly Gross Income for 'Active Distributors' was $65. . . . Approximately 46 percent of all distributors of record were found to be active."

The central theme is, however, that the opportunity for producing significant wealth in network marketing does exist. A committed distributor can learn the mechanics of network distribution and make significant income and experience other benefits as well. Anyone can be successful. Most people, however, will not define their specific goals and make the necessary commitment of time and energy to achieve them.

The Myth of Saturation

Critics of network marketing—some mathematical economists and theoretical statisticians, many regulators, and laypeople naïve about the network marketing process—proclaim the myth of saturation in the network marketing industry's growth. The saturation theme is as follows: If network marketing continues to grow, everyone in the world will ultimately be recruited into some network marketing company. Within the industry, enthusiastic but uninformed recruiters promote, "Here's your chance to get in on a ground-floor business opportunity, before the market gets saturated."

The dynamic social/economic/technological/cultural dimensions of change that have been documented in chapters 2 and 3 will provide the fuel for network marketing's growth in decade 2000. To review, the contemporary social fabric and personal lifestyles are bombarded with continuing structural change in the United States:

- Over two million people get married each year.

- Around four million new births occur annually with potentially dramatic impact on the family units.

- Annually, more than one million divorces are processed through the courts.

- Roughly two million high school students graduate each year.

- More than two million people die each year, often with dramatic impact on the surviving family members.

- In excess of one million undergraduate degrees are awarded annually.

- An estimated four hundred thousand master's degrees are granted each year.

- Approximately forty thousand advanced medical, engineering, technical, business, economics, social science, and other doctoral degrees are earned annually.

- Untold millions of professional, skilled, and unskilled workers lose their jobs then experience prolonged unemployment, change jobs, or change entire career fields annually.

Researchers in network marketing almost universally agree that the most critical single factor influencing a potential distributor's decision to become involved in network marketing is some dramatic change in that individual's life situation. This current, accelerated turmoil guarantees "windows of opportunity" that encourage reassessment of part-time and full-time career options by the New Professionals.

Within the direct selling and network marketing culture, there are potentially three levels of market penetration and saturation:

- Exposure to the network marketing industry message and/or an individual company's business proposition

- Trial of a new product or service as a user

- Joining a network marketing company as a wholesale buyer/user and/or business builder

Analysis of the "state-of-the-industry" in terms of market penetration and saturation reveals that several measures are relevant:

- In terms of shopping pattern penetration and product trail/usage, the 1997 Wirthlin Worldwide research study of direct sales representatives reported earlier also found direct selling has not saturated mass shopping patterns.

  - As a benchmark of shopping penetration, only 51 percent of the population have ever bought a product or service through the direct selling channel *in their lives!* Only 29 percent have made a direct sale purchase *in the past year;* only 11 percent *in the past month.*

  - By comparison, virtually everyone has made a retail purchase, and 80 percent have made a mail-order purchase.

- As another measure of saturation, at an estimated $23.1 billion in direct retail sales in 1998, the direct selling channel accounted for less than 1 percent of the total $2.7 billion of retail sales that year in the United States.

- In terms of distributor penetration, the 9.7 million direct sales members in 1998 accounted for 3.6 percent of the total 270.6 million United States population and 7.4 percent of 131.5 million employed U.S. workforce.

By all of these measures, direct selling and network marketing are clearly not saturated in the U.S. economy. The threat of saturation *is* a myth!

The Reality of Attrition

Attrition expressed as dropout or turnover is predictably high in the direct selling profession. The direct selling practitioner operates in a highly competitive environment. The network marketing "business builder" also faces the challenges of entrepreneurship. The risk of failure is a reality. The rewards for success in terms of wealth and professional development, however, can be extraordinary.

The causes of attrition are numerous and complex. Frequently, distributors enter the network marketing arena with inadequate understanding of what is involved in the process, without a clear business model and work plan, and with unrealistic expectations, performance milestones, and time horizons. The new distributors do not get adequate training and reinforcement. The "upline teaching downline" process often doesn't work because the upline individual may be an inexperienced new recruit with limited knowledge; a weak trainer, communicator, and coach; or too busy to support the new distributor adequately.

Many distributors experiment with network marketing and never have any long-term commitment or perseverance. Others achieve their short-term goals (e.g., finance a vacation, pay off a loan, buy a big-screen television) and retire. Some lack the energy level or work ethic, get fatigued, and quit. Many people are victims of organizational "fallout": They join an organization and participate for a while, then lose interest and retire; or they maintain their enthusiasm, work through various achievement/pin levels in the group, lose momentum, withdraw from the action, and disappear into the "black hole" in network marketing space.

There is no definitive information about actual attrition rates in direct selling or direct marketing. The actual statistical information about attrition in direct selling is largely anecdotal or based on narrowly focused individual studies.

- Spokespersons for several major direct selling companies confidentially reported dropout rates for direct sales persons in the 80 to 110 percent range.

- Buss reported in an article in *Nation's Business* in 1997 that "turnover for some MLM companies is 100 percent a year."

- Wotruba, Sciglimpaglia, and Tyagi, speaking to the American Marketing Association, reported that "turnover rates in direct selling range from a low estimate of 43.3 percent to a high estimate of 145.1 percent . . . depending on the calculation procedures used."

- Smith wrote in *Multilevel Marketing* that most directing selling organizations have annual dropout rates of over 100 percent.

- Wotruba conducted another survey of independent salespeople for some MLM companies and found that attrition is 100 percent a year at four direct selling companies (Mary Kay Cosmetics, Saladmaster, Tupperware, and United Consumers Club) and that the average salesperson had been in direct selling for 8.6 months.

The DSA, the source of the most comprehensive analytical industry-wide information, uses three different measures of sales force entry and exit in the U.S. direct selling community:

1. *Dropout rate*—the number of salespeople that dropped during the year as a percentage of the total number of salespeople for the year

2. *Turnover rate*—the number of salespeople that dropped during the year as a percentage of the average number of salespeople at the start and at the end of the year

3. *Retention rate*—the difference between the number of salespeople at the end of the year and the number recruited during the year, expressed as a percentage of salespeople at the start of the year

Based on these measures, the DSA reports the attrition statistics given in Table 5.1 for the direct selling industry for 1997 and 1998, the most current and comprehensive industry information available.

Tracking attrition in the network marketing industry is further confused by several other issues. No common definition

Table 5.1   *Measures of Attrition for the Direct Selling Industry*

	1997	1998
Dropout rate	34.9	35.2
Turnover rate	56.9	56.0
Retention rate	39.4	42.9

exists for an "active distributor." The time period for meeting "active" criteria also varies across companies:

- Amway, for example defines an "active" distributor as someone who has (1) attempted to make a retail sale of Amway products, (2) presented the Amway Sales and Marketing Plan to a prospect, (3) received bonus money from the company, or (4) attended a company or distributor meeting in the past month.

- Nu Skin International, in comparison, requires "active" distributors to have a minimum product purchase volume of 100 points (equivalent to $100) in the past month.

- Avon International defines an "active" distributor as someone who has made at least one product purchase over six merchandising campaigns over a three-month period.

- Many network marketing companies record all "signed-up" distributors as "active" as long as they continue to pay their annual renewal fee to the company regardless of their personal purchase or business-building activity.

- Other network marketing companies include all signed-up distributors as "active," require no annual renewal fees, and keep them on the distributor roster, independent of any product purchase or business-building activity, until they formally request deletion from the distributor list.

SEVEN MAJOR TRENDS IN NETWORK MARKETING

Now let's look at the seven major industry trends that are defining the new face of network marketing. These trends are positioning the industry for substantial growth in both product sales and the number of participants in this unique form of entrepreneurship.

Trend 1: A Powerful Distribution Channel

Network marketing has developed a powerful distribution channel uniquely adaptive to the Internet era. Product and services companies ignore it at their peril. Traditional corporations are now jumping on the network marketing bandwagon, which is bringing welcome change to both business strategies.

Marketing in the twenty-first century will be faced with a myriad of compounding distribution challenges:

- Traditional distribution channels will be glutted with the waves of new products.

- Massive overcommunication will clutter traditional newspaper, magazine, radio, television, and point-of-sale promotion channels of communications in the marketplace.

- In 1999, the advertising industry poured over $115 billion into this cacophony of communication noise and clutter with decreasing impact on consumer buying behavior.

- The consumer will become jaded, potentially traumatized, with overchoice.

- Marketing and distribution expenses, already approximating 60 to 75 percent of total product costs in some industry sectors, will continue to escalate in the face of rising new product underperformance under the pressure of oversupply.

Clearly, the marketing discipline needs an injection of communication effectiveness and distribution efficiency. Network marketing can be a powerful solution. It can accelerate the speed of product entry, rapid market trial, and consumer acceptance. Network marketing can provide efficiency of communication through the most powerful vehicle in the marketing arsenal, one-on-one, word-of-mouth communication. The channel can also provide a more direct and lower-cost distribution connection between the manufacturer or service provider and the end-line consumer.

> Network marketing provides efficiency of communication through the most powerful vehicle in the marketing arsenal: word-of-mouth communication.

Over the past twenty years, as network marketing's power as a distribution channel has been documented and publicized in the business culture, companies who had shunned it before now embrace it. They can't afford not to.

Direct Selling Companies Move into Network Marketing
Beginning in the 1980s, many traditional direct sales companies moved into the network marketing channel:

- Watkins, through "the Watkins Man," one of the oldest (since 1868) door-to-door suppliers of nutrition, personal care, household products, and home remedies, moved into network marketing.

- Fuller Brush, another venerable veteran in direct sales of household products since 1905 and in the 1940s one of the largest direct sales organizations in the world, moved into network marketing.

- Documenting this trend, the Direct Selling Association (DSA) reports that over 80 percent of direct sellers are now using multilevel marketing plans, up substantially in recent years.

Traditional Corporate America Diversifies into Network Marketing   There has also been a distinct movement of traditional corporate America buying network marketing divisions, establishing start-up network marketing organizations, or developing strategic alliances/joint ventures with network marketing companies as a planned strategy of diversification into this lucrative distribution arena. Some examples:

> The Direct Selling Association reports that over 80 percent of direct sellers now use multilevel marketing plans.

- In 1973, Gillette acquired Jafra Cosmetics, a network marketing company, as a corporate diversification. Gillette owned Jafra for seventeen years, experiencing a compound growth rate of 18.5 percent and reaching $229.5 million sales in 1997, when it was sold to a financial buyer.

- In 1977, Colgate Palmolive acquired Princess House, a crystal and housewares marketer.

- In the early 1980s, MCI and Amway developed a joint venture to feature MCI long-distance services in the Amway Personal Shopper Catalog.

- In 1982, Pre-Paid Legal Services, which had been marketing its products through traditional commission-based direct sales, added a network marketing sales force to focus on individual sales, while its in-house team concentrates on larger group sales.

- In 1984, Sprint, Inc., and Network 2000, a newly organized network marketing company, structured a joint venture to recruit new Sprint long-distance subscribers as an extension of Sprint's multichannel marketing program to carve market share from AT&T. Over a three-year period, Network 2000 captured 3 million new subscribers for Sprint through the network marketing channel.

- In 1989, Shaklee U.S. was acquired by Yamanouchi Pharmaceutical Company Ltd., the second largest pharmaceutical firm in Japan, as a diversification maneuver.

- In the 1990s, AT&T experimented in a strategic alliance with Shaklee to market telecommunications services through that distribution channel. That venture was subsequently abandoned.

- In 1991, Rexall Sundown created a network marketing arm with dedicated proprietary products, while continuing to market other products through more traditional channels.

- In the 1990s, Primerica, the descendant company of A. L. Williams, sells financial services through its independent sales force of more than 153,000 people, using a multilevel compensation plan—proving to be a major source of business for its corporate parent, Citigroup.

- In 1998, the Canadian telecom giant, Teleglobe, acquired Excel Communications, viewing Excel's chief asset as its dedicated sales force and customer base.

This blend of sales and distribution approaches will become a model for many companies, anxious to leave no stone unturned in their quest for shares of a fragmented market. In the coming years, we will see:

- Traditional companies buying network marketing companies

- Network marketing companies building more traditional distribution channels and in-house sales forces to complement their independent distributor forces

- Corporate America adding network marketing arms to their mix of sales approaches

- Companies in search of foreign markets, especially in developing countries with abundant indigenous labor, turning increasingly to network marketing approaches

Whatever it takes to unearth new customers! This also explains why the network marketing community has become a "living, breathing" target market in its own right. A growing number of traditional consumer product manufacturers and marketers are selling their products through network marketing channels to the network marketing distributors.

> It seems illogical for traditional companies to disparage network marketing companies when many of those same companies are jumping on the bandwagon.

"Exhibit A" is Amway's consumer catalogs and its Quixtar Web site, which sell a wide range of branded consumer products. For example, Amway distributors and their customers can find items sporting labels such as Adidas, Christian Dior, Disney, Frito-Lay, General Electric, Goodyear, Kodak, Rubbermaid, Whirlpool, Wrangler, and hundreds of others. Other network marketing companies such as American Communications Network (ACN), Big Planet, Market America, PricenetUSA.com, and Rexall Showcase do the same, using Internet shopping malls.

Service firms ranging from health insurance providers to auto clubs to computer manufacturers are busy and eagerly making deals with network marketing firms to supply their armies of independent businesspeople.

Mergers, Acquisitions, and Strategic Alliances   Moving parallel with the growth in the network marketing infrastructure, there has been a flurry of mergers, acquisitions, joint ventures, and strategic alliances reported across leading companies over the past several years. Some key examples:

- In spring 2000, Royal Numico N.V. announced plans to merge with Rexall Sundown, the parent of Rexall Showcase, its network marketing subsidiary, and Enrich International. These mergers follow a similar acquisition of General Nutrition Corporation by Numico in August 1999. The transactions collectively reinforce Numico's strategy to be the global leader in the nutritional supplements market. These additions give Numico a strong position in all channels of the growing U.S. nutritional market and a powerful growth platform in the United States and around the world.

- Nutrition for Life International (NFLI) announced acquisitions of Advanced Nutraceuticals, Inc. (ANI), and Bactorlac Pharmaceutical Inc. (Bactorlac). The maneuver provided Nutrition for Life, a network marketing organization selling an extensive line of private-labeled nutritional supplements and other consumer products, with captive manufacturing capacity. NFLI's strategic goal is to "foster an expanded positive awareness of our growth strategies . . . value creating potential to the investment community and potential acquisition candidates."

- Big Planet and I-Link have organized a strategic alliance in which I-Line Network marketing representatives and their sales volumes will transition intact to Big Planet. The combined I-Link Worldwide and Big Planet network marketing sales forces would market I-Link's enhanced telecommunications products and services to residential and small business markets. Big Planet would also purchase I-Link's products and services on a wholesale basis and would assume responsibility for providing customer service to existing I-Link customers.

- Fuller Brush, a longtime direct sales and network marketing pioneer and subsidiary of the CPAC financial group, entered into a joint venture with Quixtar, the Amway affiliated e-commerce Web site, as a partner store.

- Prodigy Communications Corporation, in its third acquisition since its IPO in February 1999, purchased FlashNet Communications. FlashNet's mission is "to bring the power of the Internet to the masses—affordably, reliably, conveniently." In announcing the acquisition, Prodigy reported, "In a single transaction, Prodigy acquires a talented pool of dedicated employees and significantly bolsters our infrastructure, customer service operations, and acquisition channels."

- Proctor and Gamble, the marketing giant in the United States, a longtime foe of the direct selling and network marketing industry and aggressive critic and legal attacker of Amway, has entered into a joint marketing agreement with Tupperware Corporation to promote each other's products. Brad Casper, P&G (Proctor & Gamble) vice president of Global Strategic Planning and Design, reported, "This cooperative relationship gives P&G brands the opportunity to bond with their target consumers through product experiences and the high-quality products provided by Tupperware and its representatives. . . . The relationship has proven very successful. We are looking forward to continued growth in 2000–2001."

- Pre-Paid Legal Services, established in 1972, has launched an aggressive strategy of acquisition and strategic alliances.

As a major expansion in the network marketing arena, the firm acquired The People's Network (TPN), its 30 thousand distributors, and its communication capability, the "Success Channel" on the Primestar digital satellite network. Reflecting an innovative marketing flair and his commitment to growth through strategic alliances, Harold C. Stonecipher, chairman and CEO, has experimented with numerous unique deals, ranging from the sales of Pre-Paid Legal Services by CNA, the Chicago-based insurance company; to its existing and new group account customers; to Primerica marketing legal plans through its more than one hundred thousand personal financial analysts; to a pilot program with Staples, the office supply discount retailer, to sell legal plans to its small business customers.

- Extending its diversification strategy in the vitamin supplementation market, Nu Skin acquired Pharmanex, a premier phytopharmaceutical company. About that union, Nu Skin reported, "This transaction combines the most innovative health supplement developer with the most potent distribution channel for these products. . . . The acquisition . . . reflects our commitment to product innovation and differentiation and moves us closer to becoming the world's leader in both natural health and direct selling."

- Reflecting more of that repositioning movement, earlier, Avon Products sold Discovery Toys. Avon announced, "Discovery Toys is unlikely to reach sufficient size to have a meaningful impact on Avon's overall results. . . . We are focusing our resources on our beauty business."

Summarizing this section, we may say that the strategic developments across the network marketing channel are dramatic and impressive. The marketing creativity and the organizational dynamics are reminiscent of the Fortune 100 "fast-laners." The network marketing industry is moving through a shakeout, consolidation, and repositioning phase.

Change is reality. The "lotions and potions" companies with "hail fellow/well met," backslapping, and cigar-chewing sales and marketing approaches are an endangered species. They can't compete in this increasingly sophisticated market and in the world of the New Professionals.

These cases illustrate the breadth of potential applications for this powerful distribution channel. Moreover, the migration of network marketing to the business mainstream and the corresponding migration of traditional business to network marketing has interesting implications for both communities—and for the New Professionals who consider fleeing corporate America to this industry. If tapping into the potential of this business model is good enough for companies like General Electric, AT&T, and Kodak, perhaps it is also good enough for professionals who find its income potential and lifestyle attractive but who are worried about their status, image and "what people will think."

Indeed, it would seem illogical at best—and hypocritical at worst—for traditional companies and their boosters in the media and financial markets to continue a frequent practice of disparaging network marketing companies when many of those same companies are in some way jumping on the bandwagon.

But the increasing number of marriages between network marketing and more traditional business approaches spells changes for the culture of networking as well. Many network marketers are fervent true believers in one-on-one selling and recruiting. They seek companies they deem to be fully committed to the independent distributor force.

The history of the industry, however, is replete with cases in which these sales forces have stagnated or even broken apart because of a real or perceived slight on the part of corporate management. Perhaps it was a detrimental change in the compensation plan or lavish price increases and charges for membership, materials, and training. Maybe the company failed to develop a culture in which the business leaders reached out to build, train, and motivate their downlines. Or perhaps it neglected to keep pace with the market by developing and introducing new and appealing products.

In this climate of sensitivity, many network marketers may view a company that blends different sales and marketing approaches as not fully committed to the network marketing gospel. The presence of an in-house sales force, selling products through the normal retail chain or "distributor-free" on the Web and certainly selling the company to a larger corporate parent, can spur waves of rumor and doubt. At a time of full employment (at least in the United States) and fierce competition in the industry for a finite supply of potential networkers, companies will have to skillfully demonstrate their dedication to their independent sales force even as they diversify their business strategies.

> The shift in attitude and culture in both traditional corporations and network marketing companies is an ideal situation.

For their part, devoted network marketers will have to broaden their outlook and appreciation of what their companies must do in a global economy not only to stay ahead of the competition but simply to survive.

For the New Professional, the shift in attitude and culture in both traditional corporations and network marketing companies—and the movement of each toward the best attributes of the other—is an ideal situation. It has become more acceptable to engage in network marketing approaches and more professional, appealing, and interesting once they get there.

Trend 2: The New Professionalism

Network marketing companies are dramatically increasing their investments in professional management, information systems, technologies, and strategic planning and bringing a more businesslike demeanor to their organizations. Business meetings are replacing pep rallies; business suits now outnumber people in shorts, blue jeans, and funny hats.

One of the most impressive developments in the network marketing culture has been the dramatic increase in professionalism across the industry, starting in the 1990s. Companies are adopting a more professional management style in their operations. Leading firms are investing in management tools, strategic planning processes, competitive market positioning analyses, corporate benchmarking, "best business practices" analysis, and data-based management software long associated with the Fortune 100 corporate culture.

> **L**eading firms are investing in management tools long associated with the Fortune 100 culture.

Charles King, in his role as educator, researcher, industry consultant, and expert witness in litigation cases, has had the opportunity to see confidential and sometimes very sensitive competitive information across many large and small network marketing firms. He reports that the leading network marketing companies are investing in increasingly sophisticated strategic planning activities, management processes, information technologies, and marketing research programs. The smaller firms are also upgrading their management tools within their financial resources.

Amway Corporation, for example, has an extensive, ongoing strategic planning and competitive monitoring program to help Amway in its global market expansion. The corporation maintains an extensive marketing research capability to track consumer buying behavior, explore new product concepts and consumer reactions, measure distributor motivations, and profile distributor segments at different achievement levels.

Meanwhile, Blake Roney, chairman, and Steve Lund, CEO, of Nu Skin International galvanized into a formidable management duo in shaping the destiny of Nu Skin during the past fifteen years. Nu Skin creatively applied sophisticated market segmentation analyses to identify lucrative target markets, thus founding the Nu Skin strategy of divisional diversification. Scott Schwerdt, vice president of distributor services, vice president of strategic planning, and chief operating officer at Big Planet, and the team of operating managers that executed the Roney-Lund charge typify the caliber and approach of the executive talent that has developed at many network marketing companies.

Mary Kay Cosmetics, as reported by Richard Bartlett in his book *The Direct Option,* has historically had an ongoing marketing research program. Bartlett conducted extensive marketing research probing why women join direct selling organizations and psychologically profiling different distributor groups based on their direct selling income success.— Of key interest, the research found "successful (direct and network marketing) sales people have a communication style or social style that encourages the building of relationships with their customers. . . . The most successful sales leaders have a combination of relationship and task orientation" (in their communication styles).

Network marketing firms are integrating sophisticated information technologies into their management information systems. Entire employee groups are communicating via digital cell phones. Most companies have comprehensive, satellite-based, voice mail and other corporate-distributor communication programs. E-mail and a wide range of electronic communications connections are now being used for order entry, inventory tracking, order expediting, and shipping. Three-way telephone conference calling, fax on demand, and Internet on-line product presentations and distributor training are commonplace.

Greater professionalism in the executive suite has permeated the organizational cultures of many firms. Jim Robinson attended a Rexall Showcase distributor meeting recently and found it much different from network marketing meetings he had attended in the past. He reports from the scene:

> On a sunny Saturday morning in Las Vegas in December 1998, more than 1,000 well-dressed men and women [wove] their way around the banks of slot machines and past the rows of card tables and entered the Jubilee Theater at 9:00 A.M. sharp. They were greeted by the mellow music of a saxophonist on a stage that was simply adorned with displays of Rexall Showcase International products. Shortly thereafter, Rexall Showcase president Dave Schofield kicked off this daylong series of briefings, testimonials, and training sessions with a financial and strategic overview of the company's progress and future plans.
>
> I was struck by the seriousness of purpose on display at this event. It was a business meeting, not a rally. Virtually everyone was professionally attired. There were few chants, cheers, whoops, or hollers. No one rushed the stage after the speeches to get autographs from their favorite company or distributor "celebrities."
>
> The presentations were heavy on factual information, business developments, and social trends, relying very little on what I call the "you gotta believe!" sloganeering. The biggest demonstration of enthusiasm among this group came when Schofield revealed that in response to an industry-wide drop in stock prices, including Rexall Sundown's, the company would be revaluing stock options at a lower level, making them more attractive.

Clearly this atmosphere marks a departure from the one normally associated with network marketing. Both authors frequently attend meetings of salespeople for companies such as Amway, Big Planet, Cell Tech, Excel Communications,

Kaire Nutraceuticals, Mannatech, Nu Skin, Nutrition for Life, Pharmenix, Prepaid Legal Services, and others that are similar in tone and demeanor. As the industry moves more into the mainstream, this style will likely become the model for the future.

Motivation, excitement, and even fun are all critical components to building a successful team, be it made up of employees in a traditional company or independent distributors in a network marketing concern. Yet increasingly, new entrants, particularly those from the professional world, are saying, like Sergeant Joe Friday used to do on *Dragnet*, "Just the facts, ma'am."

As it seeks to build its distributor force beyond today's population, network marketing's challenge is to retain its professional, upscale, serious demeanor while opening itself to potential recruits from other walks of life. Indeed, while the Rexall Showcase Las Vegas attendees appeared evenly split along gender lines with a broad cross-section of ages, little ethnic or income diversity was readily apparent—at least at this meeting. The children and babies seen disrupting other network marketing conferences with their cries and antics were nowhere to be seen here.

> Network marketing's challenge is to retain its professional, upscale, serious demeanor while opening itself to recruits from other walks of life.

Still, the maturing process underway among network marketing sales forces will likely pay off for the industry in the long run, even if in the short run greater numbers of less serious recruits could be signed up faster using the more inspirational, take-it-on-faith approaches of the past.

Network marketing's growing professionalism is happening overseas as well. The annals of network marketing's move into Asia and Latin America, particularly in developing countries, are filled with dramatic stories of thousands of poor but hopeful recruits standing in the rain and beating down doors to sign up for a small sliver of the American dream. But now a more cool-headed approach is taking hold. Dave Schofield, of Rexall Showcase, reports, for example, that during a meeting with new and potential Hong Kong distributors last year, they peppered him with detailed questions about Rexall Showcase's market capitalization and future business strategies.

Making the transition to a more businesslike approach should also pay dividends as network marketing companies confront government regulators in the United States and abroad. Unfair as it may be, a company whose management and finances are hidden from public scrutiny, which operates under a veil of secrecy while at the same time whipping thousands of citizens into a frenzy over its business opportunity, is likely to trigger the suspicions and paranoia of many governments, ranging from state attorneys general here and the more authoritarian regimes abroad.

Trend 3: Global Expansion
Network marketing companies and participants alike will look overseas for their greatest sales and recruiting opportunities, building exciting and lucrative multinational business from their corporate headquarters and home offices. Opportunities for foreign travel, exposure to different cultures, and sophisticated international commercial transactions will further enrich the network marketing experience for New Professionals.

Ninety-four percent of the world's population does not live in the United States. Obviously, then, most of the markets, consumers, and distributors of the future exist outside U.S. borders.

Industries across the board have been recognizing this new global economic reality. Exports now account for nearly one-third of the entire U.S. economy, a dramatic increase over the past twenty years. These international opportunities are not simply confined to the largest corporations. More medium- and smaller-sized businesses are getting into the act—and statistics show that, on the whole, firms that are engaged in international business pay higher wages, are more profitable, and are less likely to go out of business than those who do not participate.

> Statistics show that firms engaged in international business pay higher wages, are more profitable, and are less likely to go under than those not engaged.

For network marketers—who take pride in a business ethic whereby you build your prosperity by helping others build theirs—the opportunities to apply that ethic on a global scale, particularly in developing nations, are tremendous. Today more than 33 million people participate in direct selling businesses all around the world. Direct Selling Association president Neil Offen estimates that number could soar as high as two hundred million over the next ten years.

Many network marketing firms have already extended their reach around the globe. It is of no small significance that a company like Amway, whose name was derived from that of its incubator company (which was called the American Way), operates in fifty-three markets worldwide and makes some 70 percent of its sales outside the United States!

Amway is not alone. Nu Skin operates in thirty countries. Mary Kay is in twenty-eight. Enrich sells its products in fourteen nations, and Forever Living can be found in sixty-three.

Reigniting the Asian Miracle Let's look again at Asia, which is a principal focus of network marketing's aggressive international expansion strategy. Even in the face of its recent economic crisis, Asia's potential for many industries, and especially for network marketing, is enormous.

In his recent book *Megatrends Asia,* futurist John Naisbitt wrote, "The Asian continent now accounts for half the world's population. Within five years or less, more than half of these Asian households will be able to buy an array of consumer goods—refrigerators, television sets, washing machines, computers, and cosmetics. And as many as a half billion people will be what the West understands as middle class.

"That market is roughly the size of the United States and Europe combined."

Naisbitt identified other developments that make Asia a natural prospect market for a company offering products that focus on a healthy, modern lifestyle:

- The number of Asians in poverty has decreased from 400 million to 180 million since the end of World War II, even while the population has increased another 400 million.

- The growing middle class, not including Japan's, will have amassed $8 to $10 trillion in annual spending power in the early years of the twenty-first century.

- Currently, more than eighty million mainland Chinese earn between $10,000 and $40,000 a year. In South Korea, 60 percent of those who describe themselves as middle class make over $60,000 a year. One million families in greater Bangkok, Thailand, earn over $10,000 annually.

Naisbitt's analysis was completed before the financial crisis slammed many Asian economies. No doubt some of his projections have been slowed and skewed by that crisis. But as we assess Asia's prospects for recovery and its viability as a market for networkers and New Professionals, it is important to keep several factors in perspective:

- Even in the face of global financial turmoil, economies like those of Taiwan, Singapore, and China are still growing, albeit at reduced rates of growth.

- Most analysts believe the worst is over in Thailand, Korea, and Hong Kong. They are on their way back.

- Asian cultures have long traditions of entrepreneurship that make even weakened economies choice targets for network marketing. Furthermore, many industry leaders feature product lines related to health, beauty, and aging. There is strong consumer demand for these products in Asia.

- Economic insecurity traditionally spurs rather than dampens interest in network marketing opportunities. This is particularly true in Asia, where the social safety net is far less developed than in Western economies. A modern economy like Hong Kong's, for example, does not even have a government-sponsored unemployment insurance program. If you're out of work, you're out of luck.

The *Far Eastern Economic Review* focused on the example of Thailand: "Decades of rapid economic growth have left officials unprepared to deal with the swelling numbers of unemployed created by Thailand's recession. Averse to expensive Western-style welfare systems, the government faces growing anger over its perceived indifference to unemployment."

Even in the face of such criticism, don't look for fiscally strapped governments in the region to try to play catch-up now. "Thailand, like the rest of Asia, has been reluctant to cast the sort of costly social safety net often provided by the West," the magazine continues. An economic adviser to the Thai prime minister quoted by the *Review* then discussed an interesting alternative approach: "Thailand does not aspire to emulate the Western unemployment insurance scheme. . . . Rather than handouts, the present administration prefers soft loans toward the establishment of small-scale businesses."

The magazine was quick to point out that the standard "soft loan" envisioned by the prime minister's office is just $235, which it says won't go far toward the creation of small businesses. In fact, we know of only one kind of small business you can get off the ground with that kind of money—a network marketing business!

The *Review* also reported that elsewhere in Asia "necessity is the mother of invention for . . . laid off workers as they flock to become their own bosses." For example, China's economic reform program, which centers on the closing or restructuring of inefficient, money-losing state-owned firms, could generate an astounding 17 million layoffs of urban workers throughout the country. The government is actively encouraging affected workers to start small enterprises and gives great prominence to those who have succeeded in the hope that others will follow their lead.

> Economic insecurity traditionally spurs interest in network marketing opportunities.

Several years ago, the magazine reported, one Shanghai couple lost their jobs at a manufacturing facility. With a young son to support, they made ends meet by cleaning restaurants and office buildings at night. As soon as they were able to save enough money, they started their own cleaning business, securing several contracts at prime Shanghai office towers. The company now employs thirty-five people, nearly all laid-off workers, and the couple clears $2,500 in profits a month. "I only wish I'd been laid off earlier," says the husband.

The fact that many Asians are responding to adversity by becoming entrepreneurs is one more reason that the Asian miracle, chronicled so frequently through the 1980s, will be rekindled. Hundreds of millions of aspiring middle-class Asians, seeking both fresh opportunities and products to match their new, more upscale lifestyles, make this region a prime target for network marketing.

> **H**undreds of millions of middle-class Asians make that region a prime target for network marketing.

Just look at Taiwan. As noted earlier, this prosperous island economy of 21.5 million people is already home to well over 2.7 million people, over 10 percent of the population, engaged in direct selling, who collectively generate between $1 and $2 billion in annual sales. That's an astoundingly high percentage of the population that has embraced this business model.

The Promise of Japan   Japan, the second largest economy in the world and the most important country in Asia, is today suffering its worst national crisis since the end of World War II:

- The economy not only stopped growing, but in 1998 it also actually shrunk. Evidence in 1999 indicated a sluggish recovery.

- The banking and financial systems, burdened with more than $1 trillion in bad debts, are in need of serious reform.

- The political system, heavily reliant on consensus and back-room deals among interest groups, often seems incapable of decisive action.

- A nation that revolutionized the automobile and consumer electronics industries is now playing catch-up in its embrace of information technology.

- The implicit lifetime employment compact, under which Japanese professionals would remain with one company their entire working lives in exchange for income and retirement security, has fallen victim to American-style layoffs.

- The distribution system contains multiple layers of intermediaries, causing Japanese consumers to pay exorbitant prices for the basic staples of life.

- Inefficient land use policies, which this crowded country can ill afford, have forced most families into residences that are exceedingly small by Western standards and typically located up to two hours away by train from their places of work.

No wonder many leading observers have found a crisis of confidence and spirit among the Japanese. But it would be a mistake to underestimate the Japanese.

Consider the achievements of this remarkable people. Approximately 127 million Japanese inhabit an island country smaller than California—a state considered crowded with its 36 million residents. This population density, coupled with the island nation's geographic isolation, has given rise to a strong emphasis on social organization rather than individual initiative. Japan is a mountainous country and home to virtually no natural resources. Its entire oil supply and many other essentials of an industrial economy must be imported.

The ravages of fire, earthquake, and war have on a number of occasions during the twentieth century forced Japanese society to rebuild itself almost completely. Just over fifty years ago, the major urban centers of the country were reduced to rubble. Within a generation, the Japanese had rebuilt their country and within two generations had become a world economic powerhouse.

Japan will reemerge again, but it will be a different Japan, one that combines the best qualities of its hardworking, consensus- and team-oriented culture with new entrepreneurial approaches to career, business, lifestyle, and commerce.

And that's where network marketing comes in. All the trends driving this industry and this company forward in the United States are even more pronounced in today's Japan:

- The aging of the Japanese demands different approaches to health and retirement security.

- Economic dislocation and the lack of fulfillment in the corporate and professional worlds find many looking for alternative incomes and more satisfying entrepreneurial careers.

- An overregulated, overpriced economy is squandering national and consumer wealth, prompting the Japanese to seek more efficient ways to buy and sell and do business.

A society steeped in tradition and slow to change is today readier than it has ever been to try a different path. Pioneering companies like Amway, Herbalife, and Nikken understood years ago that certain aspects of Japanese culture are very much in sync with their kind of business—selling based on relationships, families, and an intricate series of networks. Today Japan is home to an estimated 2.5 million direct sellers, who account for approximately $30+ billion in annual sales, nearly 40 percent of the world's total. With other companies such as Mannatech, Nutrition for Life, and Rexall Showcase entering the market, those numbers are going to go way up. Let's look more closely at how and why.

> All the trends driving this industry forward in the United States are even more pronounced in today's Japan.

For years, experts have tried to reconcile the fact that while Japan's overt trade barriers—tariffs and quotas—were low by global standards, trade deficits remained stubbornly high. The number one complaint from frustrated exporters and marketers was that the rigid Japanese distribution system simply froze them out. They could get their products past the shores of Japan, but not into the stores of Japan.

What these U.S. companies may not have realized is that many domestic Japanese companies, particularly smaller start-up products and services firms, faced similar barriers. For Japanese consumers, the result has been artificially high consumer prices—the highest in the world. As *Fortune* magazine once described it:

> Even when the economy was booming, Japan had one glaring problem: a distribution system as labyrinth as a shogun's palace. Everything a consumer bought—made in Japan or imported—had to weed through the books of as many as half a dozen middlemen. Some of them never took possession of the products, but all extracted a toll, creating the world's most exorbitant prices. A bottle of 96 aspirin tablets cost $20, and not just because of the strong yen.

Richard Johnson, who heads Amway's operations in Japan, has explained the challenge this way: "It's not so much that the government or society has said foreign products can't be distributed. It's rather that the major manufacturers have created a very disciplined distribution channel that doesn't permit any outsiders in, be they foreign or domestic."

He then goes on to cite the beer industry as an illustration of the kind of "discipline" he was talking about: "Up until a short time ago, Kirin Brewery Co. basically dominated the wholesale network. It was very hard to introduce a new product, regardless of all the advertising a company did, because then bars could only order what their wholesalers would provide. And the wholesaler might say, 'If you want a case of Sapporo or Suntory [other brands of Japanese beer], you've got to take ten cases of Kirin."

Given that network marketing is based on the notion of bypassing the normal distribution chain, this form of business represents nothing less than a direct, frontal assault on the Japanese business establishment. In the case of Amway, Richard Johnson recalls, "Our start-up was very difficult. We did very little business in the first five years."

Yet with increasing fervency, the supposedly complacent and organization-minded Japanese have embraced direct selling and the entrepreneurial business opportunities it carries with it. "All the ferment, and the new willingness of Japanese consumers to give American innovations a chance, are creating opportunities for U.S. companies to transplant to Japan successful business strategies from back home," explained *Fortune*.

> The supposedly complacent and organization-minded Japanese have embraced direct selling and the entrepreneurial business opportunities carried with it.

But economic insecurity and dislocation also help explain the motives of Japanese network marketers. "Many of the distributors are refugees from the stultifying, hierarchical world of Japanese big business," observed Yumiko Ono in the *Wall Street Journal*. "They want to work for themselves and be paid according to their performance, not according to their seniority. The growing number of people who do marks a big change in Japanese society."

For many Japanese, the current economic crisis has ruptured the traditional compact between employers and employees. University graduates struggle to find the jobs they were all but promised when they entered school. Middle-aged men find themselves laid off with few prospects for being rehired. Again, these are familiar circumstances for Americans during times of economic slowdown, but for the Japanese they are unheard of in the post–World War II era. Yet other employees are not pushed out; they want to jump out! They seek a bigger, more interesting challenge in their professional lives rather than simply don the company uniform and work one job at one firm every single day from age 25 to 60.

The yearning for more satisfying career options has grown especially strong among Japanese women. Japanese homemakers have long held sway over their country's consumer economy, controlling the household purse and purchasing decisions, carefully parceling out allowances to their "salaryman" husbands for their bowls of noodles at lunch and after-work beers and snacks with colleagues.

However, for all the immense collective spending power enjoyed and exercised by Japanese women, it has proved to be a boring dead-end existence for many. For a brief period in early adulthood, Japanese women experience some measure of freedom: higher education away from home, perhaps an international trip to Hawaii or California with classmates, a job in a nice office in Tokyo. Then, for most women, comes marriage. One or both spouses leave home in the predawn darkness for the 90-minute train ride to work and return exhausted long after dark. If the wife works, she will likely return first to care for children and take care of the house. While conditions are changing for working women in Japan, the glass ceiling in the corporate world remains a formidable and foreboding barrier. Meanwhile, her husband will typically arrive home much later, long after the children are asleep, after an evening of fraternizing with coworkers, which is deemed an important and almost obligatory part of a man's career.

Economic insecurity and vigorous questioning about the quality of life received in exchange for all those hours of commuting, working, and socializing have sparked great interest in alternatives like network marketing. Explains one Japanese Amway distributor to the *Wall Street Journal,* "People are starting to wonder what they could do as a single gear in a company. They want to have fun. They want to do something. But they have nothing. When they join Amway, there's something that clicks."

Forbes magazine has assessed network marketing's appeal: "[The] be-your-own-boss pitch may be greeted cynically in the United States, but in regimented Japan it finds a willing audience, especially among housewives and frustrated salarymen."

* * *

The stage is clearly set for a boom in network marketing in Japan—but it is hardly alone. From mainstay international markets for the industry like Canada and Australia and the European Union to the emerging economies of Latin America, Eastern Europe, and Russia, network marketers are finding tremendous opportunities to expand their businesses and sales organizations. Dozens of top networkers have told us that it is the potential for international expansion that excites them the most about their businesses. Going forward, it is sure to be a powerful magnet drawing many New Professionals to network marketing.

The idea that you can build an international organization of distributors from your home office is a far cry from the old stereotype of door-to-door, person-to-person sales. Instead of loading up the trunk of your car and driving products all around town, you are conducting international commerce all around the world.

The benefits extend well beyond the opportunity to multiply one's income. The opportunity to travel the world and learn about other languages, cultures, and business traditions is also highly prized. Many network marketers retain close ties to their ethnic roots or country of origin. Their businesses allow them to reconnect with their roots. And, their knowledge of the country's culture and language as well as the presence of relatives there often give them a marketing "leg up" as they expand their businesses.

Trend 4: Network Marketing and the Internet

While the explosion of e-commerce will threaten many businesses, network marketing will empower and be empowered by it. Advances in on-line communications technologies will wring out the more distasteful, labor-intensive, administrative aspects of network marketing from the sales and recruiting process, allowing networkers to concentrate more fully on building home-based, international businesses.

The Internet, the explosion of e-commerce, and the rapid development of affordable information and communications technology are revolutionizing network marketing in several ways.

First, it is making the execution of the business more efficient and user-friendly and thus more desirable for New Professionals. Transactions that used to take hours of painstaking, time-consuming work and often physical labor are now accomplished with the push of a button or the click of a mouse.

Old-timers in the industry remember the days when they communicated with customers and prospects on a totally face-to-face basis. This approach clearly retains its marketing power and will always be a strong feature and selling point of direct sales approaches. Yet it consumes tremendous blocks of time and thus severely limits the business-building capabilities of busy people—particularly professionals who want to start as part-timers.

Ordering products and filling out applications used to be done by hand and then mailed or phoned in to the company headquarters. Products were often picked up at a warehouse and then personally delivered by the network marketer. Calculations of commissions, overrides, and bonuses were processed at company headquarters by hand, with checks mailed out in batches through the regular U.S. mail.

How things have changed! Industry leaders and rising stars have invested heavily in technology to make life as simple and efficient as possible for their independent distributors. In many cases, orders and downline applications can be submitted electronically. Order fulfillment, including packaging and shipping, is handled by the parent company—the distributor who sells a product to a customer thus never has to personally touch that product.

Technology is also being used to improve training, to motivate and inform, and to multiply the impact of a networker's recruiting efforts. Voice mail, teleconferences, satellite broadcasts, blast faxes, e-mails, Web sites, and other techniques are quickly being perfected at many top companies in the industry. The Internet has become a major source for information, criticism, and gossip about the industry. Some two hundred thousand Web sites have been identified by "browser count" directly related to the network marketing topic.

Industry guru Richard Poe has dramatically chronicled the impact of various technologies on network marketing his series of "Wave" books published by Prima. "The most advanced network marketing companies today stress simplicity above all. They use computers, management systems, and cutting-edge telecommunications to make life as easy as possible for the average distributor," he writes. In Poe's conception, technology has brought forth a new phase of individual entrepreneurship that marries old-fashioned relationship selling with cheap, easy-to-use information and communications technologies.

A senior executive at IBM recently observed that it is possible today to build and run a profitable multinational business from a home office equipped with a phone, a computer, a fax machine, and a modem—and we've met many networkers who have done just that! The biggest bookstore in the world, she further observed, is not really a store at all. It's a "virtual" bookstore on an Internet Web site called Amazon.com.

What has empowered today's entrepreneurs and puts so much business potential within their grasp is the speed at which new communications technologies are made available and accessible to the average person. While technology is becoming ever more complex in what it can do, it is at the same time becoming simpler to use and cheaper to buy.

Consider that the capacity of the microprocessor is doubling every fifteen to eighteen months and will continue to do so for the foreseeable future. That IBM executive illustrates the impact of this development by recalling that just ten years ago she attempted to perform a particularly complex function on the largest mainframe computer her company had to offer—the kind of computer that used to fill an entire room—and "brought it to its knees." Today, she does the same function with ease on a laptop computer at her desk!

Success magazine has summed up the marriage of network marketing and entrepreneurship and technology this way: "[Multilevel marketing] is creating a whole new marketplace outside the box of TV advertising, storefronts, inventory, and middlemen, and has the power to render the conventional retail world obsolete. That power arises from the union of modern technology—computerized record keeping and telecommunications—with the ancient art of schmoozing."

And John Fogg, editor of *Upline,* pinpointed the role technology can and should play in building a network marketing business when he observed, "All of the tools and technology free you up to focus on that one most intangible part of this business, which is relationships with your

> **While technology becomes ever more complex in what it can do, it becomes simpler to use and cheaper to buy.**

people. Your job is to develop your people and support them in building your business."

With companies assuming much of the burden for order taking, processing, and shipping, the distributor, as Fogg indicated, is freed to build his or her organization. In addition, these technologies give the business a more modern feel, helping it break away from the image direct selling companies have had in the past—in which being in the business meant your garage, den, and car trunk would be filled with boxes of product and precious hours would be spent delivering them.

> As companies establish global computer systems and international expansion plans, distributors will make money and grow businesses while they sleep.

Technology has thus become a critical component in the industry's ability to attract more upscale, better-educated, busy professionals. As companies establish global seamless computer systems and international expansion plans, distributors will make money and grow their businesses even while they sleep—because they be "open" for business in all time zones, twenty-four hours a day, seven days a week.

E-Commerce and Network Marketing   If network marketing had frozen in place from a technological perspective, relying on "old tools" such as in-home sales meetings, in-person product demonstrations, and hand-processed order taking—not to mention requiring the distributor to retrieve and deliver product personally—the e-commerce revolution would have posed a serious threat to this industry.

Likewise, if companies had failed to develop computer-ized systems for crediting distributors with sales made over the Internet—even when that distributor has no personal in-volvement in a particular sale—e-commerce could have blown network marketing out of the water.

Why? Because the Internet is a global community, and without a method of tracking and crediting sales to individual networkers when they are made on the Web, they would have little incentive to send customers to that Web site. Their only hope would be to try to retain their customers using the old time-consuming methods of product order and delivery—that would fly in the face of the speed, choice, and convenience e-shopping has to offer. It is a strategy doomed to failure. Without an appropriate response from the network marketing industry, e-commerce had the potential to destroy the concept of the individual network marketers' customer bases and sales organizations.

Instead, what the industry has done is transform itself into a lucrative and even invaluable asset to e-commerce. In the process, the e-commerce explosion is making network marketing stronger and more highly prized than ever.

What the e-commerce sector is all about now is "fingers and eyes." How many fingers can you get to click on your address? How many eyes can you find to look at your Web site? You can have the best home page, product selection, and price offering but if no one goes to your site, you won't make it. As we discussed regarding trend 1, the Internet is in the process of overturning many tried and true marketing approaches. Any strategy that breaks through the noise and brings real customers—dedicated, repeat customers—to your site is worth its weight in gold.

Network marketing is one such proven strategy. Many of its customers choose products not only for their quality and value but to help themselves or their friends and relatives build their businesses and advance in their organizations.

High-tech efficiency and capability combined with the high-touch personality of relationship selling that this industry is renowned for is a marriage made in heaven. Product and service companies in and out of network marketing are quickly comprehending the power of this union.

On Wednesday, September 1, 1999, at 4:37 P.M., Quixtar.com, the e-commerce arm of Amway, the nation's largest direct selling company, opened its virtual doors for business. As documented by Coy Barefoot in his Prima bestseller *The Quixtar Revolution*, the site received some twenty million hits on that opening day and has been registering some thirty to forty million hits every day since. This traffic makes it one of the most successful e-commerce sites in the short but spectacular history of the World Wide Web.

> High-tech efficiency and capability, combined with the high-touch personality of relationship selling, is a marriage made in heaven.

The site allows shoppers to fill their carts with ease with thousands of products ranging from breakfast cereals to big-screen televisions. However, those registering as shoppers or Quixtar/Amway distributors must input the referral number of an existing independent business owner. This step ensures that networkers get appropriate credit and commissions for sales and recruits, and it anchors new distributors to an existing up-line so that he or she can benefit from the training and motivation that experienced Amway business builders have to offer. Those arriving at the Quixtar site without a referral number can follow a simple point-and-click process to secure one.

Quixtar/Amway leader Jim Dornan explained the benefits that e-commerce brings to network marketing, and vice versa:

Sixty percent of each dollar that consumers spend on the Internet goes toward marketing and advertising. . . . That's two-thirds of every dollar going to nothing but trying to attract eyeballs.

Now in the old economy 60 to 80 percent of every dollar was spent on various middlemen: wholesalers, brokers, retailers, overhead. . . . Now advertising has become the biggest expense because you have to somehow get customers to find your site on the Net. And the way the Net works, that's not easy. And even if they find you, who's to say they will ever come back?

But then here we come along. Yes we've got great convenience and service and name brand products. But we do our advertising by word of mouth. We don't dump two-thirds of every dollar into the lap of some advertising company. We take that money and funnel it into a compensation package to pay our [independent business owners] for their word-of-mouth referrals.

It's a brilliant plan. It gives us ownership and a stake in the venture. We're not just customers. We're partners. E-commerce may represent the new economy. But Quixtar signals the next phase of e-commerce.

Amway is a leader but it is hardly alone in this fascinating story of network marketing's embrace of Internet technology:

- Rexall Showcase International recently announced it would move much of its recruiting, product sales, and business-building efforts to its Rexall.com site and encourage new and existing distributors to do the same.

- Shaklee Corporation, the venerable network marketing consumer products company founded in 1956, has created Shaklee.net, which will allow its sales force to own their personally customized fully functional e-commerce sites.

- American Communication Network (ACN) has launched the ACN Global Mall for ACN representatives working with iMart, an Internet-only e-commerce company, for a broad range of product alliances and backroom support operations.

- Avon, the direct-selling giant with a network marketing component, is developing a multidimensional Internet Web site strategy. Avon will continue to use its classic avon.com as its public relations, consumer, and generalized sales representative communication vehicle and product sales/order site. The firm reports it has a high-tech Web program "under construction" that will significantly improve sales representative efficiency based on expanded support for e-mail messaging, customer purchase analysis, personal sales performance monitoring, planning, and so forth.

New Professionals excited about the potential of technology to increase their personal productivity and multiply their career options will find today's network marketing industry a tech-friendly place, perhaps even more so than the traditional business world. According to Richard Poe, in *Wave 4,* "Rank-and-file networkers display an intimacy with cutting-edge technology that puts most corporate executives to shame. They work each day in the decentralized, virtual workplace that most managers and organizational scientists only read about in books."

Still, direct selling's embrace of the Internet has been an evolutionary process. The industry first saw it as a threat to its carefully guarded structure of sales and distributor "territories" and organizations. Companies also worried about their ability to standardize and then monitor and assure the integrity of distributors' sales techniques and recruiting claims. Later it viewed this technology as a way to speed the process of collecting and fulfilling product orders. Today, it has grasped the power of the Internet as a sales and recruiting pipeline, while underscoring to the marketplace as a whole that it is network marketing that can help solve companies' number one dilemma in the Internet Age: how to inform, gather, and retain loyal repeat customers.

For these reasons, we believe network marketing is an industry uniquely adaptive to the new Internet economy. Those who are not will undoubtedly become the industries of the past. Network marketing is an industry of the future.

Trend 5: Network Marketing Gets Respect

Long considered a kind of "lunatic fringe" of business, network marketing is being increasingly accepted as a legitimate and promising part of the economic mainstream, as evidenced by its growing recognition in the media, academia, and professional arenas.

When Charles King began his research on network marketing in 1990–1991, the first step was to do the classic academic "literature search" of the business press. Several conclusions quickly emerged.

First, there was virtually no descriptive, analytical content about the channel. In the *Business Periodicals Index,* the major library reference to the business-related periodical literature, there was essentially no coverage of the direct selling category. There were no key words dealing with direct selling, multilevel-marketing, MLM, network marketing, network distribution, or referral marketing.

Second, in the leading college marketing textbooks, passing reference was made to selling, salesmanship, and the selling process. In the textbook topic indexes, there were no references at all related to the field of multilevel-marketing or network marketing. Among specialized business library collections related to selling, very limited information was available about the MLM or network marketing industry, its size measured in sales volume or number of distributors, the primary products distributed, or the major individual companies.

Third, the intraindustry trade news was largely commercial advertising focusing on distributor recruiting, company products specifications and claims, personal development, and training and sales aids. Editorial content in the trade press revolved around industry personalities and trade folklore. Hard factual content about the industry was very limited.

Most of the industry information that was available focused largely on criminal exposés and highly visible consumer fraud stories—for example, litigation surrounding the Dare to Be Great, the Koscot Interplanatory, Inc., and the Holiday Magic cases; Ponzi schemes; chain letters; and pyramid scams.

Today, by comparison, the U.S. market has experienced and information explosion that is continually expanding. At least three major periodicals focus exclusively on the network marketing industry: *Upline* magazine, a monthly magazine about industry events and personalities; *Money Maker's Monthly,* a tabloid-type newspaper; and *Network Marketing Lifestyles* magazine, a human interest news magazine, currently published every two months. Success magazine also gives the network marketing industry periodic positive and supportive news coverage. (For a list of major industry information resources, see the appendix.)

While each of these publications has its own unique editorial style and mission, they are all actively seeking factual industry news and analytical content. Particularly important, too, the readers are also seeking hard news, competitive information and market data.

In addition, in recent years, the perspectives of the general news media have changed from the accusatory attitudes of the 1980s to early 1990s. While the news coverage will dependably report on industry misdeeds, the editorial viewpoint is becoming more balanced. Journalists are presenting broader stories with more factual, reflective, and informative content. In recent years, major, well-balanced feature stories have appeared in leading publications such as the *Wall Street*

Journal, Fortune magazine, *Forbes, Money* magazine, the *Chicago Tribune,* the *Chicago Sun Times,* and other major regional newspapers across the United States.

In addition, an expanding library of network marketing–focused trade books covering a gambit of industry topics written by professional journalists and industry practitioners is developing. At its Web site, Amazon.com lists over 130 titles that deal directly with the network marketing industry.

Prima Publishing has created a niche as the leading trade book publisher in the network marketing field. Prima has developed the largest and most prominent stable of network marketing writers in the industry, including Richard Poe, John Milton Fogg, coauthor James W. Robinson, Mark Yarnell, Rene Reid Yarnell, and Scott DeGarmo. The publisher has fifteen network marketing titles in print and four more under contract. Of those in print, six have earned bestseller status on the book charts. Prima reports it has sold over 1,280,000 copies in the network marketing category.

Several entrepreneurial writers also compile and market current, topically focused print and on-line newsletters such as *Fortune Now* by Tom "Big Al" Schreiter, *MarketWave Alert Letter* by Len Clements, *MLM Insider* by Rod Cook, and *MLM Woman* by Linda Locke. (Major books and newsletters are also listed in the appendix.)

Aggressive network marketing companies also complement the trade literature with their own house organs and web sites that focus on industry developments relevant to their market niches, including company/product information and sales/marketing ideas.

Academia Recognizes Network Marketing   In addition to the media and publishing worlds, the academic community is also becoming increasingly aware of the economic power of network marketing as a distribution channel and as a potential part-time or full-time professional career path.

In 1994, Charles King, professor of marketing, University of Illinois at Chicago (UIC), and Mark and Rene Reid Yarnell founded the UIC certificate seminar in network marketing, coordinated by Sandra King. The program was the first certificate seminar in network marketing ever offered by a major institution of higher education. The program is titled "Network Marketing: Planning, Building and Managing a Distributor Organization" and centers on applying proven skills of entrepreneurial management taught in colleges of business administration to the network marketing practitioner. The program, moving into its sixth successful year in 2000, has been conducted twelve times in the United States, Korea, and Australia, with over twelve hundred participants earning certification.

Topics covered in the seminar are continually reengineered from program to program to guarantee the content includes the latest technologies relevant to the evolving network marketing landscape. The content focuses on three major topic modules: (1) developing a business plan based on specific performance objectives for a network marketing distributor; (2) the tactical skills necessary for implementing the plan and building a distributor organization; (3) managing the distributor organization as an ongoing business operation over time.

Building on the original founders and seminar leaders, the instructors have been expanded to include specialists in new topic areas—for example, use of the Internet in network marketing, lead generation and follow—up, current legal issues, and new developments in compensation plans. The community of highly qualified network marketing industry leaders who can also qualify to teach as generic industry UIC guest speakers is growing.[1]

---

1. If you would like more information about the UIC Certificate Seminar in Network Marketing and future program dates, go to the seminar Web site, www.netwkmarketing.org or www.netwkmarketing.com. You may also contact Professor Charles King directly at (630) 668-1251 or via e-mail at kings63@bigplanet.com.

Charles King has actively championed the network marketing concept within the academic community since 1994. While network marketing is *not* taught at the Harvard Business School, King, who holds his doctorate from the Harvard Business School, has lectured about network marketing to students from the Harvard Law School, the Harvard Association of Law and Business, and the Harvard Business School Marketing Club.

Broader involvement of the leading universities in the United States will require establishing a platform to support academically conducted research on the network marketing business model. Today, a still-conservative and skeptical academic community lacks understanding of the network marketing channel and has inadequate information to evaluate and endorse the industry. This can change. King has developed a proposal for an industry-funded Network Marketing Institute. The institute could serve as a research center and a centralized industry information clearinghouse and be administered through a consortium of research-oriented colleges and universities.

In January 2000, Utah Valley State College launched a survey course titled "Opportunities in Direct Selling." Designated as a pilot program, the course discusses the impact of direct sales on society. More specifically, it covers "the basic terminology of the industry, the distinctions between legal and illegal activities, the history of direct sales, compensation plans, and ethics." The course includes discussion, lecture, guest speakers, presentations, and group activities. Other universities, including the University of Texas–El Paso, are reportedly exploring how they can become involved with the network marketing industry.

The State of Network Marketing Industry Trade Associations

To the New Professional evaluating alternative career tracks, a key question is, Who is looking out for the respectability and professional credibility of the network marketing industry?

The maturity and stability of an industry is often most clearly reflected in the structure of its industry trade associations. Trade associations emerge in response to the challenges facing professions, businesses, and industries. They deal with such issues as legal status of the industry; legislative relationships and regulatory jurisdictions; education and professional standards and certification; industry information and specific marketing research; industry marketing, advertising, and image development; financial structures and organizational frameworks; operating results analyses and identification of "best business practices"; and technological and scientific developments. The more comprehensive the industry's trade association infrastructure, the more professional talent and resources are available to focus on these complex industry issues.

The network marketing industry currently has three highly organized and well-funded formal trade associations and professional support groups:

- The Direct Selling Association (DSA)

- The World Federation of Direct Selling Associations (WFDSA)

- The Multi-Level-Marketing Association International (MLMIA)

The Direct Selling Association (DSA)   The DSA is the national trade association of leading firms that manufacture and distribute goods and services sold directly to consumers. Neil Offen, president, reports that at the end of the association's fiscal year 1999, the DSA had approximately 180 direct selling/network marketing corporate members and 225 suppliers. The group represents an estimated 90 percent of industry sales volume in the United States and operates on a budget of approximately $5.35 million. Reflecting conservative concern for the DSA's financial stability, the DSA board of directors is committed to maintaining a reserve to cover at least one-third of its annual expenses. At the end of 1999, the DSA had a "member equity" reserve fund of well over $2 million.

The mission of the association is "to protect, serve and promote the effectiveness of member companies and the independent business people they represent. To ensure that the marketing by member companies of products and/or the direct sales opportunity is conducted with the highest level of business ethics and service to consumers."

Toward this goal, the association has developed a code of ethics defining ethical business practices and consumer services. Every member company pledges to operate within these standards. Membership in the association is considered to be a hallmark of credibility among manufacturers in the direct selling industry.

In terms of association services, the DSA is an information clearinghouse for the direct selling industry. The association conducts the annual Direct Selling Growth and Outlook Survey, which tracks direct selling sales volume and profiles the infrastructure of the direct selling sector. The DSA also conducts the annual National Salesforce Survey that explores the attitudes, motivations, experiences, and demographics of the direct selling sales force. In addition, the association periodically does major in-depth, benchmark studies of the direct selling industry, such as the 1997 Survey of Attitudes Toward Direct Selling.

The Direct Selling Educational Foundation (DSEF), funded with more than $1.1 million per year, is another major educational initiative among the DSA programs. The DSEF mission is "to serve the public interest with education, information and research, thereby encouraging greater public awareness and acceptance of direct selling in the global marketplace." The DSEF focuses on key gatekeepers and opinion leaders among consumer advocate groups, government officials, university professors, and students to promote direct selling as a legitimate distribution channel and a potential professional career path.

Within its broader association role, the DSA also has a broad array of programs in education, government relations, member services, organizational administration, international programs, and communications.

The World Federation of Direct Selling Associations (WFDSA)
The WFDSA, founded in 1978 and headquartered in Washington, D.C., with funding of roughly $800,000 per year, is a nongovernmental, voluntary organization representing the direct selling industry globally as a federation of national direct selling associations from fifty-two countries or territories. The United States Direct Selling Association serves as the secretariat for the federation.

The WFDSA's mission is "to support direct selling associations in the areas of governance, education, communications, consumer protection and ethics in the marketplace and to promote personal interaction among direct selling executives regarding issues of importance to the industry." The WFDSA facilitates exchange of information among its members, fosters high standards of direct selling practices based on the United States Direct Selling Association's "Codes of Conduct for Direct Selling," and promotes global cooperation across the network marketing community.

Key contributions of the WFDSA are its compilation of direct sales statistics from member associations in the report "International Statistical Survey: Worldwide Direct Sales Data," global education about direct sales working through the United States Direct Selling Educational Foundation (DSEF), and the triannual World Congress of Direct Selling.

The Multi-Level-Marketing Association International (MLMIA) This group was organized in 1985 as a professionally managed, nonprofit trade organization representing the rapidly growing network marketing industry by a small group of experienced and successful network marketing practitioners. Its mantra is "We Connect You to Resources That Enhance Your Ability to Compete!"

The MLMIA promotes itself as the specifically focused "central information source" of the network/multilevel marketing industry, the largest component of the direct selling community. It defines its primary goal as "to continually provide education and to re-educate its members" on the changing competitive environment surrounding the network/MLM industry.

The MLMIA focuses its activities on "the protection, support and promotion of the individual opportunities and entrepreneurial aspects of the network/multi-level-marketing industry." It works at continually developing and improving tools and services, spreading the knowledge base in the industry, and helping members acquire and master the business skills necessary to succeed. The MLMIA reports that it has developed, facilitated, and nurtured strong connections between the network marketing industry and the outside influence centers that impact the industry's operations. Those influence centers include regulatory agencies, educators, the press, and the general public. MLMIA is committed, for example, to fostering educational programs with accredited universities and colleges in the fields of selling, marketing, and entrepreneurialism. Within these influence centers, MLMIA works to be recognized as a source of unbiased network industry data and information.

The MLMIA offers memberships in several categories:

Corporate membership—for network/multilevel marketing companies.

Support membership—for industry supplier companies including advertising and promotion agencies, data-based management and information management specialists, sales, and motivational trainers.

Distributor membership—for independent distributors

Affiliate membership—for new start-up manufacturers who want to get acquainted with the MLMIA but do not have the managerial time or financial resources to commit to full association involvement

Each membership category has a council that is responsible for representing the needs and interests of their colleagues. The councils are elected by the members of their respective sections and are coordinated by the board of directors of the MLMIA, which establishes the policies, programs, services, and overall strategic plans for the association. The MLMIA is the only professional organization in the industry that supports such a diverse constituency.

> Network marketers have a fully developed infrastructure of support to help them succeed and to document the legitimacy of their industry.

MLMIA has also established affiliate associations in Canada, England, Malaysia, Hong Kong, and Australia as a part of MLMIA's continued international expansion efforts. Through these affiliate associations, a worldwide network of people and businesses in network marketing are connected internationally.

From media coverage to published materials, from academic programs to trade associations, present and future network marketers now have a fully developed, and growing, infrastructure of support and knowledge to help them succeed and to document the legitimacy of their industry. This was not the case just a few years ago.

Trend 6: Network Marketing Goes "Public"

In a dramatic demonstration of network marketing's maturity and confidence, as well as its aggressive pursuit of capital and market share, a growing number of companies are entering financial markets. This not only empowers them with funds for product development, acquisitions, and aggressive growth but also pulls the industry out of the shadows of private ownership and creates additional inducements for New Professionals such as stock options. A particularly significant development in reinforcing the credibility of the network marketing industry has been its entry into the public financial markets.

In recent years, the direct selling industry and, more specifically, a klatch of network marketing companies have "invaded" the publicly traded stock exchanges. In an article in *Network Marketing Lifestyles,* Duncan Maxwell Anderson counts at least forty network marketing companies listed on the New York Stock Exchange, the American Stock Exchange, NASDAQ, and the Over the Counter Bulletin Board (OTCBB). (For trading symbols, see next page.)

What does this development mean to New Professionals investigating the network marketing industry?

First, the Securities and Exchange Commission (SEC) has defined very rigorous requirements for companies applying for listing on the public trading exchanges. Most private companies cannot or choose not to adhere to those criteria.

Second, the managerial/intellectual time and financial commitment required for a company to qualify to go public can be staggering or impossible for most start-up, early-growth, or medium-sized companies. The firm going public must complete an arduous planning process that includes:

- Creation of detailed vision and mission statements describing the firm's competitive position and growth goals

- Preparation of a comprehensive business plan outlining the firms' operational strategies and procedures

- Development of an initial start-up financial statement with three- to five-year projected financial pro forma statements

NYSE Companies

Amway Japan Ltd.	AJL
Amway Asia Pacific Ltd.	AAP
Avon Products, Inc.	AVP
Excel Telecommunications, Inc. (Teleglobe, Inc.)	TGO
Kirby & World Book (Berkshire Hathaway Inc.)	BRKa
Nu Skin Enterprises	NUS
Partylite (Blythe Industries, Inc.)	BTH
Pre-Paid Legal Services, Inc.	PPD
Primerica Financial Services (Citigroup Inc.)	C
Sara Lee	(SLE)
TIME-LIFE Direct	TWX
Tupperware	TUP
Westbend (Premark International)	PMI

AMEX Companies

Advantage Marketing Systems	AMM

NASDAQ Companies

Beauticontrol Cosmetics Inc.	BUTI
Changes International (Twinlab Corp)	TWLB
Dynamic Essentials (NBTY Inc.)	NBTY
FlashNet Communications	FLAS
Fuller Brush and Stanley Home Products (CPAK Inc.)	CPAK

- Organization of a management team to showcase to the investment world

- Generation of audited financial records, ideally prepared by a "Big Five" accounting firm for analysis by the SEC

- Establishment of relationships with financial and legal consultants and members of the Wall Street community

Herbalife International	HERBL
HMI Industries	HMII
I-Link (Medcross Inc.)	ILNK
Kaire International (Natural Health Trends Corp)	NHTC
Mannatech	MTEX
Nutrition for Life International	NFLI
Reliv International	RELV
Rexall Showcase International	RXSD
Usana Inc.	USNA
Usborne Books at Home	EDUC

OTCBB

Akahi.com (US Assurance Group)	UASG
Cell Tech International	EFLI
Envirotech International (ETI International Inc.)	ETICE
Futurenet	FNET
Market America	MARK
One World Online.com Inc.	OWOL
Royal Body Care (Globenet International)	ROBE
Sportsnut.com International Inc.	STSN
Travel Dynamics Inc.	TDNM
Warpradio.com	WRPR
Voyager Group (Voyager Group Brazil Ltd.)	VYGP

- Financial briefings and associated "road shows" to introduce the initial public offering (IPO) to investment analysts for their evaluation and endorsement

- A commitment of months to years in the planning and implementation of the IPO process

- Financial expenses estimated in the $700,000 to $1,000,000 range

Because of the rigor of this going-public process, firms that do get successfully listed on the public stock exchanges have survived the classic bath of fire—a very open and public examination and almost ritualistic initiation process.

Those network marketing companies that do get listed on the public exchanges, therefore, have often achieved a higher level of organizational sophistication and professionalism compared with many of their private cohorts working in the "confidentiality cloak" of the nonpublic community. These companies, at least at the time of their IPO, represent sound business organizations. Their future fate, of course, lies in the uncertainties of the market.

> Network marketing companies listed on the public exchanges often achieve a high level of organizational sophistication and professionalism.

Third, once a company does go public, it must routinely comply with the detailed reporting requirements of the SEC for the rest of its public life. The public company must continually monitor and self-police its business practices in terms of the law and industry standards.

Any reported inappropriate business conduct can focus the investigatory power and negative sanctions of the SEC on the offending firm. SEC actions against a firm typically have a severely negative impact on the company's image and stock market value.

Fourth, publicly held network marketing companies have a broader array of incentives to offer distributors, such as stock options. Going public can signal a company's intent to aggressively raise funds in financial markets that today are flooded with capital—funds that can be used to develop new products, upgrade systems and technologies, and enter new markets around the globe. All of these strategies can produce a more professional, profitable, and resource-rich parent company—just what the striving networker needs to make his or her home-based business a real winner!

The movement of network marketing to Wall Street has not been entirely smooth. Some companies believe their stock value is seriously hampered by prejudices that stock analysts and Wall Street pundits harbor against the industry. Indeed, it could be said that with the possible exception of some elements of the news media, the greatest remaining repository of ignorance and unfair stereotyping directed at network marketing resides on Wall Street. Thanks to the painstaking efforts of the pioneering executives with public companies who have spent endless hours educating analysts and investors, we are gradually seeing these attitudes change.

Trend 7: The Development of Innovative, Proprietary Products and Services

Network marketing companies are investing heavily in research and development, enhancing product quality, pioneering new industries, and contributing to significant scientific, medical, and manufacturing breakthroughs that benefit society and the economy as a whole. This is further enhancing the industry's attractiveness and credibility.

In 1969, Oklahoma insurance salesman Harland Stonecipher was driving to a meeting when his car was struck head-on by another vehicle. Even though the accident was not his fault, Stonecipher, who suffered serious injuries, was saddled with crippling legal expenses. Yet he found that as an average citizen, he didn't know how to access lawyers or the justice system in order to properly defend himself and fight back.

While recovering from his injuries, Stonecipher decided he wanted to protect his family in the future with the kind of legal protection plan that was readily available in Europe. He discovered this product didn't exist in the United States and came to believe that if it did, middle-class Americans would have access to the justice system previously reserved for the very rich. Over the next thirty years, Stonecipher created the network marketing firm Pre-Paid Legal Services, which today provides more than eight hundred thousand Americans with unlimited access to top attorneys for as little as $15 a month.

Harland Stonecipher did more than start a company; he pioneered an entire industry by bringing to the marketplace an innovative product not previously available in this country. Because the product was (and to a large extent still is) unfamiliar to most Americans, he found that the kind of face-to-face selling and personal testimonials that network marketing brings to the sales equation was the best way to go.

Stonecipher is one of a group of network marketing executives who are bringing an intense focus on innovative and high-quality products to an industry that has been known more for its single-minded pursuit of sales recruits. Leading companies are now investing heavily in research and development and are forming alliances and even mergers with strong research-oriented organizations. In the process, they are enhancing the credibility of the entire industry. After all, it's hard to argue that companies are "phony pyramid schemes" when you visit their headquarters as we have done and see state-of-the-art laboratories filled with scientists and researchers or manufacturing facilities as technologically sophisticated as anything you might find in Silicon Valley. Other examples include the following:

- *Nu Skin*—In 1998, Nu Skin acquired Pharmanex, a leading research and development company of natural health supplements. Pharmanex created proprietary products through pharmaceutical-level research and development. In 1999, the company announced the establishment of the Nu Skin Center for Dermatological Research at the Stanford University School of Medicine. The center will focus on scientific investigation, dermatology research, patient care, and training and will conduct clinical trials on new products.

- *Shaklee*—Following up on the previously mentioned acquisition of Shaklee by the Yamanouchi Pharmaceutical Company, in 1997 the two firms opened a state-of-the-art Yamanouchi Shaklee Pharma Research Center located in the Stanford Research Park.

- *Mannatech*—This company has made breakthrough discoveries in carbohydrate technology and turned them into a line of proprietary nutritional supplements.

- *Melaleuca*—This Idaho Falls company regularly recruits highly qualified scientists and lab technicians from university, government, and corporate laboratories. Its R&D team is engaged in hundreds of projects at any given time to develop industry-leading consumer products.

- *Mary Kay*—The cosmetics firm has been a pioneer in animal-free product testing and has invested heavily in breast cancer research and scholarships for women seeking degrees in business.

In these and many other ways, network marketing firms are starting to play a major role in improving and increasing the line of products and services available to consumers. The days when a company's product was almost incidental to its core activity of recruiting networkers and selling "dreams" are coming to a close. New Professionals will find industry leaders as passionate and committed to quality products as they are about the business opportunity they offer. If they are not, it's time to start asking questions about that company.

> Network marketing firms are starting to play a major role in improving and increasing the available line of products.

A NEW BUSINESS AND WORK MODEL
FOR THE TWENTY-FIRST CENTURY

As these seven trends gain momentum, network marketing's greatest contribution to society in the United States and around the world will be to spur the creation of a new business and professional model that will change the culture of commerce and work in companies and organizations both in and out of the industry. Whether you choose to join a network marketing company or not, you will benefit from this new business model and the cultural changes network marketing is promoting.

Despite the condescension that remains in the attitudes of many so-called business experts, network marketing today is having a profound impact on the entire business world. The most successful marketing companies in the future will be those that employ a blend of the best features of both the network marketing and more traditional marketing approaches.

> The most successful marketing companies will be those that employ the best features of both the network marketing and the more traditional marketing approaches.

As much as they have disparaged direct selling in the past, consumer product and services companies are realizing they can no longer afford to ignore the potency of face-to-face (or phone-to-phone and computer-to-computer) selling. They crave the customer loyalty that is increasingly hard to come by with traditional advertising and marketing approaches. Changing demographics are causing an overall shortage of workers. Regulations are driving up the cost of maintaining those workers they do find.

Again, these companies look with envy to the successful network marketing companies where a dedicated sales force works with no guarantee of income and no traditional employee overhead.

With mass media multiplying and with consumers becoming increasingly segmented, how do companies reach them? How do they cut through all the noise? How do they appeal to a public that is spending less and less time watching the major television networks and reading the daily newspapers, while spending more time logging onto the Internet, watching videos, and channel-surfing around one hundred to five hundred different channels? During those times when the nation does come together, such as on Super Bowl Sunday, how many firms can afford the price of admission to a rarely unified market—$1 to $2 million for a single thirty-second commercial?

The smart companies have come to understand that network marketing is an important part of the answer. *Inc.* magazine has observed:

> From the top of Inc.'s 500 companies to the bottom are product and service companies that have adopted multi-level marketing to control overhead, create means of distribution, and build a national sales force on a budget. All of these companies have tapped into a growing contingent of displaced workers, professionals worried about their future, at-home moms and couples—all looking to get into business for themselves.

As for network marketing companies, what do they need from the more traditional companies? Answering that question requires some understanding of the environment in which these companies operate today.

- It is a highly competitive environment. With full employment and relative prosperity in the United States, the pool of eager participants in these businesses is limited, and the distributor forces that do sign up turn over continually.

- The regulatory environment is becoming more complex, particularly in the international arena that some companies are counting on for a significant share of their future growth. Despite vast improvements in business ethics, these companies are viewed with suspicion in many countries. In 1998, for example, China overreacted to abuses by fraudulent domestic operators by shutting down for a time the entire direct selling industry! Other countries require network marketing concerns to invest heavily in local manufacturing and other facilities before allowing them to sell products and recruit distributors.

- The development of unique products and services to be sold through network marketing is becoming increasingly expensive. To be competitive, you need capital. To keep on top of the competition, you need experienced executive management that understands changing markets. You need batteries of lawyers to handle all the inevitable liability issues and to keep the class-action lawsuit vultures at bay.

Network marketing is gradually shedding its less attractive qualities, including its legacy of hype and exaggeration. At the same time, it is bolstering the already considerable strength of its one-on-one distribution channel with Internet technology. It is a more professional industry, and the higher standards it has set for itself are producing a more positive image in the media, business academia, and financial markets. It has become a global marketing force as well as a major player in research and product breakthroughs. It is incorporating the best features of the American corporate establishment: professional management; productivity investments in R&D, technology, and human resources; public ownership and stock incentives for its participants; and a global marketing prowess.

At the same time, network marketing is responding effectively to the worst: stultifying corporate bureaucracies; massive layoffs even in good economic times; slow salary growth and insecure retirement income; and an oppressive lifestyle that demands frequent travel, long commutes, and endless hours of work, leaving little room for family and leisure pursuits.

By positioning itself as such an attractive alternative, network marketing has helped fuel the rise of the New Professionals, professionals who demand more from their careers than traditional corporations or even other forms of business ownership have been willing or able to offer. But they are starting to now, thanks in good measure to the positive pressure that network marketing, with its new face and new business model, is bringing to bear on the marketplace and the fierce competition for people, products, and ideas.

Companies That Are Leading Network Marketing into the Future

Network marketing is a rich and varied industry, full of interesting and diverse business models, marketing strategies and product mixes-vastly different from the two-dimensional image that observers in many quarters may have.

In chapters 6 and 7, we look at the business models and strategies of a group of companies, selected from the hundreds of firms that will represent the industry in the next decade. The purpose of the analysis is two-fold. First, it illustrates our theme that network marketing is a rich and varied industry. Second, it will help New Professionals who are considering the industry to begin the process of choosing the right company for them.

The company profile information reported in chapters 6 and 7 is taken from the trade references, company promotional literature, and the very informative company Web sites, which we acknowledge as a key source for much of the factual information presented in the profiles. We have also

conducted extensive personal interviews with distributors
and executives from many of the featured firms featured.

The target companies have been categorized into two
well-defined segments:

- **The Pathfinders:**

    These are the leading, large, well-established, special-
    ized, and focused traditional network marketing firms
    and industry icons that have blazed many trails for the
    industry and persevered through its many trials. For
    purposes of this review, we have defined these compa-
    nies as members of our "Billion Dollar Club"—that is,
    firms whose revenues approximate or exceed $1 billion.

- **The Pacesetters:**

    These are the rising stars that are also specialized and
    focused, including relatively new and start-up compa-
    nies. These firms are exploring new product and serv-
    ice mixes, new compensation programs, new ways to
    integrate technology into their business, and new ways
    to blend network marketing with traditional market-
    ing approaches. Their significance to the industry may
    be greater than their current size or impact. But al-
    though they are interesting companies to observe, full
    of potential, they are not necessarily guaranteed to be-
    come members of the "Billion Dollar Club."

THE PATHFINDERS: NETWORK MARKETING INDUSTRY LEADERS

The industry leaders are characterized by relatively long
track records of success in network marketing, large sales
volumes, and distributor organizations, and stable management, and they are often publicly traded on the financial exchanges. As an admittedly arbitrary cutoff, we also use
annual retail sales volume in the range of $1 billion or more
as evidence of market impact and significance.

Amway

It is hard to overestimate the impact Amway has had on virtually every aspect of network marketing, American business, and the triumph of U.S.-style entrepreneurship around the world. Its founders called it their "crazy idea," and it sure seemed that way back in 1959 when partners Rich DeVos and Jay Van Andel started a new company literally at the ground level—in the basements of their family homes in the predominantly Dutch American community of Ada, Michigan.

Rich and Jay, as they were and are commonly known, had already been close friends, business partners, and fellow adventurers for nearly twenty years. They date the beginning of their association, which now spans more than a half a century, to when they were teenagers. Jay's father had given him an old Ford Model A but had little money for gas. Rich needed a ride to the high school they both attended but had no transportation. He paid Jay a quarter a week for gas, and thus one of the world's most lucrative and enduring partnerships was born.

> Network marketing is a rich and varied industry, full of interesting and diverse business models, marketing strategies, and product mixes.

As a son and grandson of immigrants and children of the Great Depression, Rich and Jay were deeply motivated by the desire to achieve economic self-sufficiency and independence. Like so many others, they had to find a way to do this with virtually no start-up funds.

"There had to be another way for people like us, who wanted a business of our own to get started," DeVos later wrote. "Here we had a knack for sales and plenty of ambition, but we certainly didn't begin to have the capital resources needed to carve out our niche in the precarious marketplace we now pictured."

Rich and Jay's early business ventures in the years immediately following World War II—a flying school and a drive-in hamburger stand among them—were reasonably successful. But the partners questioned their long-term potential for growth. The turning point came in 1949 when Jay's second cousin told the pair about a business he had entered selling a nutritional food supplement for a company called Nutrilite. Nutrilite was founded by Carl Rehnborg who, as a prisoner in a Chinese detention camp in the 1920s, survived by eating cooked plants and animal bone. Rehnborg later returned to the United Sates with a strong belief in the health benefits of vitamins and nutritional supplements. In starting Nutrilite, he was not only an early pioneer in alternative health and fitness but in many respects the founding father of network marketing.

Not only did the Nutrilite products have a somewhat captivating allure, but the company had a unique marketing approach. Distributors sold the supplements directly to consumers. They also were empowered to recruit and train other salespeople to work with them as members of their sales organization. The distributors earned income off the products they sold directly to their customers and earned an override commission off the sales made by the salespeople they had recruited and trained in their sales group or "downline."

Rich and Jay were quickly convinced that this was the winning formula. They invested $49 for a sales kit and some products and set out to recruit distributors, drawing on the presentations skills they had honed in their other ventures. Within the first year, their distributorship grossed $82,000; they quadrupled that sum the very next year. They were soon among the most successful Nutrilite distributors in the United States.

Business growth continued throughout the 1950s. But by 1958 internal conflicts within Nutrilite's management prompted the pair, along with the major distributors in their organization, to develop their own distinct organization and line of products while continuing Nutrilite sales. The American Way Association was established that year and the Amway corporation the following year, with corporate headquarters in the basements of the DeVos and Van Andel homes.

But what to sell? In 1959, the partners purchased the rights to an all-purpose cleaner that was concentrated and environmentally safe. Today L.O.C. (Liquid Organic Cleaner) is still listed as product number one in Amway's now extensive catalogue of offerings to consumers.

With a proprietary product and a marketing plan that put business ownership well within the reach of ordinary people, Amway began its meteoric rise. DeVos and Van Andel are among the wealthiest people in the United States, and it is no exaggeration to say that they moved American-style capitalism down to the retail level all over the world. Today Amway's annual sales stand at $5 billion, generated by some three million independent business owners in fifty-three markets around the globe.

> Look at virtually any aspect of the rise and development of network marketing, and you will see Amway's fingerprints.

Look at virtually any aspect of the rise and development of network marketing, and you will see Amway's fingerprints. For four decades it has been the pathfinder, clearing the way for other companies—and the lightening rod, drawing such criticism that some Amway distributors hold back on identifying the company they are associated with in the initial stages of recruiting a prospect.

Amway's system of rewarding achievers with increasingly difficult "pin levels" (ruby, silver, gold, diamond, etc.) is widely imitated throughout the industry. With its Canadian launch in 1962, followed by Australia in 1970, England in 1971, Hong Kong in 1973, and then West Germany in 1975, it was "going global" when much of the network marketing industry were still learning how to crawl here at home.

While the parent company remains in the private hands of the two founding families, Amway Japan and Amway Asia Pacific held public offerings on the New York Stock Exchange (NYSE). When the firm's Japan business went public in the 1980s, it became only the tenth Japanese company to be listed on that exchange.

Building on its historical entrepreneurial positioning in the 1980s and 1990s, Amway has a clearly defined marketing strategy for moving into the decade of 2000–2010.

- Amway was founded in 1959 by Jay Van Andel and Rich DeVos. The founders' families still maintain ownership of Amway and its two publicly traded companies, Amway Japan Limited and Amway Asia Pacific Ltd. (NYSE).

- Amway has a forty-year history. During that time, the company has repeatedly responded to competitive, organizational, and legal challenges and experienced sales growth and profitability.

- The Amway "market basket" includes a broad range of thousands of basic, high-quality, competitively priced national brands and private-label consumer products.

- The Amway sales strategy is targeted at "redirecting" consumer spending: switching consumers from a previous brand to the Amway brand without necessarily increasing their personal spending.

- Total sales are heavily based on wholesale buyer consumption by rank-and-file Amway distributors, most of whom are not active Amway network marketing business builders. Therefore, sales emphasis is placed on "increasing the number of stores"—Amway distributors—who are using the products and services.

- Another goal is increasing the number and volume of Amway products the individual customer buys—the idea of "share of total customer purchases" across the Amway product and service mix.

- Amway has been a network marketing leader measured by global sales of over $5 billion at estimated retail value and number of distributors, three million worldwide and approximately one million in the United States in 1999.

- Gross margins on the major product categories support the distribution system and the compensation plan for distributors.

- In terms of profitability, the firm has been a stable income earner based on net profit on sales in its public companies, Amway Japan Limited and Amway Asia Pacific Ltd.

- In terms of outlook, Amway currently operates in over eighty countries and territories and plans for continued in-market growth and further global growth.

Leadership has carried its price, but even Amway's own mistakes and external pressures have helped others avoid those errors and manage through outside pressures. The company suffered protracted legal problems in Canada. Back-and-forth litigation pitting the company against its more traditional consumer product rival, Proctor & Gamble, has fed unfair stereotypes depicting a cultlike culture in the organization.

Policing the conduct of wayward but powerful distributor groups has not always been easy, and their actions have at times generated negative press coverage and legal liabilities.

In 1998, after investing tens of millions of dollars in Chinese production facilities and business building, the government there shut Amway and other direct sellers down for a time—a sobering message to all network marketing companies making big investments in countries with centrally planned or capricious governments.

As discussed earlier, the Federal Trade Commission's investigation of Amway to determine whether the business was a legal pyramid no doubt produced some sleepless nights and heart-stopping moments for the company. But the 1979 ruling not only was favorable to Amway; it also set the ground rules by which network marketing companies are judged to this day.

Through it all, Amway pushes itself and the industry to the next frontier. We can see that in its bold move to its Quixtar e-commerce site. Because its range of products is so broad, Amway devotees seem to concern themselves less with particular product or service niches and more with the business model itself. One result is the oft-repeated scenes of frenzy when Amway enters into new, developing markets abroad. It is not unusual to see thousands of poor people crowding into stadiums, weathering the heat and rain, eager to buy into a small piece of the American dream.

There's a reason that business journalists writing about other network marketing companies frequently describe them as selling their product or service in an "Amway-style" system: because they know virtually all of their readers have heard of Amway. For fans and critics alike, the company re-

> Amway devotees seem to concern themselves less with particular product or service niches and more with the business model.

mains the standard by which network marketing is judged. And it is why competitor companies trying to make their mark often do so by explaining to prospects how they are "different from Amway." For all these reasons, we believe the company will continue to be network marketing's trailblazer and lightening rod. It will also continue to be very, very successful all around the world.

Excel Communications

The intersection of the network marketing distribution channel and long-distance telephone communication expanding to the broader area of telephony may be one of the great collisions in the evolution of both of these twenty-first-century phenomena.

In the early 1980s, AT&T fought the final legal battles against deregulation of the long-distance telephone industry and the loss of its monopoly on the supply of long-distance service across the United States. In 1984, AT&T lost to the United States Department of Justice.

The long-distance telephone market was now open. MCI, a fledgling entrant in the foray of the deregulated long distance telephone market, launched an array of marketing strategies using telemarketing, direct sales, direct mail, television advertising, affinity programs, and more to penetrate the AT&T presence and take market

The Pathfinders

- Amway: www.amway.com

- Excel: www.excel.com

- Forever Living Products: www.foreverliving.com

- Herbalife: www.herbalife.com

- Mary Kay: www.marykay.com

- Nikken: www.nikken.com

- Nu Skin Enterprises: www.nuskinenterprises.com

- Primerica: www.pfsnet.com

- Shaklee: www.shaklee.com

share from AT&T. One of those involved a strategic alliance with Amway Corporation to sell long-distance services to Amway distributors and make it part of the Amway story. Overnight, MCI had market exposure to hundreds of thousands of Amway representatives and their network marketing contacts. A major market penetration beachhead had been secured for MCI through network marketing.

Sprint, a Kansas City–based "near-follower" in the long-distance telephone market invasion, also pursued a multi-channeled marketing strategy. One of those channels involved a strategic alliance with a newly formed network marketing company, Network 2000, founded by an entrepreneurial opportunist, formally a sales/marketing promoter in the cable television industry.

Network 2000 was organized specifically to sell Sprint long-distance service subscriptions through a network marketing compensation program. In three years, Network 2000 signed up an estimated three million subscribers to Sprint long-distance service. The Sprint–Network 2000 alliance ultimately unraveled in an acrimonious legal battle. The network marketing channel, however, had proven its power and had hit another home run!

The battle of the Big One (AT&T) and the Small Two (MCI and Sprint) in long-distance telephone service was joined. The combat was destined to be bloody and the casualties high. AT&T's market share in long-distance service would erode from 90 percent in 1984 to 50 percent over the next decade. Enter Excel Communications into the long-distance telephone market melee. The company's founder Kenny A. Troutt grew up in a poor neighborhood in East Saint Louis, Illinois. But with a knack for entrepreneurship and athletic ability, he was able to lift himself out of poverty through youthful business ventures and an athletic scholarship.

Upon graduating from Southern Illinois University, Troutt moved to Nebraska and established successful real estate and construction companies. During the energy boom, he developed a successful oil and gas exploration company in Dallas. But due to the boom and bust cycles of Texas industry, his hold on financial success seemed tenuous at best, and he began a search for the next "big idea." He found it.

In 1988, recognizing the opportunity created by the AT&T breakup, Troutt launched Excel as a regional reseller of long-distance telephone service. He combined forces with Stephen R. Smith to design a powerful network marketing program as the company's primary distribution channel.

In twelve years, Excel Communications grew to the fourth largest long-distance company in the United States, based on revenue and capacity, with a ranking in the Fortune 1000 and 1998 revenues of $1.3 billion. The company offers its subscribers residential and commercial long-distance services, dial-around services, calling cards, Internet access, and paging services. More recent developments include international expansion and a foray into wireless communication. The products are marketed nationwide to residential and commercial customers under the Excel and Telco subsidiaries—principally through a devoted sales force of network marketers called independent representatives.

Excel is leading the network marketing push across the new frontier of services. Its growth from a small regional reseller of excess long-distance calling capacity to a member of the "Billion Dollar Club" has been rapid, to say the least:

- In 1988, President and CEO Kenny A. Troutt founded Excel Communications Inc.

- In 1989, Excel U.S. began operating with the network marketing business model.

- In 1993, Excel U.S. reaches more than $30 million in revenues.

- In 1995, Excel U.S. reaches more than $500 million in revenues.

- On May 10, 1996, Excel U.S. becomes a public corporation, trading on the NYSE.

- In 1997, Excel U.S. reaches over $1.4 billion in revenues.

- In 1997, Excel U.S. acquires Telco Communications Group.

- In November 1998, Excel Communications Inc. merges with Teleglobe Inc., making Excel the fourth largest telecom carrier in North America.

- On March 1, 1999, Excel begins international expansion with the launch of Excel Canada.

As Excel looks to the future, expect the company to continue its aggressive use of diverse strategies to fuel its market expansion and product development. You could say the company's credo is "Do in one year what others do in ten." For example, instead of slowly building a physical phone network, Excel began by simply buying excess calling capacity from the majors. The customer base it built provided the cash to then buy its own network later on. Instead of laying a years-long foundation to enter foreign markets, the company's merger with Canada's Teleglobe allowed it to shortcut that process as well. In today's business world, particularly in the arena of communications technology, can it really be done successfully any other way?

Now Excel is also acquiring the top management talent needed to execute these aggressive global strategies. It recently named Christina Gold as vice chairman and CEO of Excel Communications. Gold joined Excel following a distinguished twenty-eight-year career at Avon Products Inc. While at Avon, Gold held a number of key positions in executive management including executive vice president, global direct selling development, president and chief executive officer of Avon Canada, as well as president of Avon North America, where she is credited with the company's turn-around. In 1997, she was named one of the "Top Twenty-five Managers of the Year" by *Business Week* magazine.

On November 10, 1998, Excel completed its merger with Teleglobe. As a result of the merger, each share of Excel common stock was exchanged for 0.885 shares of Teleglobe capital stock. (Teleglobe stock trades on the Toronto and New York stock exchanges under the symbol TGO.) On February 15, 2000, Teleglobe agreed to be ac-quired by BCE, Canada's top communications company, but both Teleglobe and Excel will continue to operate under their own names in Montreal and Dallas, respectively.

> You could say Excel's credo is "Do in one year what others do in ten."

Excel's plunge into the world of high global finance and corporate consolidation presents a new paradigm for the individual network marketer. Some may wonder how one fits into an international conglomerate whose network marketing division is described as a "unit" of the overall company.

Yet on April 1, 2000, no such questions were apparent as Excel staged a hugely successful "relaunch" of its business opportunity. The company drew tens of thousands of its quarter million active North American network marketers to some eleven thousand sites that were linked through a live simulcast. Participants heard about Excel's new products (wireless and local calling), new markets (the United King-dom in the fall of 2000), the company's first national adver-tising campaign, and a more lucrative compensation plan. Coauthor Jim Robinson, who attended the meeting, de-scribed it as highly enthusiastic, with no apparent diminu-tion of the energy that has brought Excel so far so fast.

Forever Living Products International

Forever Living is the world's largest producer of aloe vera and bee products, including nutritional drinks, supplements, skin care products, and cosmetics. The Forever Resorts Division has diversified into recreation property management, with an emphasis on relaxation and healthful living in natural settings as support to the Forever Living distributor organization and as an alternative profit center.

Forever Living Products International is another pathfinder network marketing "billion-dollar" company with its own differentiated market positioning strategy built on three dimensions:

1. **Product niching built around aloe vera and beehive technology**

2. **Vertical integration in natural product production and final product formulation**

3. **Diversification into recreational property management as a support platform for the Forever Living distributor organization and as an independent strategic profit center**

Forever Living Products was founded in 1978 by president and CEO Rex Maughan, formerly a vice president of Del Web, the Phoenix-based real estate developer. Maughan was introduced to several network marketing companies by his friends in the mid-1970s. In 1978, the entrepreneur decided to target the natural health and personal care consumer with a unique new product concept, aloe vera.

Naval Ghaswala, executive vice president, and Linda Marena, marketing manager, document the history of Forever Living. The company has enjoyed substantial growth since its inception, expanding from $700,000 in the launch year of 1978 to $256 million in 1990 to over $1.1 billion in

1999. The distributor sales force totals over 5.5 million members worldwide.

The firm earned the distinction of sixth place on *Inc.* magazine's list of America's fastest-growing companies in 1997. In the same year, Rex Maughan was listed on the *Forbes* magazine's "400 Richest People in America" list. In 1999, Forever Living was ranked as the number one private company in Arizona by *The Business Journal,* a Phoenix-based business periodical.

The product focus is on aloe vera. According to company research, aloe vera, a medicinal herb, has been used in various applications for various purposes since the time of the ancient Egyptians. To benefit from aloe vera, the gel can be taken internally for its nutritional effect, or it can be combined with other ingredients to produce topical creams and lotions to nourish and improve the quality of the skin. The aloe vera products were the first to receive the International Aloe Science Council Seal of Approval for consistency and quality.

To control the quality of the natural product and assure a steady supply, the firm has organized a extensive enterprise with plantation acreage in southern Texas, the Dominican Republic in the Caribbean, and Mexico. The company maintains close quality control in its corporate manufacturing plants in Texas and the Dominican Republic.

The company also operates one of the world's largest bee facilities in the high Sonoran desert of Arizona, where the area's clean environment and abundant variety of flowering plants make it a good source for natural bee products. Company researchers have secured patents for their methods of producing pure bee products—products such as Forever Bee Honey, Forever Bee Pollen tablets, and Forever Bee Propolis, an effective natural antibiotic.

In 1981, the firm diversified into recreational property management operated by the Forever Resort Division. Originally intended as a complement to the Forever Living Distributor organization, this division has become a powerful profit center in support of the other Forever Living network marketing programs

Entering the decade of 2000, the Resort Division is strategically positioned to capitalize on the growing recreational vacation market and to provide vacation incentives to the Forever Living Distributor community. Maughan initially purchased Callville Bay Resort & Marina on Lake Mead and Cottonwood Cove Resort and Marina on Lake Mohave, both in Nevada. The Resort Division has expanded to include a network of properties in Alaska, Arizona, California, Colorado, Florida, Indiana, Georgia, Kentucky, Missouri, Texas, and Wyoming. ''

Forever Living offers a business opportunity both popular and familiar to many network marketers. Its marketing plan gives distributors three areas of income:

- **Personal sales:**

  Retailing to your customers, this will give an immediate income of 35 to 48 percent as your business grows.

- **Team-leading bonus:**

  For developing a team of people like yourself, wishing to earn an extra income, you will be paid a bonus of between 3 and 18 percent on their sales.

- **Royalty bonus:**

  If successful over a period of time, networkers will receive a passive income from the teams that they have helped to become businesses in their own right. The additional passive income of between 2 and 9 percent offers long-term residual income.

The company also runs a company car program and offers incentives for international travel and profit sharing.

Forever Living Products is globally diversified, marketing its products in sixty-five countries. Reflecting the global orientation of the product line, the products also feature the Kosher and Islamic Seals of Approval.

Forever Living Products International is a leader among the many network marketing companies that target a health-conscious market worldwide with exclusive products. The company's uninterrupted growth, staying power, and status as one of the industry's select members of the Billion Dollar Club are testimony to its product focus and marketing prowess.

Herbalife

Herbalife is a multinational nutrition company with sales of almost $1.7 billion a year. The company was born from the personal tragedy of Mark Hughes. When Hughes was eighteen years old, his mother died of an accidental overdose of prescription diet pills. That convinced the charismatic company founder to dedicate his life to helping people lose weight and improve their health safely and effectively.

In February 1980, Hughes launched Herbalife International. Sales the first month were $23,000. By the end of the first year, sales skyrocketed to $2 million.

Now a public corporation traded on the NASDAQ exchange, Herbalife started in Beverly Hills, California, where its world headquarters is now located. With an aggressive expansion attitude, Herbalife currently operates in forty-six countries and plans new country openings in the coming years. In addition to its international expansion efforts, Herbalife is increasing its community activities through the Herbalife Family Foundation, which is involved in a myriad of social causes and charitable programs.

Herbalife is a member of the Direct Selling Association and claims more than 750,000 independent distributors worldwide. The company emphasizes herbs and other natural ingredients in weight loss, nutritional, and personal care product lines. Its exclusive formulations appeal to the growing consumer interest in herbal and natural products—particularly in the all-important markets of Asia.

Herbalife invests heavily in communications technology. Through satellite television, fax systems, telephone conference calls, and now the Internet, Herbalife provides technologies to make the business-building and sales process for network marketers as efficient as possible.

> Herbalife provides technologies to make the business-building and sales process for network marketers as efficient as possible.

This has helped attract and retain New Professionals such as Ron Rosenau, whose story is highlighted on the company Web site.

Before becoming an Herbalife distributor, Ron was a successful stockbroker and financial adviser, earning a six-figure income in the United States.

"Although I was making a decent living," he says, "my job created a lot of tension and stress in my life. I didn't like having to answer to my clients or my boss. And because of time constraints, I couldn't travel or plan my day the way I wanted."

Ron's dissatisfaction with his job prompted him to answer an ad in the newspaper about Herbalife's business opportunity. Eventually he experienced great results with the products, which convinced him to give up his career and go full-time with Herbalife. Many of his clients and friends took notice and followed his example. Now he has an international organization, and the prospects for continued growth appear bright.

"Because of Herbalife," he says, "I am able to change people's lives nutritionally and financially. I am now able to do what I want, when I want, which includes travel and frequent golf games. I may have an incredible lifestyle, but one thing I never lose sight of is the fact that Herbalife is the vehicle propelling me here."

As one of the mainstay network marketing companies to capitalize on booming interest in weight loss and natural health products, Herbalife has blazed trails for the many network marketing companies that feature these product lines. As a pioneer, it has also at various times in its history found itself the target of bad press and controversy. Investors and industry watchers have also been perplexed at times by the actions of founder Hughes. For example, in 1999, he announced his intention to buy up stock and take the company back into the realm of the privately held firms. In spring 2000, he announced that he was dropping the effort due to the lack of suitable financing. Just weeks later, Hughes died of apparently natural causes at the age of forty-four. Company management was shocked and saddened by the tragedy, but acted swiftly to ensure business continuity.

Herbalife is nothing if not resilient. Its aggressive international expansion in response to flagging domestic demand is a good example. The penetration it has achieved of late in the Japan market is nothing short of breathtaking. Herbalife is a competitive company with a timely product line, ideal for those who want to build organizations extending to Russia, Japan, and throughout Asia.

Mary Kay

Like other major network marketing companies, Mary Kay Inc. achieved its initial identity and momentum from an extremely charismatic and visionary founder, Mary Kay Ash. Her story is the stuff of legends.

Company historians report that in 1963, after a successful career in direct sales, Mary Kay Ash retired for a month. During that month, she decided to write a book to help women succeed in the business world. Sitting at her kitchen table, she made two lists: one contained the good things she had seen in companies for which she had worked; the other featured the things she thought could be improved.

When Ash reviewed the lists, she realized that she had inadvertently created a marketing plan for a successful company of her own. With her life savings of $5,000 and the help of her 20-year-old son, Richard Rogers, she launched Mary Kay Cosmetics on September 13, 1963.

Mary Kay Inc. has since grown from a small direct sales company to the largest direct seller of skin care products in the United States and the best-selling brand of facial skin care and color cosmetics in the United States (based on most recently published industry sales data). The company now has more than half a million independent beauty consultants in twenty-nine markets worldwide. Mary Kay Inc. was featured three times in the annual *100 Best Companies to Work for in America*.

In 1980, Mary Kay's husband Mel died of cancer. She then turned her attention and commitment to funding research and awareness to fight the disease. In 1996, she established the Mary Kay Ash Charitable Foundation, a nonprofit public foundation that funds research into leading cancers affecting women. Mary Kay became chairperson emeritus of Mary Kay Inc. in 1987.

The company's growth and success has been steady and impressive:

- **1963:** Mary Kay Ash establishes Mary Kay Cosmetics Inc.—a 500-square-foot storefront in Dallas with the help of her 20-year-old son, her life savings of $5,000, and nine beauty consultants.

- **1964:** Mary Kay becomes one of the first cosmetics companies to introduce skin care products exclusively for men. Today, Mary Kay claims a 17 percent share of the men's skin care market.

- **1969:** Mary Kay awards the first pink Cadillacs to the top five independent sales directors. Groundbreaking and construction begins on the Mary Kay manufacturing facility.

Today, it is one of the largest cosmetics manufacturing facilities in the Southwest, measuring the size of approximately three football fields.

- **1971:** Its first international subsidiary opens in Australia.
- **1976:** The company is listed on the New York Stock Exchange.
- **1978:** A Canadian subsidiary opens.
- **1979:** Mary Kay's first independent beauty consultant surpasses the $1 million mark in commissions.
- **1980:** Mary Kay opens its doors in Argentina.
- **1981:** The founder's autobiography, *Mary Kay,* is published, selling more than one million copies.
- **1983:** As Mary Kay Cosmetics Inc. celebrates its twentieth anniversary, annual sales exceed $300 million at the wholesale level.
- **1985:** Mary Kay returns to private, family ownership in a leveraged buyout.
- **1986:** Mary Kay opens a German subsidiary.
- **1987:** Mary Kay Ash is named chairperson emeritus.
- **1988:** Mary Kay opens a subsidiary in Mexico.
- **1989:** The company takes leadership position in the cosmetics industry by ceasing animal testing.
- **1991:** Retail sales top $1 billion.
- **1992:** Mary Kay Inc. debuts on list of Fortune 500 companies.
- **1993:** For the second time, "The Hundred Best Companies to Work for in America" cites Mary Kay Inc., which is one of only fifty-five companies to appear in both

editions. It is also listed as one of the ten best companies for women. Sales exceed $1.4 billion at the retail level. Mary Kay opens in Russia.

- **1994:** Sales surpass $1.5 billion. Operations expand to twenty-two markets, including Japan.

- **1996:** The company experiences its tenth consecutive year of record sales. Wholesale sales surpass $1 billion, equating to more than $2 billion at the retail level. The company enters China.

- **1997:** Operations expand to twenty-six markets, including the Ukraine and Czech Republic. For the fifth consecutive year, Mary Kay becomes the best-selling brand of facial skin care and color cosmetics in the United States, based on most recently published industry sales data.

- **1998:** In honor of its thirty-fifth anniversary, Mary Kay modernizes its career car fleet with the addition of the new "Mary Kay edition" white GMC Jimmy sport utility vehicle and a new shade of pink for Cadillacs. The Mary Kay fleet, the largest commercial fleet of GM passenger cars in the world, includes nine thousand cars valued at more than $140 million.

- **1999:** Operations expand to twenty-nine markets, including Hong Kong and El Salvador.

In the United States, Mary Kay is a drug-manufacturing operation registered by the Food and Drug Administration (FDA). This allows the company to manufacture and distribute certain products classified as over-the-counter drugs, such as sunscreens and acne treatment products. The company develops, tests, manufactures, and packages the majority of its own products. Most are manufactured at the Dallas site, which is more than 275,000 square feet of floor space.

In April 1995, a manufacturing facility in Hangzhou, China, opened to serve Mary Kay subsidiaries in Asia's Pacific Rim, and another facility in La Chaux-de-Fonds, Switzerland, opened in January 1997 for the European region, including Russia.

For many years, Mary Kay has emphasized that it is a direct selling company, not a multilevel marketing company. Mary Kay spokespersons reported to the authors, however, that they do use a multilevel compensation plan, which pays on two levels of downline organizations. The fact that Mary Kay is probably better known to the average consumer for the products it makes rather than the direct selling and network marketing approaches it uses to sell them reveals the product-driven focus of this dynamic international company.

Nikken

Nikken is one of the largest network marketing/direct sales companies in the world. Nikken's industry positioning is dramatic based on performance benchmarks provided by company spokespersons, including:

- $1.75 to $2 billion in global sales projected for 2000

- Solid sales growth in the United States—from $3 million in 1989 to over $600 million in the United States and Canada in 1999

- 300,000 distributors in the United States and Canada and several hundred thousand more worldwide

- A customer base in Japan that includes one in eight Japanese homes, making it one of the top providers of health care products in Japan

- More than 30 million customers worldwide

- A wide selection of therapeutic products, ranging from bedding and clothing to nutritional and skin care supplies

- Sufficient capital to sustain future growth

In 1973, Nikken founder Isamu Masuda visualized a company that would help people achieve total wellness. Two years later, he formed Nikken in Fukuoka, Japan. Nikken—the company, the products, and the business opportunity—is built on a corporate philosophy centered on Masuda's concept of total wellness. This concept extends well beyond the scope of physical health, to encompass five key areas of life to be brought into a state of balance. These five areas are known in Nikken as "The Five Pillars of Health":

1. **Healthy body**

2. **Healthy mind**

3. **Healthy family**

4. **Healthy society**

5. **Healthy finances**

The company prides itself on being an innovator that applies cutting-edge technologies to help people enjoy freedom from discomfort, more restful sleep, enhanced athletic performance, more complete nutrition, and healthier-looking skin. Nikken's cutting-edge technologies include the following:

- Advanced Sleep Technology
- Ten Steps to a Great Night's Sleep
- Far-Infrared Technology
- Comfort Technology
- Flexible Kenko Technology
- Magnetic Water Technology
- Breakthrough Bioavailable Nutrition
- Swiss Botanical Skin Care
- Kenko Pet Technology

Today, the company has a global presence in full operation in nineteen countries, including Japan, Hong Kong, Taiwan, the United States, Portugal, Thailand, Spain, France, Canada, Mexico, England, Sweden, Holland, and Germany. The company reports that Nikken Europe has been experiencing substantial growth in 1999. Finland opened its doors in March of that year, and with the opening of Ireland in late October 1999, Nikken has now increased its European market unit to ten countries. In addition, by adding Taiwan to the list of Nikken countries in October 1999, Nikken distributors now have six market units to choose from—in addition to Japan—when expanding their business internationally':

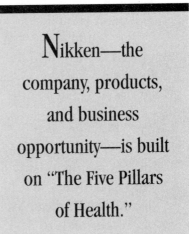

Nikken—the company, products, and business opportunity—is built on "The Five Pillars of Health."

1. **North America (United States, Canada, Puerto Rico, Dominican Republic)**

2. **Europe (United Kingdom, Sweden, Netherlands, Germany, Portugal, Spain, Italy, France, Finland, Ireland)**

3. **Mexico**

4. **Philippines**

5. **Hong Kong**

6. **Taiwan**

Currently, Nikken's North American operations are supported by its U.S. headquarters in Irvine, California, and by two distribution facilities in Toronto and Vancouver, Canada.

All of Nikken's offices and factories are linked to the head office via a sophiticated communications network. As mentioned in the last chapter, its eNikken Internet initiative has put many sales and business-building functions on-line.

We call this company the "silent giant" of network marketing. It doesn't make a lot of marketing noise in the United States—it just makes money! In a marketplace, particularly in Japan and Asia, that has grown somewhat skeptical of upstarts, Nikken's long track record, good reputation and focus on a healthy, holistic lifestyle position it well as populations of Japan and the West age.

Nu Skin Enterprises

Nu Skin Enterprises, Inc., has gone from a small U.S. startup to a multinational corporation with nearly $1 billion in yearly sales. In 1984, Nu Skin cofounder Blake Roney had just finished college when he pulled together a small group of professionals to develop a line of premium personal care products, containing only beneficial ingredients.

Beginning with less than $5,000 of start-up capital, Blake Roney, Sandie Tillotson, Nedra Roney, and several associates founded Nu Skin in June 1984 with twelve personal care products. In the company's beginning stages, with very limited capital, the founders negotiated with an Arizona company to formulate the skin care and hair care products, provide ninety days' credit, and ship the products in ten-gallon containers to Nedra Roney's apartment. There, the founders distributed products from Roney's living room, filling plastic containers and baby food jars with personal care products by hand.

Nu Skin says it opted to distribute its products through person-to-person marketing so a trained sales force could educate consumers one-to-one about the products' unique benefits. It also wanted to avoid the high cost of traditional consumer advertising and the wholesale-middleman infrastructure.

By 1991, Nu Skin International had grown its sales at a double-digit monthly growth rate, reaching $500 million in annual wholesale volume. Nu Skin was one of the fastest-growing network marketing companies in history.

In 1992, Nu Skin introduced the concept of "divisional diversification" as a cornerstone of its business model to the network marketing industry. Typically, network marketing companies introduce new products by merely adding another product line extension to the sales catalog or "product story."

To fuel continued growth, Nu Skin diversified into the vitamin, nutrition, and weight control product category by organizing a whole new division, Interior Design Nutritional (IDN). The new division targeted a niche market segment, the health- and nutrition-conscious consumer. IDN developed a differentiated strategy and a new distributor organization for marketing to the new customer.

The new division, funded by Nu Skin, offered the growth opportunity of a start-up venture without the high financial and organizational risk of working with a new company on a steep learning curve. By 1996, IDN was doing an estimated $200 to $300 million in wholesale sales volume.

Entering the decade of 2000, Nu Skin offers over two hundred products across three distinct strategic business units (SBUs) or business opportunities:

1. **Nu Skin, which markets premium quality face, body, and hair care products**

2. **Pharmanex, a company that markets natural and preventative nutritional supplements**

3. **Big Planet, a company which provides Internet technologies and services**

Nu Skin   Nu Skin is a leader in the creation and distribution of personal care products, with an emphasis on skin care. As already mentioned, it was founded in 1984 and has since expanded into more than thirty markets worldwide, with products being sold by over five hundred thousand active distributors.

Pharmanex   Pharmanex was founded in 1994 by pharmaceutical scientist Dr. Michael Chang and entrepreneur Bill McGlashan Jr. Their vision was to create beneficial products that apply the methodologies and disciplines of Western pharmaceutical science to natural products, producing dietary supplements of proven safety and efficacy.

Today, with more than sixty scientists on staff and more than one hundred fifty collaborating scientists at leading academic centers around the world, Pharmanex has developed nutritional products and a future research capability that have attracted top investors. In 1998, Pharmanex joined with Nu Skin Enterprises to help spread its product and business benefits throughout the world through network marketing.

Big Planet   Big Planet declares that its mission is "To leverage the emerging global Internet opportunity, the best in new technologies, and the privatization of public services to create an extraordinary business opportunity for our Independent Representatives and an exceptional integrated Internet experience for our customers with the Device, the Connection, and the Destination." It has set out to create the first internetworking company by combining the explosive growth of the technology and communications markets with the natural affinity of individuals and organizations to do business with people they see, know, and trust. The company believes it can accomplish this goal by providing customers with competitively priced, nationally recognized products and services combined with premium-quality service and support. Big Planet maintains strategic relationships with partners including Qwest, SkyTel, Cisco Systems, and Sun Microsystems, among others.

Products include:

- *Internet access*—a premium Internet connection with flexible access plans to suit any individual profile

- *iPhone 2050*—a fully integrated telephone and Internet device

- *Long-distance service*—competitive calling plans and rates for residential and commercial use

- *Wireless service*—phone services and paging from industry leader SkyTel

- *Dynamic Web Page Builder*—software to help customers create professional-looking Web sites

Divisional Diversification: The Future   Blake Roney, chairman of Nu Skin, emphasizes the firm's continual commitment to the divisional diversification strategy:

> Our business model is based on a simple concept: to provide compelling business opportunities for entrepreneurs around the world. . . . We are constantly identifying and capitalizing on important demographic and business trends. . . . This divisional approach to direct selling is creating strong sponsoring environments for our distributors, enabling them to focus on the business they are passionate about while buying and selling across all divisions. . . . We offer distributors the most compelling suite of direct selling opportunities in the marketplace.

Steve Lund, president and CEO, emphasizes that the "goal of our strategy is to enable Nu Skin, Pharmanex, and Big Planet to grow into billion-dollar enterprises." The three different brands offer unique and complementary business opportunities that set Nu Skin apart from its direct-selling competitors.

Today, with products licensed in thirty countries, Nu Skin is a rapidly growing network marketing company with more than half a million distributors worldwide. Its distributor force reflects many of the qualities of the New Professional. More than half of Nu Skin distributors have studied at a university, and many have received advanced degrees. To attract these individuals, Nu Skin emphasizes its seamless and global compensation plan, allowing its distributors to build an international sales network while receiving one check in the distributor's local currency.

Nu Skin Enterprises' business approach raises an interesting question: Can a network marketing company successfully house, under the same corporate roof, two units devoted to health- and youth-conscious consumers (Nu Skin and Pharmanex) and an Internet-based communications services company (Big Planet)? Since network marketers must choose which set of products they want to market, will the cross-pollination of product sales (in other words, Nu Skin distributors choosing Big Planet services for their personal and business communications needs) be sufficient to risk the brand-name confusion and marketing diffusion that could arise?

Company strategists no doubt reason that the key to the successful distribution of their skin care products depends on successful network marketers—and the key to successful network marketing in the future will be state-of-the-art communications. Therefore, the combination makes a perfect marriage. It's a bold and exciting move that business watchers in and out of the industry will monitor closely.

In the 1999 annual report for Nu Skin Enterprises, Inc., Roney summarizes the company's position on this topic: "By implementing our divisional strategy, we have laid the foundation for success. We are building on that foundation to enjoy renewed growth in 2000 and beyond." Nu Skin Enterprises is publicly traded on the New York Stock Exchange (NUS) and maintains its corporate headquarters in Provo, Utah.

Primerica Financial Services

Primerica was founded on the philosophy of "buy term and invest the difference." The theme was, buy lower-cost term life insurance, compared with whole life, and invest the savings. In 2000, Primerica sells life insurance and other financial products to more than six million clients though an independent sales force of more than 140,000 personal financial analysts who earn commissions not only on their own sales but also on those of the people they recruit to sell. To support the "Invest the Difference" theme, Primerica offers security investments to its representatives through PFS Investments in the United States and PFSL Investments Canada, Ltd.

While the size of financial service companies cannot be measured in the same manner as product companies, by all standards, this company belongs in the Billion Dollar Club. In 1998, it sold term life insurance policies with a face value of $57.4 billion, resulting in direct premiums of $1.06 billion. It also marketed $2.94 billion in mutual funds, $652 million in variable annuities, and $1.46 billion in direct consolidation loans.

The company traces its routes to 1977, when retired high school football coach A. L. Williams founded the company that bore his name until its sale in 1989. Today the Duluth-based Primerica is a unit of Citigroup, providing one of the most dramatic illustrations of the growing acceptance of network marketing on the part of the corporate establishment. It also reflects another critical trend we're seeing in network marketing: the increasing use of the business model to market services as well as products.

Network marketing will benefit greatly from moving into an arena "where the action is"—namely, financial and other services. The financial services industry, grappling with the same market fragmentation as other sectors, will benefit from the one-on-one sales approach network marketing offers. And fair or not to the companies that emphasize household and personal care products, New Professionals will find what they see as a more sophisticated set of product offerings a strong lure into an industry they never considered before.

Primerica's behemoth parent clearly understands the power of the network marketing channel and is using that channel to distribute not only life insurance but a whole range of financial products. Primerica is now putting an international expansion strategy in place that will soon bring it to potentially lucrative markets such as Germany and Spain.

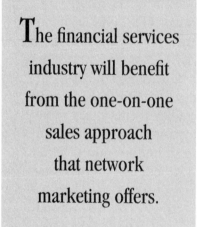

The financial services industry will benefit from the one-on-one sales approach that network marketing offers.

Network marketing is moving headlong into the service sector and Primerica, thanks to its gutsy founder and now accepting corporate parent, is leading the way.

Shaklee Corporation

Shaklee is recognized as an industry pioneer and a trusted name in health and wellness with retail sales in the 750 million range and over 500,000 distributors worldwide.

Even though the most recent sales figures available show annual revenues considerably lower than $1 billion, we have included Shaklee among the Pathfinders due to the firm's stability, longevity, and consistently significant size and impact. Shaklee Corporation calls itself "a diversified consumer products company that includes multilevel marketing, research and development technology under the Shaklee name and direct marketing, agricultural, and wholesale and retail store operations through its subsidiary, Bear Creek Corporation." It is indeed a respected industry pioneer in nutrition as well as network marketing, even predating Amway.

Dr. Forrest C. Shaklee, Sr., and his two sons, Forrest, Jr., and Raleigh, founded the company in 1956 as Shaklee Products in Oakland, California. In 1960, it introduced its first household product, Basic-H—a phosphate-free, concentrated, and biodegradable all-purpose cleaner.

After achieving substantial domestic growth in the 1960s, the company turned its sights to the international arena, opening Shaklee Japan and Shaklee Canada in 1976. Its business success also allowed it to invest heavily in research and development as well as manufacturing facilities, which in turn fueled the development of new nutritional, sports, and personal care products. The company has carefully nurtured an environmentally sensitive outlook and has also been named official nutrition consultant to the U.S. Olympic Team.

> Shaklee has associated itself with high-visibility projects and events it believes are consistent with its mission.

In 1986, Shaklee acquired Bear Creek Corporation and also provided the nutritional products consumed by the Voyager pilots when they became the first to fly around the world nonstop, nonrefueled. The opening of Shaklee Mexico came in 1992. In 1997, Shaklee and its new corporate parent, Yamanouchi Pharmaceutical Co. Ltd., broke ground for a new pharmaceutical manufacturing plant in Norman, Oklahoma. And as mentioned in the last chapter, Shaklee and Yamanouchi Pharmaceutical Co. Ltd. also opened the Yamanouchi Shaklee Pharma (YSP) Research Center located in the Stanford Research Park, Palo Alto, California.

Unlike other network marketing companies, Shaklee has, through much of its history, associated itself with high-visibility projects and events it believes are consistent with its mission and expose its products to wider audiences. One can see this strategy in its sponsorship of Earth Day activities—not a customary occurrence for corporations—as well as its ongoing sponsorship of athletic events and feats of courage and persistence such as powerless around-the-world flight.

Through its investment in research and product development and its corporate marriage with Yamanoughi Pharmaceuticals, this Pleasanton, California, firm, after nearly forty-five years, has built an impressive infrastructure around innovative products, substantial access to capital, and strong company ethics, making it a solid choice for many network marketers.

CHAPTER

7

Rising Star Companies That Are Making Their Mark

Recall that the goal of chapters 6 and 7 is to document that the network marketing industry is a rich and varied industry, full of interesting and diverse business models, marketing strategies, and product mixes. Chapter 6 profiled the pathfinders-the large, well-established, focused icons who were pioneers in the development of the industry. These icons achieved sales approaching or exceeding a billion dollars.

Chapter 7 continues that review but shifts the focus to the pacesetters-the "rising stars." These companies are elusive and continually changing. New firms are entering the industry and others are exiting. Therefore, any list will need continual updating, and ours here should not be considered exclusive or all inclusive. Nor should the failure of a company to appear on this list necessarily mean a judgment against it.

The criteria used for inclusion in the list, therefore, are subjective. In general, the firms listed are believed to:

- Provide consumer-oriented products/services
- Be structured around a network marketing compensation plan
- Have been in business at least two years
- Report annual sales at least in the range of $40-$50 million per year
- Have a unique strategic direction with growth potential
- Be accessible and willing to share information about the firms with the authors

We cast a broad net for rising star companies. We pursued many. Some didn't respond to mail, e-mail, or phone calls. Others wouldn't provide information about their businesses. Undoubtedly, there were other, potentially qualified firms whose names we never identified.

The firms profiled as pacesetters or rising stars are presented as representatives of the varied business models and strategies operative in the network marketing industry entering decade 2000.

To be sure, in the heady world of e-commerce and instant wealth, new start-up network marketing companies can be potentially romantic and exciting. They may represent the next Microsoft of the network marketing culture in the new millennium.

More likely, based on history, the new start-ups will be undercapitalized and will lack financial "staying power," have high enthusiasm and energy but no organizational structure, be undermanaged, and represent the hundreds/thousands of new start-up companies that occupy the network marketing graveyard. Time will tell.

ACN INC.

ACN Inc. entered the long-distance telephone market with a distinctly different positioning strategy compared with its predecessors, MCI and Sprint. MCI and Sprint used a multi-channel strategy for market penetration, *including* network marketing. ACN Inc. pursued network marketing as *the* channel of distribution and has committed to that venue.

Founded by five entrepreneurs in 1993, ACN markets telecommunications services throughout the United States, Canada, the United Kingdom, Germany, Denmark, the Netherlands, and Sweden. In its short life, it has grown from a $2 million start-up company to a $100 million firm that has attracted some three hundred thousand network marketers. Like Excel Communications, its initial focus was marketing cheaper long-distance service directly to consumers, but it has now attempted to branch out to other services, such as electricity. Greg Provenzano, president and CEO, reports, "With just nine states deregulated, ACN Energy has attracted over 125,000 customers and is currently ranked as the fourth largest independent reseller of energy in the United States."

ACN sees its main focus on gathering customers, not on building telecommunications systems or utilities of its own, in the image of Excel and Teleglobe. In a deregulated environment, customer acquisition is and will continue to be the critical strategy for market position. The company boldly projects that its revenues will reach $1 billion in just several more years—and with its founders' many years of prior experience in network marketing, direct sales, and corporate marketing, they just may do it!

New Professionals anxious to build businesses in the $1 *trillion* global telecom market will want to take a close look at this feisty Excel competitor.

AVON PRODUCTS, INC.

How can a company that was founded in the nineteenth century (1886) and now has $5.8 billion in annual retail revenues be considered a rising star in network marketing? Or an even better question—why do we place it on this list rather than make it a member of the Billion Dollar Club?

Avon would belong at the top of any list of direct-selling companies, for most of its vast business is conducted in that fashion—independent representatives sell products to customers and earn commissions. But unlike network marketers, they do not build multilevel sales organizations.

The company has done quite well, using the single-level direct approach. Some 2.8 million representatives (the proverbial Avon ladies and others) distribute the world's best-selling single brand of cosmetics, fragrances, and toiletries in 135 countries. They also sell an extensive line of fashion jewelry, apparel, and gifts.

> Avon has recently become a prime example of a more traditional direct-selling company moving to embrace the power of network marketing.

Despite its legacy of spreading entrepreneurship around the globe, not to mention the power of its brand name, Avon has recently become a prime example of a more traditional direct-selling company moving to embrace the power of the network marketing engine. Through its Leadership Division including some 12,000 network marketers, Avon now offers a multilevel marketing plan for distributors wishing to focus on particular product lines. At the same time, it has announced a first-ever global advertising campaign to strengthen brand identity as well as a heavy investment in Internet sales and business-building services for its independent businesspeople. That's a great combination of steps backing up the company's sales representatives.

Despite a halting economic performance in recent years, the venerable Avon is positioning itself to offer a powerful basket of assets to the network marketer. This is a company that knows how to make person-to-person selling work.

That's how it became number 308 on the Fortune 500 list of America's biggest corporations. For all these reasons, we see Avon, nearly 115 years old, as a rising star worthy of consideration by New Professionals!

CELL TECH

In the early 1970s, teacher Daryl Kollman began to notice that the children in his classes couldn't sit still and could hardly concentrate. Daryl and wife Marta later concluded that junk food made up a large part of the students' diets, and they set out to find a "perfect" food that could undo what they saw as the harmful effects of a poor diet. After extensive research, in 1974, they decided that this food was algae.

Daryl and Marta first tried the labor-intensive, artificial method of growing freshwater *Chlorella* in the deserts of New Mexico. After years of experimentation growing varieties of freshwater algae, the Kollmans discovered an exclusive source for the most remarkable blue-green algae of all: *Aphanizomenon flos-aquae*. They found it growing abundantly in a natural environment that proved to be

The Rising Stars

- ACN: www.acninc.com
- Avon: avon.avon.com
- Cell Tech: www.celltech.com
- Changes International: www.changesinternational.com
- FreeLife International: www.freelife.com
- Jafra Cosmetics International: www.jafra.com
- Life Plus: www.lifeplus.com
- Mannatech: www.mannatech.com
- Market America: www.marketamerica.com
- Melaleuca: www.melaleuca.com
- Morinda: www.morinda.com
- Nature's Sunshine Products: www.naturessunshine.com

More Rising Stars

- New Vision: www.newvision.com
- Noevir: www.noevirusa.com
- Nutrition for Life: www.nutritionforlife.com
- Oriflame: www.oriflame.com
- Oxyfresh: www.oxyfreshworldwide.com
- Pre-Paid Legal: www.prepaidlegal.com
- Princess House: www.princesshouse.com
- Reliv International: www.reliv.com
- Renaissance, the Tax People: www.thetaxpeople.net
- Rexall Showcase International: corp.rexall.com
- USANA: www.usana.com

the richest producer of biomass on the planet: Upper Klamath Lake in Klamath Falls, Oregon.

In 1982, the Kollmans began harvesting what they called Super Blue Green Algae (SBGA) and used it as the signature product for their new network marketing company. Cell Tech, frequently dubbed "the blue-green algae company" in Klamath Falls, was born. A high-tech harvesting and processing plant to dry the algae at low temperatures and preserve virtually all enzymatic activity was designed and built.

Cell Tech has since grown to become a multimillion-dollar company, harvesting millions of pounds of algae each year. It is then used to make the firm's popular nutritional supplements and personal care items that are sold by thousands of network marketers throughout the Untied States and Canada.

The Cell Tech corporate vision has been evangelistic toward "teaching the world about the benefits of Super Blue Green Algae as a dietary supplement." The Cell Tech distributor family is a mix of hard-core health-conscious, product benefit–focused users who are socially and environmentally conscious and a smaller cadre of active business builders.

Entering year 2000, Marta Kollman, CEO, and Justin Straus, vice president of marketing (a mother and son team), reported that Cell Tech will post sales in the $40 to $50 million range at year end through a distributor organization of 70 thousand active members.

Over the next three to five years, Cell Tech is driving to reenergize its sales growth through a variety of aggressive programs. At the research and development level, the company will continue to sponsor applied medical research on Super Blue Green Algae in conjunction with the McGill University/Royal Victoria Hospital, the University of Illinois, the Massachusetts General Hospital (affiliated with Harvard Medical School), and the University of Mississippi. The research studies will be used to credibly validate the nutritional value of Super Blue Green Algae and broaden the customer user base. In applied product development, the research findings may identify new product concepts Cell Tech should develop.

For the Cell Tech business builders, corporate emphasis will center on simplifying and supporting the distributor recruiting and business building process. The "breakaway" distributor compensation plan is being reviewed and will be updated and enhanced.

A new state-of-the-art Web site has been built and will continually be enhanced. It will ultimately be a corporate information center, a product information catalog, a distributor training platform, an order entry/tracking/follow-up resource, and an internal organization communication channel. For traditional field sales support and training of distributors, the company has a new product catalog and related distributor support materials under development.

With global population now exceeding six billion, innovative methods to improve both the food chain and the environment through natural foods like algae will be needed more than ever. The Kollmans were ahead of their time back in 1974. Now Cell Tech appears ideally situated to help address one of the twenty-first century's greatest challenges—feeding and maintaining the health of a hungry world.

CHANGES INTERNATIONAL

Changes International was founded by Terry and Scott Paulson, a father and son team, in 1994 with a very limited nutritional product line, a unique 15 percent first-level and 45 percent second-level commission structure still in place today, and high entrepreneurial energy. The firm grew to $40 million in three years.

In 1997, the Twinlab Corporation purchased Changes International for a rumored $12.5 million to become part of the corporation's multichannel distribution strategy. Changes International was to be the direct sale/network marketing vehicle for taking an array of Twin Lab products to the mass consumer market.

Twinlab's mission is to become "the top supplement manufacturer in the world." The company has a complete line of vitamins, herbs and nutraceuticals, antioxidants, fish and marine oils, sports nutrition supplements, phytonutrients, beauty aids, and a publishing subsidiary, Advanced Research Press, Inc., that features *All Natural Muscular Development,* a sports and fitness magazine, and health- and fitness-related books, audios, and newsletters.

Current production has the flexibility to manufacturer one thousand products in more than two thousand SKUs in distinct dosage forms: liquids, powders, capsules, and tablets. To support planned growth, the firm has a major capital expenditure program under way to boost production capacity to supply products to every channel.

In distribution, the firm is expanding into or acquiring all four major distribution channels for nutritional supplements: health stores, the mass market, direct sale, and mail order. Twinlab is also committed to establishing a presence overseas.

Most immediately, Twinlab has launched an aggressive push into the mass market. The firm reports "about a 1 percent market share in stores such as Rite-Aid and Target. There is plenty of room to grow share to 15 percent. . . . [T]hat would put its products in up to 47,000 outlets." In the beauty aids segment, Twinlab acquired the Bronson mail-order catalog subsidiary to develop that market.

Ross Blechman, president and CEO, reviews his distribution philosophy:

> We are now in every channel of distribution from the core markets, with increased presence in chains like GNC, Whole Foods, and Wild Oats, to our opportunities in the mass market, with Changes International in direct selling (network marketing) and now Bronson in mail order.
>
> It is also important to tailor products for the needs of each channel. . . . Products for health stores have different formulas and packaging than products for mass retail.

Blechman emphasizes, "I don't believe you can take exactly the same product in health food stores and retail and be successful in the mass."

Twinlab also has the financial firepower to support this growth model. The firm has averaged 25 percent sales growth per year. Year 2000 sales are estimated in the $350 to $400 million range, with strong profit performance.

Following the Twinlab acquisition of Changes International, Steve Coggin, a thirty-year veteran in the direct sale industry with experience at Avon, Fuller Brush, and, most recently, Melaleuca, was appointed president and CEO. Coggin's mandate was to convert the under organized start-up firm into a structured "growth platform" for Twinlab's penetration of the network marketing channel.

Over the ensuing 1997–2000 period, Coggin reports that Changes International has been completely reengineered.

A professional management team has been developed.
The Customer Service Department has been restructured
around a new focus on "customer satisfaction." The manufacturing and logistics systems have been overhauled. A
new computer system with associated information technology innovations has been installed. A new web site has
been developed for accessing/transmitting information,
training the distributor organization and automating in-
bound order processing though the Internet.

Changes expanded its product line to thirty-one products in 1999, with another ten additions scheduled for year
2000. The firm's "shopping basket" has been diversified
across the nutritional supplement category and into personal
care products.

Coggin reported that Changes' sales have grown from
$40 million in 1997 at the time of its acquisition to a tar-
geted sales plan of $55 million in 2000. The "active" distrib-
utor force, building on over 225 strong "business builders,"
totals over 72,000 members. Coggin summarizes by saying,
"Over the 1997–2000 period, the company has built a
strong infrastructure to support dramatic growth as a 'rising
star' in the network marketing industry over the next three
to five years."

FREELIFE INTERNATIONAL, INC.

FreeLife International, a health and wellness network marketing company, was launched in March 1995 by Presi-
dent/CEO Ray Faltinsky and Chief Operating Officer Kevin
Fournier. In the early 1980s, Faltinsky's mother was healed
of a crippling case of osteoporosis through the use of nutritional supplements. He became determined to start a
company that could extend the benefits of nutritional supplements around the world.

But how best to accomplish this goal? While preparing a
graduate thesis on direct selling, he realized that word-of-

mouth sales would be the most effective way to spread the word about the power of nutritional supplements. Teaming up with Fournier, the partners spent several years making plans, raising capital, and organizing a team of leading nutritionists to develop a strong product line.

The company spokespersons emphasize the company's strategy has been built on several key elements:

- A comprehensive product line based on innovative nutritional concepts in a continuing process of improvement and expansion. More recently, the company has added skin care products as well as a clinically proven natural treatment to promote joint health.

- Leading-edge Internet technology reflected in its Web site, FreeLife.com, in support of the distributor organization as both a marketing and sales tool and as an intra-organization communication medium

- Extensive corporate-driven field training in local markets in cooperation with local area directors

- A lucrative compensation plan that is routinely updated to respond to changing marketing conditions and distributor needs

From its beginning in March 1995, FreeLife has built a distributor force of over one hundred thousand members across the United States and Puerto Rico and has reported impressive sales results.

The message is clearly being heard by New Professionals such as Dr. Matt Silver, a former family practitioner.

"As a family practice physician involved in managed care," Dr. Silver states on the company Web site, "I had a solid and secure income that was trading time for money. I was also increasingly frustrated by the stress and long hours of medical practice. After joining FreeLife, I was able to retire from my practice in less than two years with a true residual income that is greater than what I made as a physician, and that continues to grow.

"In addition, I now enjoy the tremendous benefit of time freedom, which has greatly improved the quality of my life. I'm able to spend more time with my family, travel, and enjoy a lifestyle that even most physicians would be envious of."

The company now looks forward to an international expansion as well, all part of the mission of its founders to become "the world's largest health and wellness company, helping millions all over the world enjoy optimal health, well-being, and providing the opportunity for a more abundant life."

The exuberant energy of FreeLife as well as its products should carry it a long way.

JAFRA COSMETICS INTERNATIONAL, INC.

Jafra Cosmetics was founded by Jan and Frank Day in 1956 during the "pioneering" era of the network marketing industry. A brief time line highlights some key historical milestones for Jafra:

- Posting sales of $3.9 million in 1973, Jafra was purchased by the Gillette Company, the consumer products leader. The purchase by the prestigious Gillette organization has been heralded by network marketing industry evangelists as an endorsement of the network marketing channel by "mainstream" corporate America and a landmark credibility statement.

- After seventeen years as a Gillette subsidiary, Jafra sales had increased at a compounded annual growth rate of 18.5 percent to $229.5 million in 1997.

- In 1998, Jafra was acquired from Gillette by Clayton, Dubilier & Rice Fund V Limited Partnership (CDRJ).

- Sales and financial performance after the CDRJ Investments acquisition have been impressive. For 1999, annual sales were $290.5 million, up 17 percent over the $248.3 million sales performance in 1998. Ronald Clark, chairman and CEO, commenting on year-end results, said that 1999 "was a terrific year. We completed a number of initiatives that enabled us to more than double our operating profit for the year. We made substantial improvements to both our product cost structure and our promotional sales strategies. We were able to increase our gross margin to 71.7 percent for 1999, compared to 68.2 percent for 1998."

Jafra Cosmetics International, Inc., described itself during its acquisition by the Limited Partnership in 1998 as "a multilevel direct seller of premium skin and body care products, color cosmetics, fragrances, nutritional supplements and other personal care products." Based on 1997 sales of $229.5 million, the share of major product lines involved color cosmetics, 29.1 percent; skin care, 25.2 percent; body care and daily use products, 18.9 percent; fragrances, 16.3 percent; and other (sales aids and promotional materials), 10.5 percent.

The Jafra marketing strategy reflects another distinctive, target market approach built on several well-defined, key market positioning elements:

- Jafra targets middle-income, value-oriented consumers who seek a fresh, diverse, and quality product line.

- The Jafra consumer enjoys the convenience, flexibility, and low-key atmosphere of shopping at home, the personalized recommendations of her sales consultant, and the try-before-you-buy sales policy of the company. Consumers are believed to be loyal to the Jafra brand.

- Jafra products are positioned to appeal to a relatively wide range of market categories, demographic groups, and lifestyles.

- Jafra employs a "fast follower" product development strategy that minimizes research costs and focuses development on products that have already proven successful in the marketplace.

- In terms of price positioning, Jafra price points are generally at the higher end of the mass market category but slightly below prestige brands such as Clinique. Jafra prices are in line with Mary Kay but higher than Avon, which targets the lower to middle mass market.

- Jafra focuses on two key company sales revenue drivers: number of sales representatives and sales or productivity per sales representative.

Worldwide, Jafra has roughly 292,000 sales representatives, up 18 percent over 1998. The representatives reportedly sell, on average, approximately $1,000 annually. Using this formula, Jafra sales in 2000 are estimated to be $292 to $300 million or more.

The company, however, is committed to increasing the number of sales representatives through focused recruiting. Sales representative productivity will be increased through expanding the company's products, better-targeted marketing support campaigns, and the acceleration of new product introductions to enhance the firm's "market basket."

Another component of sales productivity is sales force retention. Jafra reports its "sales representatives have been affiliated

> Jafra employs a "fast follower" product development strategy, minimizing research costs and focusing development on products that have already proven successful.

with the company for an average of four years." The company believes this is one of the highest retention records in the network marketing industry.

Fundamental to the success of the Jafra strategy is the expansion of the senior management team who have significant direct selling experience. In his fourth-quarter and year-end 1999 report, Gonzalo Rubio, president and chief operating officer, announced a series of senior executive additions, all of whom had broad direct selling expertise. "We believe these executive appointments will help us strengthen and diversify," he said.

LIFE PLUS INTERNATIONAL

Life Plus International traces its routes to 1982 when pharmacist J. Robert Lemmon and corporate executive and network marketing leader Tim Nolan joined forces. They acquired VM Nutri Inc., which had been manufacturing nutritional supplements since 1936, and combined it with Multiway Associates, a network marketing arm that they founded. The nutritional supplements and personal care company we know and are impressed with today is the product of those two endeavors.

Lemmon came to the business with an extensive background in European-based natural therapies. He combined this experience with his own theories and formulas to produce products ranging from herbals and nutritional drinks to the company's popular Forever Young system, which combines supplements with external therapies to produce younger-looking skin.

Nolan ensures product quality and the viability of the business opportunity, which has been embraced by thousands of network marketers. "Are we control freaks?" he asks. "When it comes to manufacturing, you bet we are! We make certain our standards are maintained. . . . From the raw materials we buy, to the finished products we sell, Life Plus meets or exceeds all federal guidelines and regulations."

The company points to its in-house manufacturing operation as a big plus for distributors, as well as its communications network. No inventories are required, and if stocks run low, the company can simply produce more. In addition, the professionalism of the well-trained experts who answer consumer and distributor questions about the product content and protocol is fiercely upheld.

This product-driven company appears well positioned to continue to benefit from the frenzy of interest among baby boomers in natural health and personal care products.

MANNATECH INC.

Mannatech is a publicly traded company on the NASDAQ that develops and sells proprietary nutritional supplements and topical products. It boasts over half a million independent associations; operates in the United States, Canada, and Australia; and is widely viewed as one of network marketing's most promising newer companies.

Founded in late 1993, Mannatech began in a twenty-thousand-square-foot building in Grand Prairie, Texas, which served as the company's headquarters. From the start, the company has focused on proprietary nutritional supplements, beginning with just two. Fueled by Mannatech's own breakthrough discoveries in carbohydrate technology and by the 1994 passage of the Dietary Supplement Health and Education Act (DSHEA), the company expanded quickly. In 1997, Mannatech moved into its new headquarters, a 110,000-square-foot office facility located in Coppell, Texas. The firm also maintains in the same industrial park a 75,000-square-foot distribution and international logistics center to facilitate rapid and accurate order shipments through a computerized process.

In 1996, Mannatech began business in Canada and in 1998 initiated operations in Australia. In just two years, the company's Canadian associates grew to roughly 10 percent of the associate base and 20 percent of sales.

Growth has been dramatic. First-year sales were $8 million. In 1998, they reached $165 million. With such momentum, as well as a highly motivated leadership team and distributor force, there is no sign of any let up in sales growth or entrepreneurial potential.

MARKET AMERICA

Market America was founded by James H. Ridinger in April 1992 around a unique business model composed of several key elements:

- The "product brokerage" process

- The "Mall without Walls"

- The network marketing sales organization and the Market America "binary marketing" compensation plan

The Product Brokerage Process

Market America searches out market-driven products, emerging trends, or new innovative product breakthroughs. The company negotiates an exclusive agreement or a proprietary product line arrangement with the manufacturer, who already has the research and development, manufacturing, packaging, and/or logistical capabilities to supply the product. Each individual product, product category, or vendor becomes a "store" or strategic business unit (SBU) within Market America.

The Mall without Walls

Market America assembles each of its "stores" under the company "marketing umbrella," which then becomes a Mall without Walls. Each store is individually packaged as a self-sufficient SBU with its own identity, trademarks, training materials, and marketing support within Market America.

Under the product brokerage process and the Mall without Wall format, the firm can zig and zag, adapting rapidly to the changing consumer and technology markets. Moreover, it can operate without the high overhead costs of brick-and-mortar retail real estate and inventory holding expenses.

The current Market America Mall without Walls includes these illustrative major stores, featuring a wide array of products:

The Success Store
Flowers
Gourmet Products
Photography
Environmental
Biotech
Automotive
Jewelry
Fragrances
Security
Internet and Communications
Home Care
Health and Nutrition
Motives: Custom Blend Cosmetics
Personal Care

The Mall without Walls added several new products over 1999, including VitaShield OPC-3 Triple Serum, Gourmet Coffees, Advanced Security Systems, and a Silver Jewelry Collection.

Network Marketing Sales Organization and Binary Marketing Compensation Plan

The sales organization is built around the network marketing business model of distributors selling product through one-on-one word-of-mouth communication and recruiting and training other distributors to use and sell the product in the network marketing channel.

The binary marketing compensation plan used by Market America reportedly was the creation of the company's founder, James Ridinger. The company reports the plan includes several "unique features" designed particularly for the Market America business format.

Selling in the Market America Mall without Walls, independent distributors can specialize exclusively in one store or several stores of their choice to maximize their commission earnings. The selling concept is similar to being a manufacturer's representative, but the distributor operates under one company, Market America, and one binary marketing compensation plan.

> Under product brokerage and Mall without Walls, Market America can zig and zag, adapting to changing consumer and technology markets.

One-on-One Marketing and Mass Customization

For the time-deprived shopper of the 2000 decade, Market America has developed the UnFranchise Business Development Centers operated by independent distributors. These centers represent a potentially powerful retailing strategy for maximizing customer satisfaction and moving more retail sales.

Under this model, distributors identify ten or more of their best customers for participation in the Preferred Customer Program. The distributor customer manager analyses each preferred customer in terms of personal buying behavior, style preferences, product category usage, and so forth, and formally collects an information file.

Market America builds an individual customer data, analyzes the data, and is able to produce exactly what customers want, for each customer manager's preferred customer group and for each individual customer. The company labels this strategy "mass customization."

Measuring Performance

Sales and financial performance for Market America reflect very strong growth and profitability. Sales in 1999 reached $110.2 million, a 26 percent increase over 1998. Earnings per share were up 31.5 percent over the previous year. Sales to date in 2000 are running roughly 20 percent ahead of 1999, with similar earnings levels. The firm has approximately eighty thousand active distributors and maintains a retention level above the industry averages.

MELALEUCA INC.

Melaleuca was founded in 1985 with just seven employees. Guided by President and CEO Frank L. VanderSloot, this Idaho Falls company now employs over 1,300 people and has annual revenues exceeding $300 million. Its growth in just over fifteen years has earned it a spot on *Inc.* magazine's list of the 500 fastest-growing companies for five years in a row.

The company takes its name from *Melaleuca alternifolia,* a tree that produces natural antiseptic oil. This substance is used in many of the firm's health care, pharmaceutical, personal care, and home hygiene products.

> M elaleuca's focus on product, research, and technology makes it a good platform for its tens of thousands of network marketers.

All told, Melaleuca markets over a hundred exclusive products geared for everyday personal and household use, with an emphasis on pure, natural ingredients that are favorable to both human health and the physical environment. The company invests heavily in research and maintains automated, state-of-the-art manufacturing and distribution facilities in both

Idaho Falls and Knoxville, Tennessee, to handle some eighty thousand orders a day. This product, research, and technology focus—along with solid financial management—makes this company a good platform for its tens of thousands of network marketers, which it calls marketing executives.

MORINDA, INC.

In 1993, Stephen Story and John Wadsworth, "food scientists" with educational backgrounds in food science and nutrition from Brigham Young University, were introduced to the fruit of the *Morinda citrifolio* plant from French Polynesia. The plant's noni fruit yields a juice that Polynesians have used for over two thousand years for its health benefits. Over the next two years, the founders developed a process of harvesting, processing, and flavoring a citrifolio juice to bring it to the market in its traditional, natural form and labeled it Tahitian Noni.

> The noni fruit yields a juice that Polynesians have used for over two thousand years for its health benefits.

In 1996, Kerry Asay, former CEO and chairman of the board of Nature's Sunshine Products in the 1970s and 1980s, a network marketing company specializing in vitamin supplements (see the next section), recognized the potential of Tahitian Noni. Asay brought a team of network marketing executives to the Morinda venture to launch commercialization of the noni product through the network marketing distribution channel. The mission of Morinda, Inc., is to create a new product category and be the undisputed world leader in the noni product.

In its first month of operation in July 1996, Morinda reported sales of $40,000. For 1999, Morinda had sales of $289 million, an average of $24 million per month, through a distributor force of four hundred thousand members. From 1996 through 1999, Morinda's progressive marketing plan has paid out more than $255 million in commissions. In 2000, Morinda estimates sales will reach $350 million with a distributor force of half a million members.

Morinda states it was the first company to introduce noni juice to the market with a patented flavoring system. Its Tahitian Noni Juice brand dominates the noni market with:

- 95 percent market share

- 38 million ounces of the juice consumed every month around the world

- Use and endorsements by Olympic and professional athletes around the world

- Official global operations in over twenty countries in North America, the Caribbean/Central and South America, Europe, and Asia/the Pacific Rim, with plans for further international expansion

Based on Morinda's seamless international operations, any independent distributor can establish a Morinda business worldwide in any country where Morinda officially operates. The corporate rules and regulations are the same across every country: In countries where Morinda has not established full business operations, the firm has contracted with Tropical Express Company, an international distribution organization, to provide Tahitian Noni brand products and limited services for personal use only. Currently, Tropical Express represents Morinda in twenty additional countries.

NATURE'S SUNSHINE PRODUCTS

Nature's Sunshine Products' evolution mirrors the challenges that face family start-up companies in the network marketing industry. The company was founded by Gene and Kristine Hughes at their kitchen table in 1972 as Hughes Development Company. Based on the business concept, the husband and wife team formulated their first product and leased a capsule-filling machine for $80 per month to begin hand production of herbal vitamin capsules. First sales were direct to vitamin stores. Then a brand name was created, and sales were expanded to a broader set of retailers.

In 1974, a multilevel compensation plan was added as an alternative for distributors. By 1975, sales had exceeded $1.5 million. The company went public with company stock. In 1976, the construction was launched for a 32,000-square-foot manufacturing facility. The new business was on the runway preparing for takeoff, hopefully for high altitude, maybe transcontinental flight.

By 1979, annual sales had grown to $10 million. The company name was changed to Nature's Sunshine Products in 1981. A wave of manufacturing expansion followed. By 1992, the company has reached the magical threshold of $100 million in annual sales. *Forbes* magazine listed the firm as forty-fourth on its list of the 200 best small companies.

In 1999, the company's sales revenue totaled $289.2 million, down approximately 2 percent due to a 22 percent decrease in the number of independent distributors (down to 530,000), increased domestic competition, and foreign currency devaluation in the majority of its international markets. Eliminating the negative impact of foreign currency devaluation, sales revenue would have increased by 3 percent.

Nature's Sunshine has positioned itself as the industry leader in producing over five hundred of the highest-quality, natural herbal supplements and vitamins available in the world. The firm pioneered the encapsulation of herbal products and aggressively promoted the virtue of herbal supplements long before the concept was fully accepted. The firm claims its products "consistently offer the highest potency, delivering ounce-by-ounce the most herbal content of any product on the market." Nature's Sunshine network of distributors and managers use the herbal products themselves and are "herb specialists," "dedicated to learning and remaining up-to-date on the latest products and news in the field." Internally, the firm maintains a staff of herb technology specialists and pharmacognosists.

Today, the company sales can be divided into five product groups: herbs, 65 percent; vitamins, 26 percent; personal care products, 3 percent; homeopathics, 1 percent; and all others, 5 percent.

Looking forward to the decade of 2000, Nature's Sunshine will focus on recharging sales growth through several primary initiatives. The research and development team will explore new products such as the new item CleanStart, a recently introduced colon-cleansing formula. A major expansion of manufacturing capacity has already been launched to support domestic and international sales growth. The Smart-Start Program has been designed to accelerate new distributor recruiting.

In 2000, Nature's Sunshine Products is focusing on the development of a greater international presence. Currently international sales represent over $105 million, approximately 37 percent of consolidated sales revenue. More than 50 percent of company distributors are from international markets.

In particular, the company expects continued strong performance in South Korea, building on the 350 percent increase in sales in 1999 over 1998. In 2000, Nature's Sunshine will relaunch its operation in Japan based on a new management team. The company will also open operations in Israel in 2000.

The company operates in several key markets, including the United States, Brazil, Japan, Mexico, South Korea, Venezuela, Canada, Colombia, Russia and the former Soviet Republics, the United Kingdom, Argentina, Peru, El Salvador, Ecuador, Honduras, Guatemala, Costa Rica, Panama, Chile, and Nicaragua. The company also has exclusive distribution agreements with selected companies in Australia, Malaysia, New Zealand, and Norway.

NEW VISION

New Vision was founded in 1995 by Lynne, Karen, BK, and Jason Boreyko, who brought a combined twenty-seven years of network marketing experience to their venture. In just over five years, the Tempe, Arizona, company has racked up $600 million in annual sales throughout the United States, Canada, Australia, and Japan.

New Vision's product line features natural health treatments and nutritional supplements. It conducts intensive research, maintains strict quality control, and has formed strategic alliances with manufacturers to broaden the scope of its offering. As a relatively new company, it has emphasized automation and information technology right from the start, making its home-based business opportunity one of the most modern and user-friendly in the industry.

> New Vision has emphasized automation and information technology from the start, making it one of the most modern and user-friendly in the industry.

The network marketing press has taken note of the spectacular splash New Vision has made from the day it opened its doors. Not too many ventures achieve $600 million in sales in just five years. This one has, and it is drawing many New Professionals who are attracted by the youth and dynamism of the company's leadership.

NOEVIR

Noevir traces its roots to Japan, where it was founded in 1978 and began manufacturing operations under the Noevir brand name. Today this cosmetics, skin care, and nutritional supplements company illustrates a central development in the globalization of network marketing—namely, an explosion of international business centered around the U.S.–Japan economic relationship.

While the two nations' traditional industries such as autos, steel, and electronics continue their rancorous competition in the marketplace and the trade policy arena, network marketing firms based in both Japan and the United States have made impressive inroads in each other's market. And with Japanese Americans as the conduits, companies on both shores of the Pacific are becoming increasingly linked in a variety of mutually beneficial business relationships and growth strategies.

As noted in chapter 4, Japan leads the world in direct sales; the United States tops the field in size of the distributor force. American companies such as Amway, Herbalife, and others count on Japan for substantial shares of their total global revenues and distributor forces. The reverse is true for Japanese firms such as Noevir and Nikken, which are expanding into other international markets, including the United States. Shaklee, for example, was acquired by Yamanouchi Pharmaceutical Company, Ltd., a leading Japanese Corporation.

Moreover, the overall performance of the world's two largest economies tends to work in a countercyclical fashion. In much of the post–World War II era, when the U.S. economy has been strong, Japan's has been relatively weak, and vice versa. Since network marketing recruiting can actually increase during bad economic times (when more people are looking for alternative income sources), companies with a big presence in both countries thus find that deficiencies in their performance in one venue can be compensated by strengths in the other.

At the same time, strong societal similarities and distinctions also make the bilateral relationship thrive. Both markets are highly affluent but face profound changes due to shifting demographics, particularly in the aging of the population and shrinking of the traditional workforce. Each country also brings something unique to the network marketing party: the United States brings a tradition of individualistic entrepreneurship not widely practiced in Japan until recently; Japan brings the Asian focus on networking and a centuries-old embrace of natural products and remedies—products that form the backbone of the offerings of many network marketing companies.

So New Professionals with ambitious business goals may indeed want to ask the following question: "Is my prospective company taking advantage of the most important bilateral direct selling relationship in the world, bar none?"

In Noevir's case, the firm claims total worldwide sales approaching $1 billion and a global sales force of one million. It has enjoyed steady and, at times, spectacular growth. Noevir's U.S. headquarters in Irvine, California, gives it a strong American presence to aid domestic distributors in their training, recruiting, and sales efforts.

NUTRITION FOR LIFE INTERNATIONAL

This Houston-based health and nutrition company was founded in 1984 by a three-person team with complementary skills and similar visions: President David Bertrand, who has guided the company's strategic direction; Executive Vice President Jana Mitcham, the firm's product pioneer; and founding distributor Tom "Big Al" Schreiter, a network marketing dynamo.

Nutrition for Life emphasizes a long-term business outlook rather than flashy hoopla. The corporate focus is on developing a Nutrition for Life "Life Cycle." The Life Cycle creates an identifiable path for achieving a healthy lifestyle that produces optimum physical and mental performance for the individual and the family. The product mix includes over four hundred products, spanning water and air filtration and purification systems, health food and weight management, vitamin, mineral and herbal supplements, skin and hair care, cleaning concentrates and disinfectants, and educational/self-development programs.

Nutrition for Life emphasizes a long-term business outlook rather than flashy hoopla.

The firm had sales of over $67 million in 1999 moving through a distributor organization of approximately one hundred thousand people. It is a member of the U.S. and Canadian Direct Selling Associations. It maintains a strong and growing international presence, operating in the United States, Canada, United Kingdom, Ireland, the Netherlands, the Philippines, Guam, and Puerto Rico. Nutrition for Life has also plunged headlong into the e-commerce revolution, making some three hundred unique products available to on-line shoppers.

In his own recent book, *Making a Difference,* company founder Bertrand explained:

> When you start your own network marketing business, you leave behind the traditional business paradigm. When you leave that world behind, you must leave behind its thinking, too. Success in network marketing is often directly related to how well you make this transition. It's not always easy—you're learning a whole new approach to business, after all. . . .
>
> So many analogies have been used to explain network marketing that I wouldn't dream of throwing in another one at this point. Suffice it to say that your network marketing business is a lot like a low-risk franchise. It combines the freedom of being an entrepreneur with the security that comes from a well-tested concept. During the last two

decades, network marketing has become a popular alternative for people who want to own their own business without putting themselves at the mercy of a high-risk start-up.

ORIFLAME

This natural cosmetics company was founded in Sweden in 1967 by Robert af Jochnick and Jonas af Jochnick. Today some eight hundred thousand independent distributors who rack up annual sales exceeding $468 million sell its products in over sixty countries.

Capitalizing on the allure of the Nordic look and lifestyle, the firm has been giving mainstays like Avon and Nu Skin a run for their money. Now, Oriflame plans to establish a higher profile through a global advertising campaign and the acquisition of a new spokesperson, international model and actress Izabella Scorupco. Yet despite its growth and ambitious plans, the company maintains a strong focus on home-based entrepreneurship backed by a small corporate hierarchy.

OXYFRESH WORLDWIDE, INC.

Oxyfresh Worldwide Inc. of Spokane, Washington, was founded in 1984 and is a privately owned company of 200 employees and sales leaders. Its exclusive product lines include oral health care, skin and hair care, weight loss, nutritional supplements, air purification systems, and pet care. Oxyfresh operates throughout the United States and Canada under an aggressive expansion plan propelled by the zeal of its president and CEO, Richard B. Brooke. The company is a member of the Direct Selling Association and therefore a signatory to the industry's code of ethics.

Like other network marketing companies, Oxyfresh is banking on the trend toward natural personal care and nutritional products and its accompanying desire for cleaner, healthier living to spur it forward. But one of its signature products, the Oxyfresh Air unit, is particularly worth noting.

The more we learn about indoor air pollution, the more we are realizing that some of the greatest remaining environmentally based health hazards occur right in the home and workplace, thanks to poor ventilation, building materials, household products, and germs spread by people and pets. With proper marketing, this company, which has already proved its mettle for some sixteen years, could ride the wave of concern and action about this problem. Oxyfresh's product line, enthusiastic leadership and distributors, and training support put it on our list of rising star pacesetters.

PRE-PAID LEGAL SERVICES, INC.

Pre-Paid Legal Services' mission is to make the law work for average Americans, just like it's supposed to, and to offer aspiring entrepreneurs a low-cost business opportunity in pursuit of that mission. The company develops, underwrites, and markets legal service plans in the United States and two Canadian provinces. These plans provide benefits including unlimited attorney consultation, will preparation, traffic violation defense, defense against automobile-related criminal charges, letter writing, document preparation and review, and a general trial defense benefit.

The cost of the basic plan is just $14.95 a month, and for that price, average, middle-class families gain access to the top lawyers in the country. Today the company serves over seven hundred thousand customers. Approximately 185,000 independent entrepreneurs sell the products.

Pre-Paid Legal is a publicly traded company on the NYSE. It is a company

- Whose revenues have grown from $60 million in 1996 to $160 million in 1998

- Whose sales rose 51 percent over five years, with earnings per share soaring 175 percent over the same period

- That has enjoyed twenty-five consecutive quarters of revenue and income growth

- With no long-term debt and a cash and investment balance of $42.5 million

- That has been named the thirty-third fastest-growing company on the New York Stock Exchange

- That ranked number 13 on the 1999 *Forbes* magazine list of the 200 best small companies in America—the fourth consecutive year it has made it into an exclusive club that applies an extremely difficult set of financial performance standards

The company's founder, Harland Stonecipher, calls it a thirty-year overnight success story. Stonecipher, the son of poor Oklahoma sharecroppers, is clearly a man with a mission.

The justice system in America is broken and it needs fixing. The legal profession in America is ridiculed and reviled—and it needs to be revitalized. Entrepreneurship in America has become too expensive—and it needs to be put back in the hands of ordinary people once again.

Hardly a day goes by when we don't hear about an alleged miscarriage of justice: rogue police officers who abuse suspects; law enforcement agencies who use racial profiling to determine who to pull over on the highway; juries that are swayed by emotion rather than facts, manipulated by hired-gun psychologists to free the guilty or convict the innocent.

The legal system today is not all that different than the way McDonald's founder Ray Kroc found the hamburger business back in 1955. We've got plenty of lawyers. They're everywhere. We've got plenty of need for their services—remember that over 50 percent of us are involved in some type of legal situation right now.

But for most Americans, the quality is questionable, the service is bad, the consistency uneven, the price is exorbitant, and access is out of reach. The McDonald's example illuminates the true nature of our problem and more importantly points us to an answer. It's not a question of having enough laws on the books, enough lawyers, or enough need for legal counsel and representation. It's all about how to get the services to the vast majority people who don't know the system or where to turn.

That's where our prepaid legal concept comes in. It's simple. What we do is gather together a whole bunch of customers and charge each of them a small monthly fee for which we promise them a specific set of services. We then pool the money they pay us and use it to retain the very best law firms in the country to provide those services for our members.

Thus, the individual member gets a much better law firm at a much lower cost than he or she could ever get on his own. Law firms who probably would never give the time of day to our individual members if they called on their own pay a great deal of attention to them because those firms have to answer to us—Pre-Paid Legal Services, Inc.—for we are one of their biggest, if not the biggest, clients.

> **P**re-Paid Legal Services is an example of a network marketing company that has literally invented a new service industry in the United States.

Pre-Paid Legal Services is an example of a network marketing company that has literally invented a new service industry in the United States. Analysts in and out of network marketing see strong potential for growth for this company because of its unique product focus in a market of great, untapped potential.

PRINCESS HOUSE

Princess House was organized in 1963 by Charles Collis to merchandise crystal products, home-decorating accessories, and collectibles. The company was organized around party plan retailing, including a six-level compensation plan for sales organization builders. Collis grew the firm to the $100 to $125 million retail sales range over the 1963–1977 period.

In 1977, Colgate Palmolive, the consumer products leader, purchased Princess House to explore the network marketing channel. With the purchase by the prestigious Colgate Palmolive organization, the network marketing industry advocates highlighted Princess House as an example of diversification by "mainstream" corporate America into network marketing as a landmark credibility statement.

Colgate Palmolive grew the Princess House successfully to approximately $200 million per year, and then sales started to erode, "bottoming" at approximately $80 million in the early 1990s. In response to the sales slump, Colgate Palmolive began to explore exit strategies. In 1994, ultimately, James Northrop and an investment group, South Street Capital, bought Princess House.

The new management team at Princess House launched a reengineering process to critique the business operation in the mid-1990s. Ultimately, a turn-around repositioning strategy was drafted. The new business model shifted the traditional, narrowly focused "crystal lady" into a broader "lifestyle consultant," focusing on home accessorizing with home enhancement products. The firm expanded its product line to include home decorative accents, giftware, collectibles, casual living products, home entertaining products, and cooking, serve, and store products.

Elizabeth DiPaolo, vice president of marketing, is developing a comprehensive market positioning strategy for implementing the new corporate direction. Successful and innovative lifestyle consultants have been identified and organized into an experimental marketing team, "Templates for Success," to contribute to the strategy design and implementation.

Statistical analysis and focused group marketing research are being conducted to craft the tactics of the marketing program. Training programs are being developed and tested to teach the how-to's for new lifestyle consultants. At the major Princess House convention in New Orleans, scheduled for August 2000, focus will be on the new strategy.

Tim Brown, vice president of sales, is responsible for field sales implementation and sales force management of the strategy in conjunction with the marketing planning team that has designed it. Brown reports that Princess House sales have turned around since the redirection in 1994, climbing into the $160 million or more range at retail in 1999 based on a field force of fourteen thousand independent lifestyle consultants.

RELIV INTERNATIONAL

Reliv International, founded in 1988 by Robert Montgomery in the St. Louis area, is a manufacturer and network marketing firm that produces and sells nutritional supplements, weight management products, and related sports drinks and foods.

Initially, the firm focused on soy technology as a cornerstone of its product line. In recent years, the company has expanded into the booming $80 billion "functional food" category. Montgomery, Reliv president and CEO, defines "functional food" as "an emerging area of nutritional science made up of food products designed to influence specific functions of the body." *Food Technology* magazine reports that functional food is the leading product trend in food technology.

In 1999, Reliv enjoyed record revenue growth for the third straight year. Net sales increased to $68 million, up 31 percent over 1998. The growth, however, was not profitable. The firm lost $1.4 million on the 1999 sales record.

The company reported that the losses in 1999 stemmed primarily from the low margins earned on the contract manufacturing operations. Over the 1997–1998 period, the company brought 90,000-square-foot new manufacturing capacity on-line to support longer-term Reliv internal growth needs. To use that added capacity most efficiently and absorb related overhead costs in the short term, the company aggressively pursued contract manufacturing in the food industry.

As Montgomery states, "contract manufacturing validated itself as a revenue generator but, unfortunately, not as a profit generator."

> **R**eliv reports that it will aggressively market its soy-rich signature products and will accelerate research and development efforts on new soy-based products.

The Reliv experience summarized an axiom in the network marketing industry: some companies can successfully manage contract manufacturing operations *and* aggressive network marketing growth. Others cannot. Reliv did not.

Looking forward into 2000 and beyond, Montgomery emphasized that Reliv will focus its business strategy on a formula that works based on the following elements:

• **Expertise in food technology.**

Reliv has been a pioneer in the development of soy protein products. In 1999, the U.S. Food and Drug Administration approved legislation that allows foods "with at least 6.25 grams of soy protein to carry labels stating that soy protein can reduce the risk of heart disease by lowering cholesterol levels." Reliv reports that it will aggressively market its soy-rich signature products and will accelerate research and development efforts on new soy-based products in its "Reliv 2000" Product Development Program.

- **The Reliv distributor network.**

  Reliv will place magnified emphasis on new sales support and compensation programs for the thirty-seven thousand members of its distributor organization. In 1999, Reliv introduced an interactive Internet system to provide a full array of e-commerce facilities for its distributors, ultimately on a worldwide basis. The Internet system will include a complete product catalog, on-line order entry, order delivery tracking, on-line sponsoring new distributors, information on the distributor genealogy and sales volumes, distributor e-mail communications, personalized distributor Web sites, linkage to corporate Web sites and e-commerce opportunities, and more.

- **International growth.**

  In 1999, Reliv successfully expanded into Mexico and, in the first quarter 2000, into Colombia. Montgomery reports the firm has opportunities to enter Europe, Asia, and Latin America and is "developing specific initiatives" to capitalize on those markets.

  Reliv is a company that its management pledges is "focusing on our core network marketing business . . . in the food technology market. . . . [W]e are focused, energized, and positioned for growth."

RENAISSANCE, THE TAX PEOPLE, INC.

Renaissance, Inc., was founded in 1995 by Mike Cooper and John Meadows as a start-up network marketing company. The original business model was built on a network marketing–driven Renaissance Buying Club Membership Program.

The initial mission of Renaissance was to identify a broad portfolio of products to feature, with emphasis on high-priced/high-margin product categories (e.g., high-end jewelry, golf equipment, hunting, fishing and camping products, etc.), establish supply sources, and offer those branded products at discounted but profitable margins through a network marketing distributor force. The venture was launched and attracted approximately twenty-six thousand distributors by 1997.

As a potential service to its independent marketing associates (IMAs) organization, Cooper investigated how IMAs could document expenses associated with their home-based network marketing businesses and use them as legitimate deductions from their income taxes. In that analysis, he recognized the enormous potential tax savings and the need for a simplified tax accounting procedure of system designed for every home-based business operator.

A new business concept was born! Cooper reports, "We decided to expand to include a tax service division called Advanced International Marketing (AIM) that later evolved into The Tax People (TTP)."

Renaissance, The Tax People (TTP) was organized in November 1997 to offer tax expertise and audit protection services through the network marketing channel. The TTP business model focuses on the 120 million American taxpayers. Taxes represent the largest single expenditure for the typical consumer—an estimated 35 percent of gross family income. Tax analysts estimate the average American taxpayer works four to five months for the "tax system" to reach his or her personal "Tax Freedom Day" to satisfy their federal, state, and local tax burdens—before earning a cent for themselves. The National Taxpayers Union Foundation, using its taxation models, estimates that American taxpayers for 2000 reached the Tax Freedom Day on May 3.

TTP contends many families are struggling financially because they don't understand the tax system and are overpaying their taxes. Jeff Schnepper, tax expert and author of *How to Pay Zero Taxes*, wrote:

The tax code is extremely complicated and changes every year. . . . Before the changes in 1998, the IRS tax code was 9,471 pages containing 1,300,000 words. The 1997 tax regulations, which are needed to interpret the tax code, consist of 91,824 pages and 5,750,000 words. This is a total of 101,295 pages and over 7,050,000 words. . . . To fill out the 1998 1040EZ tax form, the IRS sends you 31 pages of fine print instructions—and that's the easy form. . . . The amount of paper work is staggering.

Into this information maze stepped TTP. The TTP program provides both tax expertise, a formal tax accounting system, *and* a format for a home-based, network marketing business with its associated tax deductions. TTP services include the following:

- The Tax Relief System (TRS)—a detailed "paint-by-number" instruction manual outlining tax strategies and an expense documentation system for collecting and analyzing relevant tax information. The TRS has been written by experienced tax advisers and former IRS agents based on U. S. Tax Code rulings and regulations, IRS revenue rulings, and tax and district court rulings.

- The Tax Dream Team—a team of tax experts and former IRS agents to work directly with TTP members in organizing their tax information and tax reports

- The Affiliated Tax Professional Network (ATPN)—a network of over nine hundred local tax professionals who are affiliated with TTP to support TTP members as part of the TTP member benefits

- Audit protection by the Tax Dream Team and the ATPN as needed in dealing with the IRS if challenges do develop

- A home-based, network marketing business based on marketing the TTP program to other business associates, friends or family

Furthermore, TTP "guarantees in writing that following their simple business plan will provide you with at least $5,000 in additional legal tax deductions or TTP will refund the fees paid for services."

Member growth has been impressive. Following the formal start-up in 1997 and the rollout in 1998, TTP welcomed 4,648 new IMAs. In 1999, more than twenty-two thousand new members joined. Fewer than 7 percent of customers cancel within thirty days of purchasing. Of all IMAs that join, 88 percent remain active for more than six months. TTP claims its "retention rate is ten times the MLM industry average."

Todd Strand, vice president of sales, reports that sales totaled $1.2 million in 1997, $5.3 million in 1998, and $23.6 million in 1999. Current sales are running roughly $6.0 million a month, with an estimate of $65 to $100 million by year-end 2000.

REXALL SHOWCASE INTERNATIONAL

This company traces part of its roots back to 1903. A young man named Louis Liggett, who by age 26 had already organized a powerful national association of America's druggists, was riding on a train to Seattle when he first dreamed of the idea of Rexall drug stores. A forerunner to franchising, Rexall gave hard-working families a chance to own their own business but at the same time be part of a larger organization with a respected name. In thousands of communities, it gave Americans a trusted corner drugstore and even a place to socialize.

Now flash-forward to 1937. A man named Carl DeSantis was born and raised in the Miami area. He grew up in modest surroundings. At the age of nineteen, Carl began what would be a seventeen-year retail drugstore career with Super-X and Walgreen drugstores. Managing stores from Florida to North Carolina, DeSantis not only learned the nuts and bolts of running a business but also saw upfront and personally how consumers made purchasing decisions, what product pitches and presentations they either responded to or ignored, and how their tastes evolved over the years.

One thing DeSantis observed while managing a drug store in Miami Beach was the large number of "snowbirds" from the northern states who, after escaping the brutal winter for the sunshine of south Florida, came into the store in search of a low-cost product to protect and soothe their fair, sunburned skins. DeSantis and a pharmacist developed an inexpensive lotion called "Sundown" and sold it locally.

Shortly after that, he observed that a lot of calls and inquiries were coming into the store from customers looking for special blends and potencies of vitamins, particularly vitamins E, B-complex, and C. For millions of Americans, taking a daily multiple vitamin was nothing new. But DeSantis detected a growing interest in nutrition and health products, and he saw that consumers were becoming intrigued and captivated by the notion that particular vitamins and minerals were associated with particular health benefits. That savvy perception led Carl DeSantis headlong into the vitamin business in 1976.

Beginning with several vitamin products under the SDV brand, DeSantis turned a bedroom of the family home in North Miami Beach into the company warehouse. The kitchen table was the packaging and order-processing department. His wife, with a background in accounting, kept the books. Sons Dean and Damon pasted labels on bottles and prepared orders for shipping every afternoon after school. The front door was "shipping and receiving"—the UPS driver would back up to it each afternoon to pick the day's packages.

The marketing plan was simple: word-of-mouth customer satisfaction and $450 ads in the *National Enquirer.* "The ads in there were cheap in those days," the senior DeSantis remembers.

By the early 1980s, Sundown Vitamins had become one of the most popular brands. DeSantis graduated from employee to boss. The consumer's intense focus on health, diet, and fitness—a trend he detected before most—was picking up steam.

In 1985, DeSantis reports, "I just happened to be in New York at an industry meeting. I met a number of people from the major drug companies. I also found out while I was there that the Rexall drug company, which was started in 1903 in Boston, was available.

"I got together with some people I know on Wall Street and they advised me if I wanted to make a move, it would be a potentially very good one for our company."

He got on a plane the next day, flew to St. Louis, and struck a multimillion-dollar deal to acquire the name, products, and assets of Rexall. "We were able to earn back what it cost us in seven months," he says.

Rexall is one of the most respected brand names in the United States, recognized by 78 percent of the public 38 years old or older, thanks to the twenty-five thousand Rexall drugstores that one time dotted the American landscape.

"We had bought a legend with Rexall," DeSantis reflects. Acquiring the Rexall trademark further strengthened Sundown's position in a nutritional health products industry that by the late 1980s and early 1990s was growing rapidly. Today Rexall Sundown has grown from a kitchen-table family business to a more than $500 million corporation publicly traded on Wall Street and selling more than one thousand products in over fifty nations.

In 1990, company leaders, led by its current CEO Damon DeSantis, made a critical decision: to create a new network marketing division called Rexall Showcase International. This division would operate alongside the parent companies' other divisions but would have its own line of unique, exclusive products.

The network marketing division's early days were rocky. But in 1991, the arrival of a handful of premier networkers who had broken away from Nu Skin helped the company overhaul its marketing plan and gain credibility. Today Rexall Showcase International is viewed as a major emerging force in the nutritional supplements and natural health remedies field, in both the United States and Asia. And, as we have seen from some of the distributor examples cited earlier, it is a major draw for the newer breed of network marketers we call New Professionals.

Indeed, the impact of the entire family of Rexall Sundown operations on the global vitamin and nutritional supplements market can be clearly seen in the May 2000 announcement that the Dutch conglomerate, Royal Numico, would purchase the company for $1.8 billion.

> Rexall Sundown is a good example of a company that started out on a more traditional footing, acquired a powerful brand name that almost everyone knows, and then began a foray into network marketing.

Rexall Sundown is a good example of a company that started out on a more traditional footing, acquired a powerful brand name that almost everyone knows, and then began a foray into network marketing—thus reversing the process followed by other network marketing industry leaders.

"We're building on a lot of history here, and we never forget that," says Damon DeSantis. "What we're creating with Rexall Showcase International is a virtual Rexall, a Rexall without the bricks and mortar but with thousands and thousands of dots on a map, each representing an independent businessperson. Except it will be a map of the world, not just the United States. And the vehicle won't be the train that used to carry a roving display of Rexall drugs' product and franchise opportunity—the vehicle will be network marketing."

USANA INC.

Calling itself a science-based nutrition company, USANA has made its mark on network marketing through the efforts of three men:

- Myron Wentz, Ph.D., is a recognized pioneer in cell culture technology. In the early 1970's, he founded Gull Laboratories, which soon became the world's leading producer of commercially available diagnostic test kits for viruses. Turning to disease prevention, Dr. Wentz changed his focus to products designed to provide adequate cell-level nutrition, fiber, and antioxidant protection for the human body.

- In 1991, John McDonald, Ph.D., joined Wentz to create the USANA Corporation. McDonald studied antioxidant properties and formulated combinations of antioxidants, vitamins, and minerals that could reduce the risk for disease and enhance lifestyles.

- In 1992, Dallin Larsen, a top marketing executive, joined the USANA team. This expanded management team created a network marketing program.

USANA is publicly traded on NASDAQ and has charted significantly over the years. Revenues at the end of 1993 were $3.9 million, growing to revenues of $121.6 million at the end of 1998. The company reported revenues for the first quarter of 1999 of $31.3 million, which represents an increase of 19.7 percent from the $26.2 million reported in the first quarter of 1998.

As of March 1999, the company had approximately 118,000 distributors and 30,000 customers throughout the United States, Canada, Australia, New Zealand and the United Kingdom.

*   *   *

With apologies to other sound companies we could have described were this discussion longer, we hope this two-chapter survey of both the pathfinder network marketing companies and some of the rising stars illustrates the strength and diversity of the industry. While readers have likely noticed a high concentration of firms focused on nutritional and personal care products, they should have also seen a growing breadth of product and service categories as well as an intriguing mix of business strategies.

> Any doubt that the network marketing industry is a legitimate one filled with "real" companies and "real" products should now be completely dispelled.

Most important of all, any doubt that the network marketing industry is a legitimate one filled with "real" companies and "real" products should now be completely dispelled by the rich histories of some and the product-driven intensity of others. In a new era of ethereal dot.com start-ups and technology ventures whose market value belies economic rationality, it is time for other industries to answer the "legitimacy" question. While there are no doubt bad-apple shams in network marketing, the industry as a whole has long since answered that question. It's time for conventional wisdom to catch up.

Game Plan for the New Professional

In the previous four chapters, we have:

- Defined network marketing and reviewed its history

- Described its current impact in today's consumer marketplace and on the workforce worldwide

- Analyzed some dramatic industry trends that are rapidly changing the network marketing culture and positioning it for substantial growth among highly skilled, successful professionals

- Identified those companies that, because of their size, product innovations, or distinct business models, are setting the pace for this diverse industry with an impact that extends beyond network marketing to the larger business world and society

We hope you are convinced of the following points enunciated earlier:

- Network marketing is a genuine business with a long, albeit controversial, past—one that is deeply rooted in the traditions of face-to-face salesmanship, an occupation honored in many societies but for some reason disparaged in the United States.

- Industry standards in product development, marketing, management, financial systems, technology, and business ethics have risen substantially in recent years, giving network marketing a "new face" based in reality and not the customary and expected industry hype.

- The industry's impact on the economy and society extends well beyond its still relatively small claim on total sales or the workforce, attracting a broad array of individual participants for diverse reasons. It is clearly positioned as an attractive alternative professional lifestyle for workers and an effective alternative distribution channel for consumer product and service companies struggling to be heard in a fragmented, Internet-driven marketplace.

- Network marketing can be a challenging and lucrative "knowledge business," one that is international in scope, powered by new technology, rich with innovative, proprietary products—and thoroughly compatible with the New Professional's renewed focus on family, lifestyle, retirement planning, and time freedom. For this reason, network marketing is increasingly recognized as the most promising path out of the economic and social conundrums described in chapters 2 and 3.

ANSWERING THE QUESTION "WHY?"

Steve Schulz is a top network marketer and trainer for Excel Communications. At a recent gathering, Steve—aided by charts, an overhead projector, slides, and his trademark humor—moved through the explanation of his company's business opportunity with efficiency and clarity. Many in the crowd took notes; others just listened intently. Steve's explanation was simple, factual, and convincing.

Suddenly he fell silent, put down his pointer and pen, and looked out at the audience. "I can teach you how, but I can't teach you why. What you have to do on your own is figure out the why."

In others words, Steve was asking his audience to shift their focus from a dispassionate, fact-based inquiry about an industry to a more personal evaluation about its application to their own lives. We suggest you now do the same. Only you can determine whether your "why" is strong enough to lead you to this business and whether, having arrived, you find that it is the right kind of business and lifestyle for you.

So the time has now come to help you get up close and personal with what can legitimately be called the new network marketing industry. Being very "humble" authors, we can say that you now have a depth of information, arguments, and trends about network marketing that has never before been assembled in such a comprehensive way between the covers of a single book. But there is one question about this business we can't answer—only you can: "Is network marketing right for me?"

If you decide that indeed it is, that response leads naturally to another pair of personal questions: "How do I pick a company that is right for me? How do I know that the company I have chosen is a legitimate business with a workable marketing plan that gives me a reasonable shot at achieving my personal goals?"

While we may not be able to answer these questions for you, we can set out a game plan of considerations you should contemplate and a checklist of issues you should evaluate as you decide whether and how to join the ranks of the New Professionals.

A helpful way to introduce these considerations and issues is to look through the eyes of others as they have decided to embark on new ventures in network marketing. What factors drove their decisions? How did they answer the question "Why?"

After years of meeting literally thousands of network marketers, we have discovered that the answers to the question "Why do this business?" can be as varied and diverse as the people in the business.

Some have known little but misfortune their whole lives; others were sitting at the top of highly respected, professional careers.

Some just wanted to make a little extra money to pay off a few bills; others were determined from the start to make millions.

Some are high school and college dropouts; others have MBAs or law or medical degrees.

Some joined to climb out of poverty; others joined because they were already making six-figure incomes but had no time to enjoy their affluence.

> The answers to "Why do this business?" are as varied and diverse as the people in the business.

Some signed up so they could do something together as a family; others did it to save their families.

Some began as passionate believers in the power of network marketing; others believed these businesses were a sham but joined as a favor to the friend or family member who invited them in.

Yet we have also noted and documented, through facts and examples, that economic uncertainties and time pressures, combined with a significant upgrade in network marketing industry practices and opportunities, have steered the demographics of the industry in a new direction. A greater number of previously accomplished professionals—who in the past had been satisfied with their traditional careers and highly suspicious of network marketing—are asking why and finding their answer here.

As we have explained, this approach represents a significant shift in the industry. Accurately or not, fairly or unfairly, the most common answer to the why question for many pursuing in network marketing has been "Because I have no where else to go. I'm short on money, education, and income opportunities. I'm out of options."

The Direct Selling Association research cited in chapter 4 uncovers this reality: The overwhelming majority of participants in this industry did it part-time to reach modest financial goals—to buy a new car, pay off some bills, get some desired products at a discount, or earn some extra money for Christmas presents. Critics of the industry often overlook this reality as they level the familiar charge that very few network marketers actually get rich. This is true, but then getting rich in this business is a goal embraced only by a very few.

But network marketing is also heavily reliant on attracting and retaining recruits who are, after all, voluntary participants and who can join—and quit—with virtually no investment lost or penalty incurred. Not surprisingly, therefore, many industry appeals and company testimonials over the years have acquired a highly motivational and blatantly emotional appeal—and they have pushed to the forefront those participants who were down on their luck, who came from nowhere, and who have genuinely achieved astounding success . . . the "rags to riches" stories.

You have probably heard some of these stories and know of their allure, because they are expressions of the potency of the American dream. They are stories of individuals who come from humble beginnings. Many of them have suffered personal and financial setbacks or have succumbed to human frailties ranging from alcohol to gambling to philandering—until they "turned it all around" thanks to network marketing!

These are inspiring stories, particularly in our confessional culture. No matter where you come from or how low you have sunk, you can change your life, stage a comeback, and achieve your dreams. The most successful network marketing companies have built their legends around these kinds of testimonials in their effort to appeal to the broadest swath of average citizens.

But this drumbeat message has come at a price to the industry, and it is out of synch with the more analytical demeanor of the New Professional. By basing the appeal of the business on emotion rather than economics and by emphasizing its low cost, ease of entry, and simplicity of execution, those who advocate network marketing cause many successful, higher-caliber professionals to feel it is not for them. An emphasis on only the "rags-to-riches" stories and insistence that the business becomes one's all-consuming passion—a kind of substitute religion—turns off those who take a more reasoned and compartmentalized approach to life's activities.

THE NEW PROFILE OF THE NETWORK MARKETER

A number of firms are now making a conscious effort to target a different audience. Rexall Showcase International is one such company. The demographics it cites in describing its distributor force are revealing not only for the trend it signals in the industry as a whole but also for the kind of image companies like this one strive to project. According to the company:

- Distributors have an average income of $66,000, nearly triple the national average

- 20 percent earn over $100,000 a year

- 30 percent come out of the health care field

- 85 percent own their own home

- 60 percent have college degrees

- 85 percent allocate ten hours or less to the business each week, reinforcing that this is truly a part-time business

Jim Moyles has known mostly success in his professional life. He worked for some of the nation's top companies, such as IBM and Lehman Brothers, and then started his own merger and acquisition firm, often earning commissions of more than $100,000 per transaction. But after eighteen years in this field, Jim was looking for something different. Something he learned from the merger and acquisition business was that even more valuable than earning large fees is building value in a business that could be sold or given to your children.

One day a friend of his son's called to ask Jim for his advice about a business he was getting started. It turned out to be a network marketing business, and the product was a "buyer's club"–style membership. Jim was intrigued by the idea and decided to get involved. "We quickly built a team, and it was fun," he recalls.

There was just one problem. They soon found out that in Florida membership sales are off limits for network marketing companies. "I had so much fun doing this business, and I could see the potential was enormous. So I decided to learn from this experience and find the right company with the right product line. What added to my determination to find the right company is that I came to realize that multi-level marketing is a brilliant method of doing business. The challenge is to find one of those companies that have integrity and are destined to go on to long-term success.

"I discovered that if you can find such a company and you put together a team of quality people, some marvelous things can happen. First, it can create more income than anything else that you do can. This is because of the tremendous leverage. Second, it's also a better kind of income. It's residual! It becomes independent of our day-to-day activities. I now have a business that generates a seven-figure income, a business that I can give to my children or sell."

Jim Moyles came to the business of his own volition, out of his own sense of curiosity and business acumen. He was not down and out but rather doing just fine before he ever became a network marketer.

So what was his answer to the question "Why"? "It was an easy decision," he explains. "It's designed to be done on a part-time basis. Why wouldn't anyone want to diversify and develop a second source of income? As for doing this as your primary focus, you have to do a little soul-searching." Jim suggests that prospective distributors look at their career or business and, income aside, ask some basic questions. "Are you truly enjoying your business or career? Is it more fun than it was a few years ago? Is it allowing you to live the lifestyle you want? Are you in a field that is taking advantage of the trends?"

Jim's suggestion is based on simple logic and common sense. Many like him have achieved success as the professional world defines it, and most Americas routinely tell pollsters that they like their jobs. Because work is such a central part of life, to do otherwise is basically an admission that we hate our lives. Few are willing to entertain such thoughts. So instead, we whine and complain around the edges: "I'm on the road too much." "I don't have enough time to see my kids." "My company management doesn't know what it's doing."

Many successful professionals harboring such thoughts tie themselves in mental knots for their entire careers. They'll never act on the many "coulda, woulda, shoulda" plans they concocted while counting off the years in their company or organization. By the time they reach the minimum retirement age—or are offered an early retirement package—they're ready to get out and retreat. This helps explain why demographers who are rightfully concerned about the growing shortage of workers in the United States, Japan, and Western Europe should not count on longer life expectancies to produce legions of people who want to extend their working lives beyond the bare minimum. Only if financially desperate will most consider doing so. Polls regarding job satisfaction aside, most employees in traditional careers will vote with their feet by getting out the moment they can.

What the new network marketing industry presents to successful but dissatisfied people is this: an opportunity to diversify and make other choices from a position of security and strength, not weakness and despair. It suggests that if you assess your own level of happiness and financial security and find them wanting, you should not wait until you are forced to act or are too old to act. Why not do it now, alongside your current career or business, and put yourself on a path that gradually but steadily addresses the changes you want to make and build a second income and perhaps the life you really want to lead?

Dr. Tom Klesmit, a former professor of chiropractic medicine, consultant to governments, researcher, and author for professional journals, joined network marketing from an established, successful, fifteen-year medical practice.

> The network marketing industry presents an opportunity to diversify and make choices from a position of security and strength, not weakness and despair.

"Dr. Tom" was introduced to network marketing and Nutrition for Life International (NFLI) via a fax from an associate. Dr. Tom convened a meeting of his attorney, CPA, and financial advisor to evaluate the risks associated with the network marketing business opportunity. As a practicing doctor, he felt qualified to evaluate the line of vitamin supplements. Based on that due diligence, he joined NFLI in January 1996.

Dr. Tom was very clear on his why's for network marketing. As he reported, "I love patient care and the personal satisfaction I get from helping people . . . but managed care changed my health care environment. I became an administrator, a paper shuffler, a government bureaucrat."

According to Dr. Tom, "Network marketing offered me the avenue to continue helping people by using vitamin supplementation and my medical knowledge." In terms of the business platform, network marketing offered "the time flexibility to work around my professional medical practice and provided a 'willable' business to be handed on to my children."

In June 2000, Dr. Tom was among the highest paid distributors in NFLI, with a downline of between five and ten thousand distributors, including more than five hundred physicians.

Resa and Matt Salter are the epitome of the New Professionals for whom this book was written—a young family pursuing the traditional American dream.

In the 1980s, Resa and Matt graduated from college, moved to Northern California, and launched their professional careers. Matt advanced rapidly to become general manager of a commercial textile company. Resa positioned as an elementary school teacher.

After their two sons, Justin and Ronnie, were born, Resa shifted from teaching to running a small day care center out of their home so she could spend time with her young sons. After two years as day care manager, however, Resa felt it was time for a change. "It was hard work and included a lot of stress and responsibility. My energy level wasn't the same for my own two kids."

Enter network marketing. Unexpectedly, a friend introduced Resa to the personal care products of Nu Skin International and the opportunity to distribute the product line. Resa experimented by selling to her day care families part time.

After ten months, Resa's income reached $1,200 per month, equal to her day care center revenue. At that point,

Resa closed the day care operation and became a full-time network marketer. By the end of her first year, Resa was earning $2,000 per month, which got Matt's attention.

Meanwhile, Matt's career had plateaued. Although successful as a general manager, Matt was logging long work hours and the typical, long California commute. A family member of the owner had moved into his firm to be groomed as the next CEO. Advancement opportunities were now slim to none. Matt began to study network marketing and started distributing Nu Skin products to his business associates part time.

In July 1990, ten months after he started helping Resa, their network marketing income reached $12,000 per month working from home. At that point, Matt walked away from his corporate role and become a full-time network marketer with Resa.

In early 1993, Nu Skin expanded to Japan. Matt reports, "The best man in our wedding put us in touch with a businessman who had strong connections in Japan. We invested our time and capital to build solid relationships with a team of aggressive young Japanese entrepreneurs. By the end of the first year in Japan, our group had generated about $5 million in sales volume." Momentum was in motion!

Today, the Salters operate a global business involving 20,000 distributors in twelve countries, moving about $100 million in volume per year. The Salters have achieved yearly earnings in the million-dollar range.

Resa summarized the story: "Our goal has always been to have more time with our family. We've worked hard. We've made some sacrifices, but today we have a nearly perfect life style. We have flexible schedules. We can spend quality time with the kids when they need it. We have financial independence. We wake up every day and feel thankful we're in this position."

Jim Moyles believes that "never before have so many high-quality people been so unhappy with their careers and businesses. They want to take control of their lives and network marketing is the best vehicle." Could you be one of them?

John Berta found that he was. Now 51, John likes to say that he semiretired at age 40—he semiretired from his first career building and running a successful multioffice accounting, real estate, mortgage brokerage, and property development firm in the Tampa Bay area. John moved there from New Jersey more than twenty years ago after methodically picking the community in which he wanted to live and do business. "I hand-selected Tampa Bay," he says coolly.

But then John Berta is, to use his own words, a "logical" guy. He doesn't jump at things. He checks them out. He prefers facts to hype; long-term potential to a short-term quick strike. So when he found himself growing bored with his business and "semiretiring" when barely into middle age, he began to look for something new. "I basically stumbled onto network marketing," he says. "Like many professionals, I didn't see myself in it. But I did the due diligence and really checked it out, and I came to the conclusion that it is absolutely the best way for companies to efficiently distribute their products. Word-of-mouth is and always will be the strongest way to market. Network marketing takes advantage of that fact even in a technological age."

In November 1991, John joined the industry and not only achieved financial success in it but met his future wife there, too! "Today Julie and I have an organization that spans all fifty states, Mexico, Korea, Hong Kong, and Taiwan," he reports. "We work the business predominantly from our home. We spend anywhere from twenty-eight to forty hours a week, forty weeks a year."

John is convinced that network marketing is poised for substantial growth. And unlike many that poke fun at the baby-boomer generation, John has a different assessment. "I believe with the boomer generation you have people who are leaders, who are the questioning kind of people. They're going to look at the trend lines, examine what's going on around them, and make smart decisions based on the facts. They are less willing to be tied to the old ways of doing things simply because that's the way they've always been done," he explains.

"The baby boomers who are in their forties today are beginning to take stock. They know they have a good chance of living longer than generations before them. They understand that they aren't really prepared to retire in a way that allows them to maintain a good lifestyle. And they have seen more changes in business and professions in the past five years than have been seen in decades.

"They aren't stupid; they see what's going on around them," John continues. "Boomers go into the grocery store, and instead of the teenager who used to bag their groceries, there's a 70-year-old man doing it because he needs the money. And they're wondering, 'Is this what's in store for me when I'm 70?' "

John also strongly believes that as network marketing goes mainstream and comes increasingly to define the primary mode of marketing and distributing products in the twenty-first century, it will be those companies that adopt a more professional, businesslike face that will earn the greatest following. "Mine is basically a conservative, middle-of-the-road, professional company. That's the foundation we're building on," John says. "I for one only ask people to make a decision on the facts. We've never been a company of hype, a pep-rally company, and I hope we never will be."

THE COMMON DENOMINATOR

For Bob Torsey, a highly successful Excel representative, personal experience tells him that the most common denominator among people joining the business is "the desire to do something different with their lives."

"People who are totally content with their lives don't often join the business," he told us. "We attract those who for any of a number of reasons want to change what they're doing."

It's not a question of being a failure, Bob emphasizes. "We're also appealing to many highly successful people from all kinds of highly skilled professions," he explains. "They've found one rainbow. Now they're ready to seek another."

For years Bob was chasing his elusive rainbow in the corporate world. A vice president of marketing for a $500-million-plus building materials company, he was working seventy to eighty hours a week and was well paid for his efforts—until he became a victim of corporate downsizing.

Despite the rug being pulled from under him in the traditional business environment, Bob initially reacted to Excel with "arrogance and skepticism," but positive experience and income growth have changed his view. Frequently asked about his level of wealth, Bob replies in this telling fashion: "I live where I want to live. I drive what I want to drive. I pretty much come and go as I please. And I don't have all the pressure. So I guess I'm pretty wealthy!"

Recalling the daily grind of the corporate world, Bob sizes up the bottom line by saying, "I'd rather have another hour in my back pocket than another buck."

A BUSINESS WITHOUT BARRIERS OR BORDERS

Many professionals find that the barriers in more traditional careers do not exist in network marketing. There is no "glass ceiling" for women, no "color barrier" for racial and ethnic minorities, no "limited access" for the physically disabled, no "age discrimination" confronting the elderly. In fact, many New Professionals find in network marketing a refreshing restoration of meritocracy to the business world. Each individual rises or falls based on his or her efforts. This is an appealing prospect for many and a somewhat frightening one for others, for when all excuses and real and perceived barriers are stripped away, all that is left is one's own success—or failure.

Network marketing can indeed be a flexible business that allows practitioners to operate with little or no overhead or inventory according to their own schedule and lifestyle. For many professionals, the network marketing lifestyle, teamed with user-friendly communications tools and information technology, enjoys a perfect marriage. It doesn't matter where you live or where you come from, whether you have disabilities, or what your native language is—your territory is now the world.

> Many New Professionals find in network marketing a refreshing restoration of meritocracy.

Many consider it their "virtual" business: an office without walls; a warehouse without inventory; an asset without capital; a company without staff.

ARE YOU A CANDIDATE FOR NETWORK MARKETING?

Clearly, scores of New Professionals are finding in this industry qualities and advantages, beyond income potential, that they found lacking in their original careers. Even so, recall Bob Torsey's observation that those who are fully content with their lives do not often join network marketing companies. He has identified central issues to consider in your personal evaluation as to whether network marketing is right for you:

- If you are already totally satisfied with your professional career and personal lifestyle, there is unlikely to be a compelling enough reason for you to begin a network marketing business.

- If you are absolutely convinced that your current earnings and investments are sufficient and secure and that they will produce a substantial long-term income during what could be a decades-long retirement, then you don't need to worry about creating another stream of income.

- If you are happy with the pace and daily routine of your life and you're able to balance all of your priorities—from having enough time for fitness and leisure activities to spending quality time with your family—then congratulations on a job well done.

- And if you find that your current career is rewarding and satisfying, and you are content that when it's over you will be able to point to achievements and contributions you'll be proud of and remembered for, then stick with it.

If indeed your personal career and life assessment confirms all these values, then our snap response is, Write a book and tell the rest of us your secret!

But most serious professionals are not fully satisfied and want to aim higher. Whether it's the desire to bolster and diversify their finances, create more flexibility and time freedom, meet new people and try something new, or build their own business and be their own boss, most are ready to consider sensible, workable, and respectable alternatives. Network marketing is one of them.

CONFRONTING THE CONCERNS AND DOWNSIDES

But is the lifestyle attainable through network marketing one you would really enjoy and succeed at?

Suppose we posed this question to you: How would you like to work at home, commuting down the hall to your home office, wearing the most comfortable clothes in your closet, taking a break when you wanted to or needed to run an errand, attending your kids' soccer games and other daytime activities—and still earning a substantial income in a now respectable profession?

Your first reaction might be that this is probably the dumbest question you ever heard! Who wouldn't kill for such a chance?

But it's not that simple. Not every professional will react as positively to the independent, home-based business environment as the successful network marketers we have discussed. Entrants should consider that they might find the culture of work fostered in network marketing and home-based occupations too radical a departure from the pattern of their current lives. Some may not even like it.

How would you like to work at home, wearing the most comfortable clothes in your closet, taking a break when you want to—and still earning a substantial income in a now respectable profession?

Let us explain by drawing an example from the transportation world.

For years an effort has been under way in major metropolitan areas to convince more Americans to scrap their one-person-per-car commutes in favor of carpools or mass transit. Anecdotal evidence uncovered as to why this "sell" is so difficult may surprise you: Many commuters actually like the time they have to themselves in the isolated confines of their vehicle! For many it is the only time of the day when they can be alone, be somewhat anonymous, listen to music, or daydream without interruption. Others use the time to listen to books on tape, hear self-improvement messages, or even learn foreign languages.

Few want to admit that they enjoy escaping their hectic household or harried workplace. Fewer still would say doing so is actually worth the price of sitting in traffic. But those tempted by the undeniable lure of working out of their home should consider the other side to the benefits of "commuting down the hall."

Both of us have worked for considerable periods out of our homes and find a lot of distractions alongside the enviable convenience. By interchanging periods of work with periods of domestic duties, chores, errands, and the like, the day's work never seems to be finished. Technology that allows you to stay in touch with customers, bosses, and partners is invaluable, but if you're like us, you find yourself checking and responding to e-mail messages at all hours of the day (or night) seven days a week.

Those accustomed to compartmentalizing their lives, drawing sharp lines among work life, home life, and leisure time, may find these distinctions uncomfortably blurred when working out of the home in network marketing or any other business. Some people may find life more orderly and balanced by keeping the home life sacrosanct, physically leaving their place of residence in the morning, working hard and working well for the day, and then leaving it all behind when quitting time comes. Still others who do telecommute report that they feel isolated, miss the social interaction with colleagues, and worry about not being part of the action.

You should think about all these issues and judge them against your own personality and circumstances. If being self-disciplined and maintaining steady work habits are problems for you, you may encounter productivity problems in such an unstructured environment.

Although we don't doubt the network marketers who have told us about the relatively few hours they put in to make sizable leveraged incomes, we have not met a successful leader in the industry yet who isn't on the telephone or computer all hours of the day or night. There are conferences to attend on weekends and meetings to conduct in the evening, when most Americans are curled up on a comfortable sofa watching television. The leaders in these businesses appear every bit as driven as the executives and managers who run large companies. They just seem to be having more fun doing it. Indeed, maybe that's why many top network marketers don't seem to realize how hard they are really working!

The lifestyle network marketing can put within your reach has undeniable appeal. But only you can assess whether it is the right lifestyle for you. You should go into it with open eyes.

There are other issues to consider. We suggest you engage in a dialogue with yourself, focusing on the most common questions and concerns that prospective network marketers struggle with, ones often raised by their family and friends— thus bringing the added factor of peer pressure to the equation.

> The leaders in these businesses are every bit as driven as the executives and managers who run large companies. They just seem to be having more fun.

You will note that some of these issues have already been discussed in earlier chapters. Hopefully the information we have presented there will point you toward satisfactory answers.

Concern 1

I didn't get all this education and work this hard to rise in my profession simply to end up as a salesperson. Wouldn't becoming a network marketer be a big step down? Although it enjoys a proud tradition in many cultures, selling is inexplicably frowned upon by many in our status-seeking society. You see this attitude most among people with impressive-sounding jobs but modest incomes and no control over their time. Working among many highly skilled and status-oriented professionals in academia, politics, and the corporate world, the authors confront such condescension all the time.

For many from the so-called boomer and yuppie generations, building an independent business through network marketing simply doesn't jibe with their carefully cultivated image as worldly, white-collar professionals. They crave title, rank, status, and, most important, security. They seek the identity and social approval that comes from their association with a prestigious company, a big-name law firm, or an important government agency.

Yet this attitude is changing. As the security of the status jobs disappears and the frenetic, pressure-cooker lifestyles they bring lose their appeal, many upscale professionals who used to dismiss network marketing are taking a first or a fresh look. There are only so many times smart people can watch others build much happier, more rewarding lives before they conclude, "Why can't I do something like that?"

When we look at the successful people in network marketing today, we see doctors, lawyers, professors, and corporate executives as well as teachers, homemakers, real estate salespeople, and small-business owners. We see those who came to the business at a time when they were down and out and those who were sitting on top of another field but wanted something different. In short, if you're looking for someone like you who has succeeded in network marketing, chances are you'll find that person—a person willing to coach and lead you along the same path.

Concern 2

I'm not sure I'll be very good at selling. Can I do it? Network marketing is, when all is said and done, a sales profession. There's no way around that fact. If you believe you lack the ability or desire to contact people on a face-to-face basis, look them in the eye, and ask them to buy a product, service, or business opportunity—and there's no way you can change that—then this industry is not for you. But keep several points in mind as you consider this issue.

According to Harland Stonecipher, founder and chairman of Pre-Paid Legal Services, the biggest and most important sale a salesperson will ever make is when you sell yourself. Make that first and most vital sale; in other words, really believe in what you are doing and the product or service you are selling, and it won't matter how glib, slick or polished you are. The sincerity will shine through if you feel it—and the lack of it will be exposed if you don't. It is your own passion and conviction that will appeal most to prospective customers. Convey that and positive results will follow.

> Your passion and conviction will appeal most to prospective customers. Convey that and positive results will follow.

The biggest fear you will face is the fear of rejection. But if misery really does love company, in this field you'll be in very distinguished company— even the most successful salespeople in the world log more rejections than sales. When you are rejected, that doesn't necessarily mean you have failed. More often than not it was a question of timing or need on the part of your prospect.

Next, don't assume you have no experience or capability in sales simply because you have not occupied sales positions. Most jobs in most professions involve the need to persuade, and that's what sales is. If you're a lawyer, you need to sway judges and juries. If you're a government official, you need to woo voters. If you're a corporate executive, you need to convince superiors and colleagues to embrace your ideas and adopt your strategies. Even outside the workplace, we find ourselves in the persuasion business all the time— working on spouses, children, parents, friends, and others.

Unless you're a survivalist in the mountains of Wyoming, most likely you have considerable sales skills to bring to the table. You've just never thought about them in this way.

Finally, forget about the old, outmoded image of network marketing in which you envision a participant spending endless frustrating hours attending or conducting house parties, product demonstrations and pep rallies or filling out reams of order forms and hauling cartons of household cleaners and soap powder all over the neighborhood. Network marketing is becoming a high-tech, high-touch business in which advances in technology, communications, and logistics have ironed most of those time-consuming and more mindless activities right out of the process. While your personal appeals to customers and recruits will always be an essential ingredient of success, functions such as product orders and fulfillment, business accounting, and training are now accomplished with little more than a click of the mouse. This approach not only frees you from the "grimier" aspects of the personal sales profession but also allows you to concentrate on more lucrative activities such as registering new sales and recruiting new downlines.

> Network marketing is a high-tech, high-touch business in which most of the more mindless activities have been ironed out.

You will also find in quality companies plenty of sales support to assist you. Don't resist this mentoring! If you are moving into an exciting business endeavor, treat it as such by recognizing that you are not a know-it-all but more like a trainee. The only difference is that unlike most industries, you cannot get fired. You can only fire yourself.

Concern 3

My friends sneer and shake their heads when I tell them about my interest in network marketing. How do I respond when they accuse these companies of being phony pyramid schemes or when they warn, "Don't ever try to recruit me!"? Jim tells the story of when he first started writing about this growing but still misunderstood approach to business: "Some of my own associates—many of them from highly skilled professions—criticized me for writing about network marketing and condemned the companies as pyramid schemes. Finally, I got frustrated and challenged one friend to explain his remark.

"'You just called this company a pyramid,'" I said. "'Just what is that anyway?'

"'Well, it's when a company, um, you see . . . .' He stammered for a minute while trying to explain the precise meaning of his criticism, why it was bad, and how it applied to the company in question. He didn't get very far.

"Clearly both the media and word of mouth had poisoned his attitude against network companies. He had simply heard that these companies were pyramids and that pyramids were bad; therefore, the companies must be bad. Case closed."

While its reputation is improving, the fact is that network marketing still suffers from an image problem. As we have seen, some of the negative elements of that image were inflicted by the industry itself. We hope this book will help the image catch up to the new, more professional profile we see today in network marketing. Consider again these indicators of a new maturity:

- Direct selling/network marketing is catching on across America and around the world, drawing an estimated thirty-six million participants today, rising to as high as two hundred million a decade from now.

- Companies and individuals who had never considered it before are now adopting it in varying degrees.

- It is changing the way we buy and sell goods and services.

- It is providing additional income, lifestyle options, and business opportunities to millions of people who otherwise may have had none.

- While there are guarantees of success, network marketing is free of the artificial barriers present in other occupations.

- Leading companies in the industry are now publicly traded on Wall Street. Some offer stock options and health benefits. They are in business all over the world. Many have developed proprietary products in state-of-the-art laboratories and research centers.

- It leads many to the establishment of lifelong friendships and allows them to pursue a business activity with spouses, children, and relatives.

What, in fact, does constitute an illegal pyramid? U.S. federal and state laws are subject to different interpretations. But generally it is seen as an operation that is built almost exclusively on paying people to sign up as distributors—with little or no focus on gathering actual customers to buy products and services. New recruits are required to buy large quantities of a product upfront, with no opportunity to return unsold inventory for a refund. Intense pressure is applied to get them to buy expensive tapes, instructional manuals, and tickets to meetings and rallies. Essentially, participants feed off each other, with the big fish consuming the resources and energies of the smaller fish.

As reported, the entire multilevel marketing industry faced a legal day of reckoning in 1979, when the Federal Trade Commission ruled that Amway was a legitimate business and not a pyramid. The ruling set forth many of the ground rules that network marketing companies abide by today.

Yet, as we also remember from those accounts, a great deal of skepticism about network marketing remains—in part because it is still a relatively new approach for most people. Doubts are also fueled by competitors who have sunk fortunes into hiring sales forces, buying ads on television (an industry that itself has much to lose), and developing intricate retail distribution networks. They have a vested interest in keeping suspicion alive, even though many of them are migrating toward direct selling approaches themselves.

In *Wave 3*, Richard Poe draws an interesting parallel in his discussion of network marketing's bumpy road to acceptance and legitimacy:

> New ideas are always attacked and rejected at first. In its earliest days, franchising endured similar abuse from the press and from the corporate world, and for almost identical reasons. . . .
>
> The media attacked like hungry barracuda. Exposés featured destitute families who had lost their life savings through franchising schemes. Attorneys general in state after state condemned the new marketing method. Some congressmen actually tried to outlaw franchising entirely. How quickly things change! Today, franchises account for 35 percent of all retail sales in the United States.

Concern 4

Does anyone really get rich in this kind of business, except for the few at the top who got in early? Turnover is high throughout network marketing. People move in and out of the business all the time. In some cases, it's because they've achieved the relatively modest set of goals they established at the outset: to earn some extra money to pay off bills, buy a new car, or take a vacation. Others join because they like people and want opportunities to socialize and broaden their network of friends, but they never focus on making the business their full-time occupation. Some are initially attracted by the low entry fee but don't enter with a serious level of commitment. Industry leaders point out that because the cost of entry is so low, the cost of exiting is low as well, and so many people head for the exit. Some who leave network marketing have soured on the experience and believe the deck was stacked against them. The riches they envisioned didn't materialize, and they blame the company.

> As with most endeavors, you get out of it what you put into it.

It is true that most people who join network marketing never develop incomes to a level where they can leave their full-time jobs. As with most endeavors, you get out of it what you put into it. But those who do work direct selling businesses full-time earn above-average incomes. The DSA once estimated that more than half of the full-timers make over $50,000 a year. One in ten makes over $100,000.

Would it be possible for you to attain the levels of income, success, and happiness attained by the network marketers profiled in this book? Absolutely. Are there any guarantees? Absolutely not.

The question of market saturation is a hotly debated issue in network marketing. Companies that have been around a long time and have produced large numbers of wealthy distributors go to great lengths to insist that similar success is equally possible for the new distributor who joins that company today. They point to the opening of new international markets and the introduction of new products and services as reasons that you would not be "too late to the party" if you joined now. And they underscore that experience, longevity, and a proven track record, particularly in an ever-changing industry such as network marketing, offer you the stability, credibility, and support you need to get your business off the ground.

Others say that you have a superior advantage by getting in at the beginning of a network marketing venture, that there is greater teamwork and more enthusiasm because people like being part of something new and different. If you do well in a newer venture, you're more likely to be singled out for recognition and publicity by the parent company, which gives you further opportunities to lead and build your organization.

> Many New Professionals argue that the personal growth and time freedom they have earned from their businesses far outweigh the money.

The fact remains that not all of the value in this business can be calculated in dollars and cents. Many New Professionals joining the industry argue that the personal growth and time freedom they have earned from their businesses far outweigh the money on their scale of values. The fringe benefits in the business can be pretty good!

- As parents, you have more time to spend with your children.

- After a lifetime of working for someone else, you get a chance to build something for yourself and your family that might be worthwhile even if you were to make less money.

- You can face the prospect of old age with financial security and improved health, so that you don't become a burden on your children and grandchildren.

- You can make lifelong friendships among highly successful, positive people-people from all walks of life, from around the world, whom you would never have met otherwise.

- You can enjoy the satisfaction that comes with helping others to better health and more secure finances by becoming a teacher, mentor, and leader in your organization.

Most people do not become rich in network marketing, but many say they become *enriched*.

Concern 5

I'm already too busy. How could I ever find the time for a business like this? The "no time" excuse is probably the most common reason that people turn down a friend's or associate's invitation to join a network marketing business. There's no question that time poverty is a serious issue for two-income families struggling with the demands of both careers and children. However, a recent book by time-study experts John Robinson and Geoffrey Godbey suggests that most of us could find the time to undertake a new activity, like starting a network marketing business, particularly since the industry is placing a greater emphasis on providing opportunities for part-timers with full-time occupations.

> **M**ost people do not become rich in network marketing, but many say they become *enriched.*

It's a question of priorities. These researchers examined the lifestyles of ten thousand survey participants and concluded that contrary to popular belief, Americans actually have more free time now than at any other period during the last thirty years—an average of forty hours a week.

If you find that difficult to believe, consider that the study found a wide gap between people's perception of how busy they are and the reality. Study participants were asked to keep detailed diaries of their activities. When the results were analyzed, it was found that on average, working men perceived that they spend 46.2 hours on their paid, professional work. In actuality, they spent 40.2 hours. Women perceived 40.4 hours but actually worked just 32 hours.

Americans actually have more free time now than at any other period during the last thirty years—an average of forty hours a week.

What's the reason for the exaggeration? "Being busy has become a status symbol," Robinson told *Newsweek* magazine "As you say time is more important to you, you become more important yourself."

"In fact," the magazine goes on to report, "Americans are working fewer hours than they did in 1965—about five fewer hours for working women, six fewer for men."

Here's one other key finding: On average, working Americans spend fifteen of their forty free hours a week watching television. If you're one of them, perhaps it's time to reorder priorities and reexamine how readily we invoke that most common of excuses: "I don't have time."

CHOOSING A NETWORK MARKETING COMPANY

If, after evaluating the network marketing industry on a macrolevel and examining your own needs, goals, strengths and weaknesses on the microlevel, you have determined this is an industry you'd like to join, how do you choose from the myriad of companies that are eager for your participation? Let's turn to this critical subject now.

The First Step: Define Your Goal

As you size up any venture, you need to define what you want from it. Are you *equity driven*—do you want to build a business with long-term value? Or are you *income driven*—do you want cash flow?

Network marketing can help you fulfill both goals. During the three to five years of hard work it can take to build a substantial downline, you'll be equity driven. However, once your downline is in place, your investment can become a cash machine. In the earliest stages of your inquiry, however, the most important order of business is to define your goals.

The Second Step:
Research the Industry and Identify Target Companies

Hundreds of companies have come and gone in the past twenty years. The failures happen because of weak products, poor management, and not enough capital. Just a handful of companies are in the Billion Dollar Club outlined in chapter 6. A few more can be distinguished by their innovations, their longevity, a lucrative niche in a growth market, or the backing they get from a well-established parent company and/or brand name. Make sure the company you choose falls into at least one of these categories.

Since network marketing undergoes especially tough legal and regulatory scrutiny, it's also a good idea to see how your prospective company stands up to such scrutiny. Check with the Direct Selling Association (www.dsa.org) to see whether the firm is a signatory to that organization's code of ethics. Surf the World Wide Web to see what the media is saying about the company, and sample the many chat rooms and individual sites devoted to network marketing companies. If it's a publicly traded company, go to the numerous investor sites to see how Wall Street views the company.

Be fair when you perform this check. Understand that many complaints spring from disgruntled distributors who simply didn't work hard enough and are casting blame or from politically ambitious attorneys general and district attorneys who may be hyping complaints coming into their office to prove themselves champions of the average consumer.

As we mentioned in chapter 5, a growing literature about network marketing now exists. You've started in the right place by reading this book! Prima Publishing has an impressive catalogue of other helpful works, including the popular *Wave 3* (and *4* and *5!*) series by Richard Poe. For a list of the best resources, see the appendix.

The Third Step: Conduct a "Preflight" Check

Once you have identified a company to join, follow this checklist:

1. First, look at the sales history. Is the company in rapid growth or has it reached a plateau? Is it successfully creating new products and diversifying?

2. Your company should be financially stable and in the black. It should have a track record of three to five years' operation and be a member of the Direct Selling Association without current regulatory problems.

3. Look for a company known for computerized distribution, one that has embraced the Internet age.

4. On compensation, the ideal plan allows you to recruit as many people as you can onto your front line. And the better plans also pay commissions on five or more levels. Each additional level can geometrically increase your income.

The Fourth Step: Know Thy Product—and Love It!

When you're trying to sign up distributors, you need them to feel confident that the product will be easy to sell. It has to be more than good—it should be unique. And ideally it should only be available through your network company, so that distributors will know they aren't competing with retail stores. Your product should be needed by a broad segment of the population. A favored target today is the baby boom generation.

The ideal product keeps satisfied customers coming back. Frequent reorders have been crucial to the success of the biggest products. One key strategy is to get people to *redirect* their spending. Persuade people who are already using deodorant, shampoo, and long-distance telephone service to switch to your superior network source.

Most important of all, it has to be a product you can really get passionate about. You have to believe in it to be successful, because in sales, "Nothing sells like sincerity."

The Fifth Step: Be Open to Training

Don't go into this business as a know-it-all. You can draw from the success and experience you may have achieved in the business or professional world, but network marketing is a unique culture. Learn from those who have perfected this business and excelled in it.

> Learn from those who have perfected this business and excelled in it.

In network marketing, you must learn the skills of the soft sell and how to build a sales organization: inviting, presenting, closing, training, coaching, and motivating.

Network marketing is a numbers game. Rejection and personnel turnover are realities of the business. Only 5 to 10 percent of the population will be successful. The challenge is to find and develop these people.

The Final Step: Find Mentors

Once you've identified a good company; studied its reputation, product line, and compensation plan; and determined it is an organization you'd be proud to join, with products you believe can make a real difference for people, what's the next step? Find the upline supporters at your company who can help you learn to build an organization.

The Changing Recruiting/Sponsoring/Distributor Signing Environment   In the traditional network marketing world, a current distributor member would introduce you, as a potential network marketing recruit, to the network marketing concept and to a particular network marketing company. Under the traditional convention, if you decided to join that company, you would be automatically committed to join under that person's distributorship as a member of that person's downline.

Unfortunately, upline-downline marriages sometimes prove to be incompatible. Sometimes the upline member is from another community, creating a long-distance relationship. Other times, the upline sponsor is a new networker with limited knowledge for training you. In still other situations, the upline member has too little time to adequately nurture and guide you.

Interviews with disgruntled distributors who have dropped out and become victims of network marketing attrition indicate that this lack of training, coaching, and mentoring in the early life of a new distributor is a key cause for that personal failure. Although companies typically encourage the new member to search upline to other senior leaders to develop a more compatible relationship, that process frequently proves too cumbersome or simply does not work.

In the current changing recruiting/sponsoring/distributor signing environment, there is much more purposive searching and exploratory courtship between potential downline recruits and their upline candidates.

Network Distributor Organizations: A Case Study Charismatic network marketing leaders who have been powerful business builders of massive downline distributor organizations like Bill Britt of Amway, the late Ken Pontious of Enrich, Jeff Schlegal during his NSA period, Mark Yarnell formerly of Nu Skin, Dexter Yeager of Amway—are legends in the forklore of the industry. These distributor dynasties, however, have varied widely. They are very personalized, reflecting the particular personalities, business models, networking approaches, sales aids, and programs promoted by the individual leaders.

MGIWorldNet.com, a contemporary network distributor group, represents a unique organizational structure built on the professionalism and technology that have engulfed the network marketing industry over the past ten years. MGIWorldNet.com has adapted the framework and sophistication of Corporate America to the high-touch, personalized culture of network marketing.

MGIWorldNet.com was initially organized as Millennium Group International (MGI) in 1991 in Ottawa, Ontario, Canada by cofounders, Richard Santiago, Connie Barker, and Miak Getz. The MGIWorldNet.com Prospectus, published in June 2000, differentiates between the "network marketing company" and the "network marketing organization." The network marketing company "provides services and products and the infrastructure for their delivery". The network marketing organization, MGI, "is the organization of representatives responsible for building a distribution infrastructure for the network marketing company" to promote products and services to the end-line consumer.

MGI emphasizes that in this industry where coaching, teaching and organizational support is essential for success: "For serious business builders, the choice of a networking organization should be as important as their choice of a net-work marketing company."

MGI is focused on developing an integrated network marketing distributor organization that can then build strategic alliances with network marketing companies look-ing to expand their distributor force. The MGI distributor organization can maximize "efficient speed-to-market" for any potential strategic partner.

The MGI vision is "to be one of the leading network marketing organizations in the world". Its mission is to "de-velop a virtual global network that allows people to develop and prosper in a spirit of contribution and collaboration . . . make network marketing a leading distribution force . . . de-velop leaders . . . provide a model and infrastructure."

MGI is organized as a corporate entity funded by its members. It supports members' business building efforts through centralized functions where those are more efficient. Those functions involve strategic planning and development, target city operations, training, standards development and compliance, communications through the MGI Web site, voice messaging, conference calls, and training program, and financial and administrative services.

As of June 2000, MGI reports it has formal operating teams in seventeen cities across North America with an ac-tive program of expansion underway. The teams make over twenty-five business presentations weekly, with an average of fifteen hundred guests per month plus ongoing distributor coaching and training. Members have formal support for long-distance business building in any of the markets where MGI has a presence.

MGI has an integrated Business Model, which is systemati-cally followed and duplicated across the organization in every market. The membership is supported by broad range of oper-ating services in each target city. Each city operation is man-aged by a three-person local team of City Coordinator, Briefing Coordinator and Lead Generation Coordinator. These leaders manage the presentations, coordinate and deliver "power trainings," conduct post-presentation training sessions, identify and train new presentation speakers, and manage the various lead generation activities for the city.

Richard Santiago and Connie Barker, cofounders, offered a colloquial summary description of MGIWorldNet.com: "Have network marketing channel, looking for profitable business alliances." The organizational concept and operational framework are indeed unique and potentially effective.

The critical challenge, however, centers on identifying and creating strategic partnerships with powerful network marketing companies! Who are the qualified candidates?

Selecting your mentor is critical. Most of us looking back on our lives can identify several mentors who really made a difference. As a new network marketer, you'll need to add at least one more mentor to your list to really succeed. The best companies have network leaders who really want you to duplicate their success and will take the time to help you do it. The beautiful thing about this industry is that it is not only not a sacrifice for them to do so is also in their financial self-interest. The more successful you are, the more they profit.

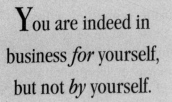

You are indeed in business *for* yourself, but not *by* yourself.

Soon you will want to follow their lead by mentoring people of your own. Network marketers identify the mentoring opportunity as one of the most rewarding features of this unique business model. You are indeed in business *for* yourself, but not *by* yourself.

CHAPTER

9

I Quit!

Let's begin the end of our discussion with a diagnostic test of your potential to be a New Professional. We call it the New Professional's IQ (I Quit!) test.

It is important that you look reality squarely in the face when answering these test questions, judging your situation and abilities as they really are. You may wish to discuss your responses with a spouse, significant other, or close friend-because those closest to us can often pierce through our defense mechanisms and help us shed our personal illusions.

After that, we suggest how you can "score" yourself and what to do next if you "passed" or if you "failed." As you will see, the questions call primarily for qualitative rather than quantitative (or even yes and no) answers. Thus, scoring will be of a similar nature.

THE NEW PROFESSIONALS IQ (I QUIT!) TEST

Test questions fall into three groups:

- Group 1: how you assess your current job and career path; economic condition and overall financial situation.

- Group 2: how you evaluate your lifestyle, degree of happiness, time management family situation, and degree of control over where and how you live.

- Group 3: how you measure your potential as a successful network marketer, for no matter how foolproof and failure-resistant network marketing companies claim their business-building model to be, the fact remains that this profession, like any other, requires a specific skill set and work attitude.

Here we go!

Group 1 Questions

- Is there a plausible possibility that your job could be eliminated?

- Could your company merge with or be bought by another firm, resulting in a downsizing program affecting you?

- If you are a business owner, could your enterprise suffer an irreversible financial setback?

- Are you generally satisfied with your income level? Can you expect reasonable, uninterrupted advances in salary and stature going forward?

- Are you adequately prepared for your eventual retirement? Will Social Security, your company pension, and personal investments allow you to approximate your current lifestyle during twenty to thirty years of retirement?

- Has your profession-be it banking, real estate, health care, law, teaching, or any other-changed since you entered it? Is it still rewarding and lucrative?

Group 2 Questions

- Do your professional obligations leave you adequate time for family, friends, and leisure pursuits?

- Do you have a bearable commute to your place of work or business, and, once there, do you work in pleasant, friendly surroundings?

- Are you living in the part of the country in which you want to live?

- Do you have a significant degree of control over your life, or do you feel trapped by routine and personal circumstances?

- Do you prize stability over uncertainty and a degree of risk over security?

- Is it vital to your self-esteem that you work for a large, well-known, prestigious organization?

Group 3 Questions

- Do you have reasonably effective communications skills?

- Are you willing to talk in front of people?

> Look reality squarely in the face when answering these test questions and judge your situation and abilities as they really are.

- Would you be able to approach friends, family, colleagues, and even total strangers with a sales pitch most won't want to hear?

- Does the fear of rejection significantly affect your behavior, including your willingness to ask people for favors, bosses for raises, and potential customers for sales?

- Do you have a sufficient degree of self-discipline to ensure that you would accomplish work tasks in a home office environment in a timely manner-resisting distractions ranging from children to pets to television to snacking?

- Would you feel a sense of isolation if for a significant portion of your professional life, you never left your house and never went to meetings or attended "power" breakfasts, lunches, or dinners?

- Would you consider it demeaning to sell consumer products or services and commingle with people whose educational, income, and class levels may be lower than your own?

- Will a negative reaction to your new profession by family and friends cause great concern or a rapid change of course?

SCORING YOUR POTENTIAL AS A NEW PROFESSIONAL

Having pondered all three groups of questions in the New Professional's IQ Test, it's now time to evaluate yourself. As noted, the questions we have posed are qualitative and subjective in nature. Thus, what you should be seeking from this exercise is a reasoned and intelligent diagnosis of your potential as a New Professional, rather than an up or down, yes or no, pass or fail grade.

Evaluating Group 1 Questions

Only you can speak to your specific degree of satisfaction with your income, your financial situation now and in the future, and the level of confidence you have in it.

Suppose you find your current career interesting, challenging, and lucrative, and you have reason to believe your job is safe. Suppose also you have a good pension plan at work, which you have buttressed with a responsible level of savings. You are less likely than most to want or need to consider starting your own network marketing business.

Even with the old work and business model changing, some portion of the workforce finds that it still works for them. After all, at network marketing companies themselves, you find corporate executives who are not network marketers. They made their bones in the traditional corporate world, were hired for the management skills they acquired there, and are promoted and paid along those lines.

However, if you are one of many who is not entirely sure of your long-term job security, who has not adequately invested for retirement, and who wants to diversify income streams in a business that costs little to begin and can be developed part-time, then network marketing-and its potential for serious long-term residual income into your retirement years and beyond-is an appealing approach.

Evaluating Group 2 Questions

Whether or not you are making a substantial, growing, and secure income in the established business or professional world, what about your quality of life? You may be in great shape financially but be otherwise stressed and unhappy. If you find yourself at the office or on the road too much of the time, missing important events involving your spouse and children, you may want to take another approach.

Seek from this exercise a reasoned, intelligent diagnosis of your potential as a New Professional, rather than a yes or no, pass or fail grade.

If you face a long commute every day, if you are tired of the endless pattern of meetings and office politics, or if you'd like to work at your own pace in casual clothes, home-based businesses can be a great alternative. And if you have school-age children at home, you would probably love to find a career option that doesn't make you choose between earning a good income and being at home for your kids virtually every day.

And how about where you live? Do you live there because it's convenient to your job or because that's where you really want to be? Home-based businesses and other forms of telecommuting let you live where you want.

These lifestyle factors are some of the most powerful considerations for New Professionals making important career decisions. Indeed, we see them weighing more heavily in those decisions than money. Money is a threshold to be crossed. Once the aspiring New Professional decides or proves it can be crossed in network marketing, then the real benefits click in-time freedom, stronger families, more enjoyable lifestyles.

However, as indicated earlier and by the nature of several of our group 3 questions in this chapter, you must truthfully consider whether the network marketing lifestyle is indeed compatible with your personality and character traits-as well as those of your family.

Working at home may leave you feeling isolated, unimportant, and uninvolved. You may lack the discipline to put in the necessary hours of concentrated work. There may be too many distractions, too many easy excuses for putting off income-producing tasks. Your personal habits may change-you may eat more or bathe, shave, and groom less. You might even fall into the habit of watching daytime TV! All of these pitfalls have been known to occur among those who telecommute or operate home-based businesses.

The flip side of that equation could also occur-you may find that your work is never done. If business challenges are weighing on your mind, how do you leave them at the office when the office is just down the hall? Instead of spending more quality time with your family, you may find yourself on the computer or the phone at all hours, seven days a week.

As good as it sounds in theory, you must honestly question whether the flexible home-based lifestyle promised by network marketing will work for you.

Evaluating Group 3 Questions

Your prior success in the business or professional world does not automatically mean you will be a good network marketer.

You must aggressively try to sell products and a business opportunity to virtually everyone you know, including family and friends, and be prepared to be rejected often. You need to have a certain "gift of gab," be a good conversation-alist, find ways to connect with different kinds of people, and communicate with passion.

Couple these skill needs with the possibility that some of the people you know may react negatively to your new en-deavor-not just rejecting your entreaties that they join your business but also expressing surprise or dismay at your ca-reer choice. If "what people think" is inordinately important to you, if you are embarrassed to sell to people, if you lack the focus to close the deal, or if rejection just eats you alive, this industry will probably not be right for you.

However, that said, many companies have worked hard at perfecting training systems and what they like to call "du-plicable" models of success. Mentoring is strong and dedi-cated in network marketing. After all, those mentors' own success is measured by how well those they train perform. So if you have a modicum of skill and the right attitudes, chances are good that you will be able to translate the skills that have made you successful in your current career into success in your alternative line of business.

THE JUGGLING ACT

Having scored yourself in each group of questions, now you must determine how to juggle all three categories of evalua-tion to determine your next move.

For example, you might be making plenty of secure money but desire a different professional and personal lifestyle. Or you may decide that your career is going the way of the dinosaurs and you need to build a network mar-keting business for the income security. You may be con-vinced that network marketing is a legitimate alternative income opportunity, that you may need the income and would enjoy the lifestyle, but have to honestly admit you just won't be good at it. Perhaps you don't really need an-other line of income, but knowing your skills, you know you'd be so good at it and can't pass it up. Besides, it might be a fun, educational, and rewarding project you can do as a family and meet many new people along the way.

You must balance all three groups of questions, weighing each realistically, to determine your viability as a New Professional in network marketing.

WHAT IF YOU "FAILED" THE NEW PROFESSIONAL'S IQ TEST?

What do we say to those whose assessment is that they failed? They don't want to, don't need to, or couldn't succeed at becoming such a New Professional?

To some, we might want to say "Congratulations!" You may have an ideal job that rewards you amply, financially and personally, and that allows you to lead a balanced life with plenty of time for family and leisure. Keep it! You may have made successful investments that guarantee a secure, comfortable retirement. Good for you! All you need to understand is that most are not like you-and thus the rise of New Professionals around you may impact you through your children, colleagues, employees, and clients. Many of them will be seeking a different kind of life, and you need to understand that.

For those who need an opportunity like network marketing but who feel impossibly constrained by the lack of time, knowledge, or ability-don't worry, this industry is not going away. The opportunity will be there should your circumstances or self-evaluation of your prospects change.

Don't overlook the fact that there are other ways to be a New Professional. You may come upon a different kind of flexible business opportunity and have the money and skills to invest in it and make it work. We have emphasized that the impact of network marketing on the broader business world is strong. It may positively change your occupation as opportunities to work out of your home and keep more flexible hours expand throughout the work environment.

Don't think you'd be good at network marketing? Perhaps your spouse will be-give this book to him or her. Let your spouse be the professional "pioneer" on this occasion. If you have children, then at least one parent will be able to stay at home, and you can join him or her later.

Indeed, its time for a confession from your authors. As much as we admire the network marketing industry on the whole, neither of us is in it. Yet we both consider ourselves New Professionals.

As a professor and business consultant, Charles has built a career that allows him to teach at the university level while remaining rooted in the pragmatic world of business. Unless he is in the classroom, keeping office hours for students or handling his other faculty responsibilities, he works at home-and travels the world for business and pleasure.

Sandra King, his best friend, wife, business partner, and an integral member of the King consulting team, is another example of a New Professional. Sandra has a master's degree in business, a twenty year marketing career in corporate America, and now manages the King consulting practice. Sandra has developed expertise as a business builder in network marketing and now coordinates network marketing educational programs around the world.

Jim spent twenty successful years in the blue-suit world of politics and corporate public affairs. Tiring of the grind of power breakfasts, boring meetings, office politics, and management hassles, he has now crafted a balanced professional package that includes a significant advisory role at the U.S. Chamber of Commerce, which he conducts mostly through phone, fax, and e-mail, and a promising writing career. Thus, he remains close to his longtime interests in politics and public policy through his relationship with the Chamber, an organization based in Washington, D.C. But he lives where he wants to live-in Los Angeles-and supplements his income with a secondary income stream from writing, which is Jim's first love.

TEN TRENDS POWERING THE RISE OF THE NEW PROFESSIONALS AND THE GROWTH OF NETWORK MARKETING

Whether you enter the ranks of the New Professionals now or later, whether network marketing is your vehicle of choice, whether you choose to travel this road another way, whether you choose to make this journey all at once or one step at a time by building a part-time business, or whether you remain in the more traditional world of work while your spouse takes these opportunities-all will find their lives impacted by the rise of the New Professionals and the growing appeal of network marketing. Ten major trends in society are powering these changes. We hope they are familiar to you after a close reading of the first eight chapters of this book.

Trend 1: Side-by-Side Economic Uncertainty and Opportunity

Corporate layoffs at the middle and senior management levels will continue to rise due to consolidation and globalization, despite record prosperity. At the same time, stock ownership has now reached 50 percent of American households. Many families earn (or lose!) more in a day from their investments than they do from a day on the job. The insecurities of the traditional workplace combined with the exciting alternative possibilities of entrepreneurship and investing are transforming the culture of work and income. The one-job, one-paycheck families of the 1950s have been replaced by the two-job, two-paycheck families of the 1990s. These will now be replaced by a cluster of income-producing activities, including direct selling.

Trend 2: Professions in Decline

Facing unprecedented competition, cost pressures, regulations, and the impact of Internet technology, service professions such as law, health care, medicine, teaching, franchising, and bricks-and-mortar business ownership will continue to change character significantly. Traditions of caregiving and personal attention to clients/customers will further give way to a green eye shade accountants' mentality, seriously reducing the level of income and personal satisfaction for many practitioners.

Trend 3: An Aging Society

The aging of society and the shrinking of the working age population will severely limit the ability of government entitlement programs like Social Security and Medicare, as well as private pension plans, to provide adequate income and care for 76 million baby boomers upon their retirement. They will become at best "safety-net" welfare programs, offering only hand-to-mouth survival to those who failed to save, invest, and develop diverse, long-term income streams.

Trend 4: Longer Life Spans

At the same time, longer and healthier lives will increase people's ability, given the right income opportunities, to stay productive and active well into their golden years. The senior market for products and services related to health, beauty, and diet-staple products of the network marketing industry-will explode. So will the attractiveness of the network marketing opportunity.

Trend 5: Job Flexibility

A shrinking workforce, combined with tremendous pressures to cut commute times, reduce vehicle pollution, ease suburban sprawl and congestion, and strengthen family stability, will force companies of all types to offer employees more flexible work schedules. The ranks of the nation's telecommuters-already 20 million strong-will grow rapidly. It will become the norm, not the exception, in many industries.

Trend 6: The Power of the Internet

High-speed, cost-efficient, user-friendly Internet and communications technology will make home-based business opportunities more effective and lucrative than ever before. Part-time business ventures conducted on the side, with spouses and children helping out, will boom, thus strengthening the family. This will lead many people into self-employment and small business ownership who have never been able or willing to consider it before. Such businesses can be built anywhere in the world where there is access to electrical power and telephone and Internet service.

Trend 7: The Growing Appeal of Network Marketing

During the past ten years, network marketing has become an established and acknowledged channel of distribution for its efficient speed to market capability. An important community of specialized network marketing companies has developed. Network marketing is being integrated into the distribution strategies of tradional, mainline marketing companies.

Network marketing is also being adopted as an alternative part-time or full-time career opportunity among the New Professionals exploring alternative career paths and income options. Network marketing is totally compatible with the renewed focus on family, lifestyle, retirement planning, and time flexibility.

Capitalizing on broader economic, lifestyle, and technological trends, network marketing will continue to enjoy substantial growth, improving its business position and image, and attracting legions of upscale professionals. Most will start such businesses on a part-time basis first and then go full-time if and when their level of success and other sources of income allow. Many will take early retirement in their initial careers, further straining the unfavorable demographic trend lines facing the economy as a whole.

Trend 8: Persistent Barriers in the Traditional Workplace

Despite a tight labor market, roadblocks to success-such as the glass ceiling, language problems facing recent immigrants, vestiges of racial and ethnic prejudice, and professional handicaps for people with disabilities, as well as unmarried or divorced mothers with young children-will continue to bedevil the traditional business world. For the most part, network marketing has been able to break through these artificial barriers, offering equal potential to all participants, with success, income level and advancement based on sales and recruiting performance only.

Trend 9: Direct Selling as an
E-Commerce Distribution Channel

E-commerce and the technology-induced fragmentation of the consumer market will force even traditional product and service companies to explore face-to-face direct selling and network marketing methods. Rather than continue to pour millions of dollars into expensive national advertising campaigns and celebrity endorsements, many firms will instead return money to a "volunteer army" of networkers in the form of product discounts and incentives to gather other customers and networkers. At the same time, branding, quality, service, and price competitiveness will continue to be important, causing many network marketing firms to blend their sales and recruiting approaches with more traditional business methods.

Trend 10: Expanding International Marketplace

Network marketing's appeal will grow even faster in burgeoning international markets than it will in the United States-especially Canada, Mexico, Japan, China, Southeast Asia, Brazil, and the United Kingdom. This explosive growth will create a gold rush of opportunities for domestic network marketing companies and their participants. In turn, the globalization of the network marketing opportunity-made possible by fast, efficient technology, travel and global movement of product, capital, and information-will dramatically increase the appeal of the industry for well-educated, culturally and economically sophisticated U.S. professionals.

WHERE IS YOUR WALDEN POND?

In the final analysis, by joining the ranks of the New Professionals, you are saying "I quit!"

But you are not quitting life or business or a hunger for personal achievement.

You are quitting a professional world that demands more from you and gives less to you.

You are quitting a work model that demands that you must choose between family and career.

You are quitting organizations whose own success and survival in a globalized economy of cutthroat competition may one day require getting rid of you.

You are quitting professions that have lost their moral compass, straying so far from the reason you joined them-to cure the sick, defend the innocent, or teach the ignorant, for example.

By becoming a New Professional, you are regaining control over your finances, your career, and your personal fulfillment. Your new company is called YOUR NAME HERE, Inc.—and you are in charge!

You decide where headquarters is. You decide what the business hours are. You decide what products or services to offer. You decide whom you want to work with.

By becoming a New Professional, you are opening your life to a myriad of new people, experiences, and opportunities to try different things. By becoming a New Professional, you are anchoring your career to the principle that the more you help others succeed, the more you will succeed.

How different that is from the old work culture most of us have endured.

In the 1840s, the writer-philosopher Henry David Thoreau retreated to a cabin he built with his own hands on the shores of Walden Pond in Concord, Massachusetts. Critics delight in pointing out that the two years he spent there was hardly a monastic existence. Thoreau strolled through the streets of the village, making conversation with friends and neighbors, helping others with chores, and enjoying home-cooked meals prepared by others. He wrote, he thought, and he explored-but he also shopped, socialized, and was very much a part of society.

Critics who claim this was a contradiction have missed the point. Thoreau simply wanted to live life on his own terms. The same is true for today's New Professionals. They are searching for their own Walden Pond-a place and lifestyle not aimed at retreat or isolation but where they can become more a part of the things they really care about, the things that really matter. Where is your Walden Pond?

Thoreau summarized it simply more than 150 years ago: "I went to the woods because I wished to live deliberately, to front only the essential facts of life, and see if I could not learn what it had to teach, and not when I came to die, discover that I had not lived."

We hope you, the aspiring New Professional, will be able to contemplate and change your own life with similar all-encompassing satisfaction.

APPENDIX
SELECTED NETWORK MARKETING INFORMATION RESOURCES

For the New Professional seriously considering the network marketing industry as an alternative business venture, a broad cross section of information references has been compiled here. The references include three sections:

- Leading trade press publications

- Selected generic network marketing–related Web sites

- Selected network marketing book references

LEADING TRADE PRESS PUBLICATIONS

The leading trade press publications include:

Money Maker's Monthly
6627 West 171st Street, Suite B
Tinley Park, IL 60477
(708) 633-8888
e-mail: editors@mmmonthly.com
www.mmmonthly.com/mmm

Direct Sales Journal
6627 West 171st Street, Suite A
Tinley Park, IL 60477
(708) 429-4444
e-mail: info@directsalesjournal.com
www.directsalesjournal.com

UPLINE Journal
106 South Street
Charlottesville, VA 22902
e-mail: customerservice@upline.com
www.upline.com

Network Marketing Lifestyles
106 South Street
Charlottesville, VA 22902
e-mail: customerservice@nmlifestyles.com
www.nmlifestyles.com

There are a number of advertising vehicles, promotional mailers, etc. that are used across the industry but those were not considered important information sources.

SELECTED GENERIC NETWORK MARKETING–RELATED WEB SITES

There are an estimated 200,000-plus Web pages that are network marketing/multi-level marketing related according to the various Internet search engines. The Web sites vary widely in terms of theme, content detail, and accuracy. New Web sites are being created and others abandoned continuously.

These Web sites have been selected as representative of the generic network marketing industry information available on the Internet. The selection is subjective and other sites may be equally informative. Many of these sites link into other Web sites multiplying the information exposure. The Web sites are listed by Web site title in alphabetical order.

In addition to these generic Web sites, every major network marketing company has its own proprietary Web site which can be a valuable source of company specific information. The authors referenced many of those sites in Chapters 6 and 7.

The authors do not endorse any of the content presented in these Web sites. Some of these sites may have not been updated recently. Others may have been deleted or abandoned since being listed here. The reader should recognize there is no control over Web site content or accuracy. In this arena, let the reader beware.

Web Site Title	URL
Direct Selling Association	www.dsa.org
Effective MLM Marketing Tips	www.mlmsecretsexposed.com
Evaluating Network Marketing Opportunities	www.pmignet.com
Fortune Now Newsletter	www.fortunenow.com
Free 2 Try Opportunities	www.free2try.com
Get Buzy International	www.getbuzy.com
IBMC Cyber Mall	www.ibmc.com
Internetwork Marketing System	www.internetwork-marketing.com
Leap Online	www.mlmnetwork-marketing.com
Millionaires in Motion	www.miminc.com
MLM 101	www.mlm101.com
MLM.com	www.mlm.com
MLM Directories	www.mlmdir.com
MLM Law	www.mlmlaw.com
MLM Legal	www.mlmlegal.com
MLM Mall	www.mlmmall.com
MLM Startup.com	www.mlmstartup.com
MLM Success Tips	www.mlmsuccesstips.com
MLM University	www.mlmu.com
MLM Woman Newsletter	www.mlmwoman.com
MLM Yellow Pages	www.bestmall.com
MLSA	www.mlsacomline.com
Multi-Level Marketing International Association	www.mlmia.com

Web Site Title	URL
Network Marketing and MLM Insider Magazine	www.cory@mlminsider.com
Network Marketing News	www.networkmarketingnews.com
Network Marketing News Online	www.onlinemlm.com
Network Marketing Resources	www.he.net
Network Marketing	www.networkmarketing.com
The Network Marketing Emporium (Cashflow)	www.cashflow.com
The Network Marketing Emporium (Catalog)	www.catalog.com
Truth About MLM Programs	www.insiderreports.com
UIC Certificate Seminar in Network Marketing	www.netwkmarketing.com
Who Is Who in Network Marketing	www.whoswhomlm.com
World Federation of Direct Selling Associations(WFDSA)	www.wfdsa.org

SELECTED NETWORK MARKETING BOOK REFERENCES

The book selections are admittedly subjective. The references, however, do present varied perspectives.

Direct Sales: An Overview by Keith B. Laggos, Ph.D., presents a comprehensive, in-depth, textbook coverage of the history and infrastructure of the direct-selling and network marketing industry.

The fast paced, very readable and enjoyable, bestselling *Wave 3* and *Wave 4* series by Richard Poe tracks the major network marketing industry developments and key milestones over the past ten years.

Your First Year in Network Marketing: Overcome Your Fears, Experience Success, and Achieve Your Dreams by Mark Yarnell and Rene Reid Yarnell outlines the mechanics of developing a network distributor organization, details the many challenges and highlights the extraordinary rewards that can be earned.

The over 65 book references, listed in alphabetical order by author's last name, cover the gambit of the network marketing industry from "how-to" procedures to specific skill development activities to case studies of some of the leading industry firms.

Andrecht, Venus C. and Summer McStravick. *MLM Magic: How an Ordinary Person Can Build an Extraordinary Networking Business from Scratch.* Ransom Hill Press, 1993.

Averill, Mary and Bud Corkin. *Network Marketing : The Business of the '90s (A Fifty-Minute Series Book).* Crisp Publications, 1995.

Barefoot, Coy. *The Quixtar Revolution: Discover the New High-Tech, High-Touch World of Marketing.* Prima Publishing, 1999.

Barrett, Ph.D., Tom. *Dare to Dream and Work to Win: Understanding the Dollars and Sense of Success in Network Marketing.* Warner Brothers Publications, 1998.

Barrier, Rusty and Tricia Seymour. *Rise to the Stars! A Daily Focus Book for Network Marketing Entrepreneurs.* Entelechea Press, 1998.

Bartlett, Richard C. *The Direct Option.* Texas A&M Press, 1994.

Bertrand, David with J. Mark Bertrand. *Making a Difference While You're Earning a Living.* New Paradigm Publishing, 1998.

Biggart, Ph.D., Nicole Woolsey. *Charismatic Capitalism.* The University of Chicago Press, 1989.

Billac, Pete and Sharon Davis. *The Millionaires Are Coming: How to Succeed in Network Marketing.* Swan Publishing Company, 1999.

Butwin, Robert. *Street Smart Network Marketing: A No-Nonsense Guide for Creating the Most Richly Rewarding Lifestyle You Can Possibly Imagine.* Prima Publishing, 1997.

Clements, Leonard W. *Inside Network Marketing: An Insider's View Into The Hidden Truths and Exploited Myths of America's Most Misunderstood Industry.* Prima Publishing, 1997.

Clements, Leonard W. *Inside Network Marketing: An Insider's View Into The Hidden Truths and Exploited Myths of America's Most Misunderstood Industry, Revised 2nd Edition.* Prima Publishing, 2000.

Clouse, Michael S. and Kathie Jackson Anderson. *Future Choice: Why Network Marketing May Be Your Best Career Move.* Candlelight Press, 1996.

Conn, Charles Paul. *Promises to Keep: The Amway Phenomenon and How It Works.* G. P. Putnam's Sons Publishers, 1985.

Counsel, John. *The Beginner's Guide to Making Money in Low-Cost, Home-Based Business . . . No Risks!* Wrightbooks, 1993.

Counsel, John. *What You Should Know About MLM Before You Join.* Wrightbooks, 1995.

Crisp, Robert E. *Raising a Giant: A Book About Becoming a Leader in Network Marketing.* Robert Crisp Enterprises, Inc., 1998.

Cross, Wilbur. *Amway: The True Story of the Company that Transformed the Lives of Millions.* Berkley Publishing Group, 1999.

DeGarmo, Scott and Louis Tartaglia, M.D. *Heart to Heart: The Real Power of Network Marketing.* Prima Publishing, 1999.

Elsberg, Sandy. *Bread Winner—Bread Baker.* Upline, 1997.

Failla, Don. *How to Build a Large Successful Multi-Level Marketing Organization.* Multi-Level Marketing International, Inc., 1994.

Fitzpatrick, Robert L. and Joyce K. Reynolds. *False Profits: Seeking Financial and Spiritual Deliverance in Multi-Level and Pyramid Schemes.* Herald Press, 1997.

Fogg, John. *Conversations with the Greatest Networker in the World.* Prima Publishing, 2000.

Fogg, John. *The Greatest Networker in the World.* Prima Publishing, 1997.

Gage, Randy. *How to Build a Multi-Level Money Machine : The Science of Network Marketing.* Gage Research & Development Inst., 1998.

Go, Josiah. *Build, Grow, and Sustain Your Network Marketing Distributor Business.* Design Plus, Philippines, 2000.

Hedges, Burke. *Who Stole the American Dream.* INTI Publishing, 1992.

Helmstetter, Ph.D, Shad. *American Victory: The Real Story of Today's Amway.* Chapel and Croft Publishing, 1997.

Helmstetter, Ph.D, Shad. *Network for Champions: What's Right About America and How to Be Part of It!* Chapel and Croft Publishing, 1995.

Higgins, Patrick and Nicolett O'Keefe. *The Future is Knowing Network Marketing.* Unlimited Horizons, 1996.

Kalench, John. *17 Secrets of the Master Prospectors.* Millionaires in Motion, 1994.

Kalench, John. *Being the Best You Can Be in MLM: How to Train Your Way to the Top in Multi-Level Network Marketing.* Millionaires in Motion, 1990.

Kalench, John. *Greatest Opportunity in the History of the World: You and the Dream of the Home-Based Business.* Millionaires in Motion, 1991.

Kishel, Gregory F. and Patricia G. Kishel. *Build Your Own Network Sales Business.* John Wiley & Sons, 1991.

Laggos, Ph.D., Keith B. *Direct Sales: An Overview.* Keith B. Laggos Publishing, 1998.

Michelli, Dena and Alison Straw. *Successful Networking: The Skills You Need to Succeed in the Business World.* Barron's Educational Series, Inc., 1997.

Moore, Angela L. *Building a Successful Network Marketing Company: The Systems, the Products, and the Know-How You Need to Launch or Enhance a Successful MLM Company.* Prima Publishing, 1998.

Nichols, Rod. *Successful Network Marketing for the 21st Century.* Oasis Press, 1995.

Paley, Russ, Walt Kleine and Evan Auster. *Network Your Way to Millions: The Definitive Step by Step Guide to Wealth In Network Marketing.* Wealth & Health International, 1999.

Pinnock, Tom. *You Can Be Rich by Thursday: The Secrets of Making a Fortune in Multi-Level Marketing.* Wildstone Audio, 1997.

Poe, Richard. *Wave 3: The New Era in Network Marketing.* Prima Publishing, 1994.

Poe, Richard. *The Wave 3 Way to Building Your Downline.* Prima Publishing, 1996.

Poe, Richard. *Wave 4: Network Marketing in the 21st Century.* Prima Publishing, 1999.

Powers, Melvin. *Make Money with Classified Advertising.* Wilshire Book Co., 1995

Rackham, Neil. *Spin Selling.* McGraw-Hill, 1998.

Robinson, James W. *Empire of Freedom.* Prima Publishing, 1996.

Robinson, James W. *The Excel Phenomenon.* Prima Publishing, 1997.

Robinson, James W. *The New Excel Phenomenon.* Prima Publishing, 2000.

Robinson, James W. *The Pre-Paid Legal Story.* Prima Publishing, 2000.

Robinson, James W. *Prescription for Success: The Rexall Showcase International Story and What It Means to You.* Prima Publishing, 1999.

Roller, David. *How to Make Big Money in Multi-Level Marketing.* Prentice Hall Press, 1989.

Schreiter, Tom. *Big Al's How to Create a Recruiting Explosion.* KAAS Pub, 1986.

Schreiter, Tom. *Big Al's Super Prospecting: Special Offers & Quick-Start Systems.* KAAS Pub, 1994.

Schreiter, Tom. *Big Al's Turbo MLM.* KAAS Pub, 1988.

Schreiter, Tom. *How to Build MLM Leaders For Fun & Profit.* KAAS Pub, 1991.

Scott, Ph.D., Gini Graham. *Strike it Rich in Personal Selling: Success in Multi-Level Marketing.* Prentice Hall, 1991.

Scott, Ph.D., Gini Graham. *Success in Multi-Level Marketing.* Prentice Hall, 1991.

Shapiro, Steve. *Listening for Success: How to Master the Most Important Skill in Network Marketing.* Shapiro Resource Group, 1998.

Shook, Robert L. *How to Be the Complete Professional Salesperson.* Lifetime Books, 1995.

Snetsinger, Patrick Michael. *Confessions of a Multi-Level Marketer (Networking from Your Heart).* Palinoia Press, 1997.

Stewart, David. *Network Marketing: Action Guide for Success.* Success in Action Publisher, 1991.

Tan, Richard and K. C. See. *52 Reasons Why People Join Network Marketing.* Conquest Resources, Australia.

Tan, Richard and K. C. See. *201 Simple Ideas to Make More $$$ in Network Marketing.* Conquest Resources, Australia.

Timm, Paul R. *50 Powerful Ways to Win New Customers: Fast, Simple, Inexpensive, Profitable and Proven Ideas You Can Use Starting Today! 2nd Ed.* Career Press, 1997.

Van Andel, Jay. *An Enterprising Life: An Autobiography.* HarperBusiness, 1998.

Ward, Randy. *Winning the Greatest Game of All.* Network Support Group, 1984.

Yarnell, Mark and Rene Reid Yarnell. *Your First Year in Network Marketing.* Prima Publishing, 1998.

Yarnell, Mark, Valerie Bates and John Radford, Ph.D. *Self Wealth: Creating Property, Serenity, and Balance in Your Life.* Paper Chase Press, 1999.

Yarnell, Rene Reid. *The New Entrepreneurs: Making a Living—Making a Life Through Network Marketing.* Quantum Leap, 1999.

INDEX

Charles W. King received his doctorate in business administration from Harvard University and is a professor of marketing at the University of Illinois, at Chicago (UIC). Dr. King is also a consultant, with more than twenty-five years experience in entrepreneurial ventures. He focuses on strategic marketing planning, competitive market positioning, and management of the tactical marketing functions in entrepreneurial ventures.

King conducts ongoing research on the network marketing industry and writes for the industry trade press. He is also a nationally recognized speaker on network marketing as a legitimate channel of distribution and as an outstanding entrepreneurial business venture. King also consults with network marketing companies and serves as an expert witness in legal cases involving network marketing.

In 1994, King cofounded the UIC Certificate Seminar in Network Marketing, the only program of its type sponsored by a major university worldwide. The UIC Seminar Program has become the standard for professional education in network marketing and has expanded into Asia and Europe and is now moving into South America.

James W. Robinson is the author of the bestsellers *The Excel Phenomenon* and *Empire of Freedom* and co-author of *The Pre-Paid Legal Story* (all from Prima). Called "the entrepreneur's advocate" by the *Washington Post,* he makes frequent media and speaking appearances in support of network marketing and free enterprise. A veteran of the California political and government scene, he is currently senior advisor to the U.S. Chamber of Commerce. He lives in Los Angeles.